Going WILD in the KITCHEN

The Fresh & Sassy Tastes of Vegetarian Cooking

Leslie Cerier

Foreword by Susun Weed

 SQUAREON PUBLISHI

COVER DESIGNERS: Phaedra Mastrocola and Jacqueline Michelus
COVER PHOTO: Getty Images, Inc. AUTHOR PHOTO: Terri Fain
INTERIOR ART: Gayle Kabaker
EDITOR: Marie Caratozzolo
TYPESETTER: Gary A. Rosenberg

Square One Publishers
115 Herricks Road
Garden City Park, NY 11040
(516) 535-2010 • (877) 900-BOOK
www.squareonepublishers.com

Library of Congress Cataloging-in-Publication Data

Cerier, Leslie.
    Going wild in the kitchen : the fresh & sassy tastes of vegetarian cooking /
Leslie Cerier.
      p. cm.
    Includes index.
    ISBN 0-7570-0091-6 (pbk.)
    1. Vegetarian cookery. 2. Cookery (Wild foods) I. Title.

TX837.C382   2005
641.5′636—dc22

                                                                                        2005008911

Printed in the United States of America

10   9   8   7   6   5   4   3   2   1

CONTENTS

To my two wonderful daughters,
Emily and Michelle.
May you be wildly creative
in and out of the kitchen.

ACKNOWLEDGMENTS

Thank you, Chris Kilham, for the name of this book: *Going Wild in the Kitchen.*

Thank you, Nava Atlas, for reading the early drafts of the book's first chapter, "Recipe for Inspiration," and for sharing a common vision in supporting organic farmers and eating locally and seasonally.

Thank you to all the organic farmers—may you thrive and multiply.

Thank you to my many catering clients and cooking students, whose questions and requests inspired many of the recipes in this book.

Thank you to Bronwyn Mills and Len Huber, who read and edited early versions of this book and taught me grammar.

Thanks goes to Rudy Shur of Square One Publishers, who believed in my diamond-in-the-rough book proposal and teamed me up with Marie Caratozzolo, his star editor, who turned me and my manuscript upside down and inside out to make this book the most complete guide to creative vegetarian cookery.

Thanks to all of the companies I have listed in the Resources section. Your products have helped me eat well and have encouraged me to create many of the wonderful recipes that are found in this book.

Thanks to Susun Weed for your Foreword and for sharing your knowledge and enthusiasm for wild foods and edible flowers.

Thanks to Alyse Bynum, Anna Abele, and Linda Tumbarello for your friendship and support.

Finally, a very special thanks to my mother, Paula Cerier, who continues to encourage me to be wildly creative.

FOREWORD

My love affair with wild food began when I planted my first (postage-stamp-sized) garden. The year was 1968; the place, the Catskill Mountains of upstate New York. I can't claim to have planned on liking wild foods. They just sort of happened to me.

You see, when the seeds I'd planted in my garden started to sprout, I couldn't tell which seedlings were weeds and which were the ones I had put there. I didn't know which ones to want and which ones to want out. So I let them all grow. And grow they did. Some of them grew very quickly and very well, whether I watered them or not, whether I wanted them or not. Those, of course, turned out to be the weeds. The scrawny ones that seemed intent on dying were the vegetables (sigh).

Fortunately for me, a friend turned me on to Euell Gibbons and his books the very next year. Imagine my surprise when I discovered that the plants everyone else was calling weeds were actually "wild foods." And that wild foods were just as edible as vegetables—and a lot easier to grow.

Soon I was cooking up delicious dishes from my garden—thanks to the weeds. At a very young age, my daughter, Justine, picked purslane and fried it with her eggs for breakfast. I harvested and cooked so much amaranth and lamb's quarters that I not only had plenty to eat, I had lots left to freeze for winter enjoyment.

Soon I stopped planting lettuce completely. It didn't make sense to work so hard for rather boring lettuce when roadsides, meadows, and my garden edges supplied me with plenty of tasty greens for salad: Sheep sorrel and curly dock, wild oregano and bergamot, garlic mustard and watercress, chickweed and mallow, dandelion and wild madder, to name but a few.

And the more I read, the more uses I found for those weeds. They were not only wild foods, but dye plants, basket materials, and—best of all—safe, simple medicines. The rest is history. I fell in love with wild foods and became an herbalist. A wild woman with her wild weeds.

Leslie Cerier is a wild woman, too, in the best sense of the word. She thinks—and cooks—in wild spiraling starbursts that embrace surprising—and surprisingly good—foods. She not only has a knack for combining flavors, colors, textures, and aromas to their best advantage, she is a fine teacher who can impart her skills to others through the written word. Aren't we lucky to have another great cookbook from her?!

Going Wild in the Kitchen offers us "fresh and sassy tastes" by walking on the wild side. But not too wild. Most of these recipes are perfectly fine without their wild ingredients. Or, for only a little effort, even novices can include a variety of superbly nutritious semi-cultivated or wild-harvested foods in their meals. So, come on into the garden with Leslie, Euell, and me. Before we're through, we may make a wild woman out of you, too.

Susun Weed, Herbalist
Author of the *Wise Woman Herbal Series*

INTRODUCTION

I've always been crazy about the great taste and wholesome goodness of organically grown foods. To me, there is nothing more appealing and delicious than fresh, locally grown vegetables and fruits. Add to that, the incomparable flavors of wild mushrooms and berries, aromatic herbs, exotic ancient grains like quinoa and teff, delectable sheep and goat's milk cheeses, tasty vegetables from the sea, and a variety of edible flowers that offer both visual appeal and distinctive flavor—and it's no wonder that I'm crazy about these natural gifts of the earth. And with Mother Nature as my ever-present guide, it's easy to go wild in the kitchen, adapting to the bounty of the season while conjuring up exciting new dishes, and reinventing old family favorites.

Sharing the skills and excitement of creative vegetarian cooking with you is my greatest wish. And whether you are a novice or experienced cook, *Going Wild in the Kitchen* will help you stretch your culinary capabilities and show you just how easy, fun, and deliciously satisfying this cooking style can be. Improvise, improvise, improvise! I'll show you how to adjust recipes according to the seasonal availability of ingredients, and venture beyond standard organic beans, grains, and vegetables to incorporate foods like wild greens and roots, edible flowers, and ancient grains into your meals. As vegetarianism continues to gain momentum, more and more of these lesser-known foods are making their way to the forefront of a health-conscious nation. And as you will see, not only do they add nutritional value to dishes, their unique tastes and textures provide flavor and interest as well.

To start you off on the right foot, the book opens with a helpful chapter called "Recipe for Inspiration." Consider it a primer, a place to turn when you have a question regarding an ingredient, a preparation method, or a cooking technique. In it, you'll find extensive glossaries that cover each of these subjects, as well as informative tables to help guide you in selecting edible flowers and wild foods, preparing various beans and grains, and experimenting with flavorful herbs and spices.

What follows next are nine chapters filled with over 150 of my favorite recipes. To kick things off, "Morning Bliss" includes a collection of delectable breakfast dishes from pancakes and waffles to smoothies and scrambles—something for everyone. Looking for a sensational soup? Whether you're craving a bowl of something light and brothy or thick and hearty, you can count on "Loving Spoonfuls" to provide you with the perfect choice. "Super Sides" and "Main Attractions" include enough mouthwatering entrées and accompaniments to keep you and your family well fed and satisfied, while "Just Desserts" offers a wonderful array of luscious treats, including cakes, cookies, pies, and more. You'll also find recipes for delicious sauces and dips, sensational salads, and appetizing wraps. There is even a chapter devoted to making your own flavored oils and vinegars.

Believe me, there isn't a recipe I prepare that is etched in stone. And although you can make the dishes in this book as presented, I encourage you to use them as springboards for creating your own unique variations. Rely on your instincts and imagination to make use of whatever ingredients are on hand or in season.

To further help you flex your sense of cooking creativity, in each chapter, I've included a "Mix and Match" chart that provides plenty of ideas for ingredient substitutions. Don't ever be afraid to add, omit, alter, or substitute.

It's time to roll up your sleeves and follow your instincts . . . time to enjoy the experience of creating healthful meals that are both satisfying and delicious . . . time to "go wild" in the kitchen!

1

Recipe for Inspiration

Go wild in the kitchen! Venture beyond the usual beans, grains, and vegetables to include an endless variety of global organic vegetarian fare to your meals. Be creative. Step outside the box and try your hand at preparing dishes with beautiful edible flowers; flavorful wild mushrooms, herbs, and berries; tangy sheep and goat cheeses; tasty sea vegetables; and exotic ancient grains like teff, quinoa, and spelt. If cooking with these kinds of foods is new to you, I'm here to help you stretch your creative culinary capabilities and show you just how easy, fun, and deliciously satisfying it can be.

Healthy, vegetarian cooking can be both taste tempting and eye appealing, generating excitement in the kitchen and broad smiles in the dining room. You just have to let yourself go. Don't be afraid to experiment. You can make just about any ingredient the star of a dish or have it share the spotlight with a supporting cast of other tasty fare. Any food that is flavored with the right blend of herbs and spices or complemented by an interesting garnish can be both exciting and inspirational.

Cooking is a daily ritual that feeds your spirit as well as your body. However, it is much more than a means to an end. It is a celebration of the earth's bounty. So let's celebrate! In the following chapters, I have offered dozens of exciting recipes that encourage you to go wild in the kitchen, incorporating lots of different and sometimes unusual ingredients into your meals. While preparing the dishes, if you run across an ingredient, preparation method, or cooking technique that is unfamiliar, this is the chapter to turn to for answers. Consider it a primer, a source for the basics. On the pages that follow, you will find extensive glossaries that cover each of these subjects. This chapter also includes a number of helpful charts and tables to help guide you in choosing edible flowers, wild greens, and roots.

It is my greatest wish to share the skills and excitement of creative vegetarian cooking with you. This chapter is designed to help you set the foundation.

ADAPTING TO CHANGE

As the seasons change, so does the availability of

3

fresh, local produce. With the fall comes crisp apples and tart cranberries, while juicy strawberries and fresh figs are the specialties of summer. But would they be so special if we could eat them all year long?

My enthusiasm for creating new recipes and preparing menus has always come from the local harvest. I take my cues from Mother Nature, who never fails to offer plenty of guidance. For instance, in June, the markets near my western Massachusetts home are filled with fresh spinach, baby red kale, arugula, radishes, strawberries, green and red leaf lettuces, mustard greens, and mizuna (a leafy green Asian vegetable similar to spinach). Also available are perennial herbs like chives, oregano, garlic chives, sage, and sorrel. Simultaneously harvested, these items become natural choices to "mix and match" for adding a flavorful spark to savory salads, quiches, dressings, scrambled tofu, sushi rice rolls, and pasta dishes. As the summer progresses, crunchy string beans, cherry tomatoes, sweet baby carrots, and aromatic basil find their way into my salads and side dishes. The sight of the season's first zucchini or plump shiny eggplant always inspires me to fire up the grill. Come fall, hearty collard greens, red bell peppers, and cilantro become my kitchen staples. When the weather turns cold, leafy kale is my green of choice, and winter squash varieties like delicata and butternut take the spotlight in many of my meals.

Along with ingredient availability, the weather is another factor that affects how and what I cook. When it's hot outside, I avoid using the stove as much as possible, so outdoor grilling is a welcome and sensible alternative. Quick-grilled vegetables and tofu, refreshing fruit smoothies, and marinated salads made with combinations of ingredients like corn, grains, and berries are refreshingly cool—perfect warm-weather fare. To beat the heat, I always cook beans, pasta, or grains in the early morning or at night when the house is cool. On cold winter days, my kitchen is host to slow-simmering soups, garlicky roasted vegetables, and spicy stews that are thick with potatoes, winter squash, carrots, and yams.

An attractive garnish can enliven any dish. For a splash of color, I may add yellow calendula flowers and bright red bee balm to my summer pasta salads, or toss some toasted nuts on a mixed green salad for contrasting texture. Chopped herbs added to cooked rice or other grains offer a delicate fragrance. The list of ideas is ever changing and goes on and on . . . simple pleasures that please the palate.

I also find myself reinventing many of my favorite recipes to keep them appealing and enjoyable. For example, I love making pies all year long, so I take my favorite pie crust and create fillings that reflect the bounty of the season. It might be apple, blackberry, or apple-blackberry in the fall; pumpkin, pumpkin-pecan, or pumpkin-date in the winter, a lemon tart or chocolate mousse in the spring, and a blueberry, peach, or blueberry-peach crumb in the summer. I also create variations for a number of the pies themselves. Instead of using only pumpkin in my pumpkin pie, I may add some sweet potatoes to the mix, or I might avoid using pumpkin altogether and use only butternut or kuri squash. Some days, I might add more cinnamon to the filling than usual; other times, I may leave out the cloves. I even alter the pie crust by using different flours, oils, and/or sweeteners.

If there is one type of dish that encourages me to "go wild," it's soup. There is nothing better for flexing my cooking creativity. During the long winter months, I keep my basic minestrone fresh and inspiring by swapping some standard soup vegetables for others. Instead of carrots, I'll use butternut squash, or I may substitute leeks for onions. As for beans, I'll toss in whatever is on hand—pinto, kidney, navy, lima, or combinations of a few varieties. Come the spring, I will swap leeks for wild leeks in soups like Basmati Rice Soup with French Herbs (page 50). Adapting my Curried Lentil Soup with Coconut Milk (page 53) to the seasons is easy and always tasty. I use fresh tomatoes, summer squash, spinach, and eggplant in the summer, and canned tomatoes, carrots, yams or delicata squash in the fall and winter.

When you take your cues from Mother Nature and make ingredient selections from fresh local bounty, improvising meals becomes second nature. On the following pages, you'll discover lots of wild plants and flowers that you never even knew you could eat! They will open up a whole new world to you and generate exciting ideas in the kitchen.

YES, YOU CAN EAT THAT

Violets? Dandelion leaves? Wild leeks? Mother Nature has certainly provided us with lots of edible plants—many more than those typically found on grocery store shelves. A wide variety of flowers, for instance, make beautiful and tasty additions to salads, sandwiches, jams, and muffins, while a number of wild greens and root vegetables can be nibbled raw or enjoyed when cooked.

When picking wild edible plants, be sure to stick with those that grow wild or come from untreated gardens. When picking plants or flowers that grow wild, choose only varieties that grow at least four feet from the road—far from any pollutants emitted by cars and other vehicles.

Be aware that most flowers sold by florists have been chemically treated and should be avoided. The tables on pages 6 and 7 list many edible flowers and plants along with when they are harvested, which parts are best to eat, and a description of how they taste.

As a general rule, it is best to pick most flowers and herbs early in the day to take advantage of their peak fragrance and flavor. If they are dusty, rinse them gently and pat dry before using. Some grow high enough off the ground to be free of dirt and don't need to be rinsed at all. Most blossoms tend to wilt quickly, so pick only what you will be using that day. And if you plan to use the flowers in a salad, it is best to add them after the salad has been tossed. Any acid in the dressing will cause the delicate petals to wilt and lose their color.

Although health food stores, produce markets, ethnic food shops, and even some grocery chains carry the majority of ingredients called for in this book, some are available only through mail order. Sources of these items are listed in the Resources, beginning on page 211.

CREATIVE COOKING WITH HERBS AND SPICES

Herbs and spices are among Mother Nature's most versatile gifts. Nothing adds more interest and taste appeal to dishes. They also support good health by reducing the need for salt. As garnishes, they add eye appeal. Herbs and spices are also different from each other. *Herbs* are the leaves of certain plants that do not produce woody stems and usually die at the end of a growing season. Basil, thyme, and cilantro are some examples. *Spices* are the twigs, stems, roots, pods, and seeds of a number of aromatic plants. Garlic, cumin, cinnamon, and ginger are considered

Edible Flowers—A Bouquet of Flavors

Flowers not only add beauty to gardens and lend a decorative touch to bouquets and centerpieces, many varieties also offer taste and eye appeal to dishes. The chart below lists a number of edible flowers along with when they are available and how they taste.

Harvest Time	Flower	Edible Part	Taste
Spring	Dandelions	flower petals leaves	honey (when young) bitter (when mature)
	Red clover	flowers	very little flavor, delicate crunch
	Violets	flowers leaves	light and sweet slightly tart
	Wild daisies	flower petals, leaves	light, delicate
Spring and Summer	Blueberry	blossoms	blueberries
	Johnny-jump-ups	flowers	mild wintergreen
	Pansies	flowers	wintergreen
Summer	Comfrey	flower petals	fresh green beans
	Day lilies	buds, flowers, pods	raw asparagus
	Purple bee balm	flowers	oregano
	Purple vetch	flowers	peas
	Red bee balm	flower petals	sweet and lemony
	Roses	petals	sweet with hint of apple, cinnamon, or mint
	Squash	blossoms	mild squash
	Sweet goldenrod	flowers	anise
Summer and Fall	Anise hyssop	flowers, leaves	licorice
	Borage	flowers	light and delicate
	Calendula	flower petals, heads	pungent
	Lavender	flower petals	lavender
	Marigold	flowers	tangy to bitter
	Nasturtiums	flowers, stems, leaves	peppery

Wild Greens and Roots

Throughout the year, a cornucopia of wild foods is available for your eating pleasure. As shown in the chart below, some are tender enough to eat raw; others are best when cooked.

Harvest Time	Greens or Roots	Edible Part	Taste
Early Spring	Fiddleheads (from ostrich ferns)	entire fiddlehead (cooked)	cross between asparagus and artichoke
Spring	Dandelion	leaves (raw or cooked)	bitter
	Garlic mustard	leaves, flowers (raw)	garlicky
	Ramps (wild leeks)	leaves, bulbs (raw or cooked)	garlicky
Spring and Early Summer	Nettles (before it flowers)	leaves (cooked)	peas or parsley
Spring and Summer	Sheep sorrel	leaves, flowers (raw)	lemony
Spring through Fall	Chickweed	leaves, stems (raw)	clean, crisp
	Lamb's quarters	leaves, stems, flowers (raw or cooked)	spinach
Summer	Mallow	leaves, flowers (raw)	okra, delicate and slippery
Early Fall to Spring	Amaranth	Leaves (cooked)	spinach
	Burdock	root (cooked)	earthy
	Purslane	leaves, stems (raw or cooked)	sweet and sour

Spice It Up!

A pinch of this, a sprinkle of that . . . the right herbs and spices can add a flavor-enhancing dimension to most foods. Go wild and have fun using them in the foods you prepare, and don't be shy about experimenting. As seen in the table below, these tasty additions, which fall into different flavor categories, are one way to help "correct" dishes that are too spicy, bitter, sour, or bland.

TASTE	FLAVOR CORRECTIONS	HERBS AND SPICES
SWEET	Balances overly bitter, sour, or spicy dishes.	Allspice, anise, cardamom, cilantro, cinnamon, coriander, fennel, saffron, and turmeric.
SOUR	Balances overly bitter or spicy dishes.	Bay leaves, caraway, chives, cloves, cumin, dill weed, lemongrass, marjoram, nutmeg, parsley, saffron, and tarragon.
PUNGENT, SPICY	Adds interest to bland dishes.	Basil, chilies, cilantro, coriander, curry, fennel, fenugreek, garlic, ginger, horseradish, mint, mustard seeds, oregano, peppercorns, rosemary, sage, and thyme.

spices. The "Spice It Up" chart above, provides an extensive listing of these flavor enhancers.

You can store most dried herbs for about a year. Spices can be stored longer. Before cooking with these flavor enhancers, be sure to smell and/or taste them to be sure they are fragrant and potent. As a general rule, it is best to add strong, hearty spices at the beginning of a dish's cooking time, while delicate herbs, fresh or dry, should be added near the end.

Every culture uses certain herbs and spices that lend unique distinction to its food. These flavor enhancers often cross borders and appear in more than one ethnic cuisine. Ginger, for instance, is commonly used in Indian, African, and Asian dishes, while dill is a popular flavoring used in Eastern European, Indian, French, and Mediterranean cooking. Cumin is standard in African, French, Indian, Mediterranean, and Mexican cuisine.

Ginger, dill, and cumin belong to a category of herbs and spices called *carminatives*. They contain volatile oils that absorb intestinal gas, relax stomach muscles, increase peristalsis, reduce flatulence, and aid digestion. Thyme, cinnamon, fennel, chilies, anise, caraway, cardamom, mint, and turmeric are other carminatives. Cooks throughout the world intuitively cooked with these herbs and spices before scientists discovered their restorative virtues.

GLOSSARY OF INGREDIENTS

The following ingredients are used in the recipes throughout this book. They are briefly defined and listed according to categories.

GRAINS

Grains are the seeds of cultivated grasses. They have been considered staple foods throughout the world for thousands of years. The table on page 10 offers additional information on cooking whole grains.

AMARANTH. High in fiber, iron, and protein, tiny amaranth seeds have a mild nutty flavor and are often used in porridge, pilafs, and puddings. Amaranth contains lysine, an essential amino acid, which, when combined with corn, wheat, or brown rice, creates a complete protein.

BARLEY. In its many forms, barley is a hardy grain used in dishes ranging from soups and salads to pilafs and stuffings. It has a distinctive nutty taste and is high in potassium, magnesium, and iron. Hulled barley is the most nutritious type, as only its inedible tough outer hull is removed. For pearled barley, the outer bran layer is also removed, making it easier to chew and faster to cook than hulled varieties.

BASMATI RICE. "Queen of fragrance" is the literal translation of this aromatic long-grain rice, which comes in white and nutritionally superior brown varieties. It is popular in Middle Eastern and Indian dishes.

BHUTANESE RED RICE. This ancient short-grain rice comes from the Himalayan kingdom of Bhutan. It is russet in color, soft in texture, and high in protein. Enjoy this rice in pilafs, salads, stir-fries, and puddings.

BROWN RICE. This chewy, nutty rice comes in short-, medium-, and long-grain varieties. Rich in fiber, protein, calcium, phosphorus, thiamin, niacin, and vitamin E, brown rice is a popular choice in pilafs and salads.

BUCKWHEAT GROATS (KASHA). Rich in calcium, iron, magnesium, potassium, phosphorous, and vitamins B and E, heart-shaped kasha is popular in pilafs, stuffings, and croquettes; it is also traditionally combined with bowtie pasta. Toasted kasha has a rich aroma and a strong earthy, almost salty flavor.

BULGUR WHEAT. A light, pleasing, quick-cooking cracked wheat, bulgur is high in iron, phosphorous, thiamin, and magnesium. It is delicious in salads, soups, stuffings, casseroles, meatless burgers, and pilafs.

FLAVOR ADJUSTING

Although the addition of certain herbs and spices can help balance dishes that are too sweet, salty, bitter, spicy, or sour (see "Spice It Up" on page 8), you can also adjust flavors by:

✔ Adding water to dishes that are too spicy, sweet, or sour.

✔ Adding salt to dishes that are too sweet or sour (not those that are too bitter).

✔ Adding a fat (oil, butter, ghee, tahini, nut butter) to dishes that are too spicy, sweet, bitter, salty, or sour.

Cooking Grains

Rich in fiber, vitamins, and minerals, whole grains are also low in fat and cholesterol free. The table below provides cooking requirements for these nutritional powerhouses. Unless otherwise specified, most grains require the following basic cooking directions.

After thoroughly rinsing the grains, place them in a pot along with the water and bring to a boil. (You can also boil the water before adding the grains.) Stir once, reduce the heat to low, and simmer covered for the required time. Do not stir the grains as they cook or they will become a sticky mass. Once cooked, let them sit about five minutes, then fluff with a fork and serve.

Grain Type (1 cup)	Water	Cooking Time	Directions	Approx. Yield	Suggested Seasonings
Amaranth	3 cups	20 minutes	Basic cooking directions above.	3 cups	Black pepper, cinnamon, cumin, garlic.
Barley, pearled	3 cups	50 to 60 minutes	Basic cooking directions above.	$3^1/_2$ cups	Bay leaf, cilantro, cumin, dill, garlic, sage.
Basmati rice	2 cups	45 to 60 minutes	Basic cooking directions above.	3 cups	Bay leaf, chilies, cinnamon, garlic, ginger, saffron.
Bhutanese red rice	$1^3/_4$ cups	20 minutes	Basic cooking directions above.	$2^1/_2$ to 3 cups	Bay leaf, chilies, cinnamon, cloves, garlic, ginger, thyme.
Brown rice, short-grain	2 cups	45 to 50 minutes	Basic cooking directions above.	$3^1/_2$ cups	Bay leaf, chilies, cinnamon, garlic, ginger, saffron.
Buckwheat groats (kasha)	2 cups	15 minutes	Basic cooking directions above.	2 cups	Bay leaf, black pepper, dill, parsley.
Bulgur wheat	2 cups	5 minutes	Basic cooking directions above.	$2^1/_2$ cups	Black pepper, chives, garlic, mint, oregano, parsley.
Carnaroli rice	$2^3/_4$ cups	20 to 25 minutes	Basic cooking directions above.	$2^1/_2$ to 3 cups	Bay leaf, cinnamon, garlic, ginger, parsley, saffron, thyme.
Chinese "forbidden" black rice	$1^3/_4$ cups	30 minutes	Basic cooking directions above.	$2^1/_2$ to 3 cups	Basil, cilantro, garlic, mint, parsley.
Grano	2 to 3 quarts	35 minutes	Add to rapidly boiling water and cook like pasta.	$2^1/_2$ to 3 cups	Cilantro, dill, fennel, garlic, mint, oregano, parsley, thyme.

Grain Type (1 cup)	Water	Cooking Time	Directions	Approx. Yield	Suggested Seasonings
Kamut	3 cups	2 hours	Basic cooking directions above.	2½ cups	Basil, cardamom, coriander, cumin, fennel, garlic, rosemary, sage, thyme.
Millet	3 cups	20 to 30 minutes	Basic cooking directions above.	4½ cups	Caraway seeds, chives, cilantro, dill, ginger.
Oats, rolled	3 cups	5 to 7 minutes	Basic cooking directions above, but stir occasionally.	2 cups	Black pepper, cinnamon, garlic, parsley, thyme.
Quinoa	2 cups	10 to 15 minutes	Basic cooking directions above.	2½ cups	Chilies, chives, dill, garlic, mint.
Sorghum (milo)	3 cups	1 hour	Basic cooking directions above.	4 cups	Chilies, cumin, fennel, garlic, oregano.
Spelt (farro)	1½ cups	2 hours	Basic cooking directions above.	2 cups	Basil, black pepper, garlic, rosemary, sage, thyme.
Spelt bulgur or spelt cous	1½ cups	5 minutes	Basic cooking directions above.	2 cups	Black pepper, chives, garlic, mint, oregano, parsley.
Teff	3 cups	20 minutes	Basic cooking directions above.	2 cups	Basil, cardamom, chilies, cilantro, cinnamon, cloves, cumin, fenugreek, garlic, ginger

CARNAROLI RICE. A bold white Argentinean rice, carnaroli has a creamy texture that makes it perfect for risotto.

CHINESE "FORBIDDEN" BLACK RICE. Once enjoyed only by emperors, this soft-textured, nonglutinous, medium-grain Chinese rice is high in protein and iron. It has a delicious nutty taste and turns a beautiful deep purple when cooked. Forbidden rice adds unique flavor, texture, and eye appeal to a number of dishes, including pilafs, salads, puddings, and risottos.

GRANO. This pearled durum wheat is high in fiber and protein. Cooked like pasta, grano is perfect in soups, stews, pilafs, and salads. It is also delicious mixed with pasta sauce.

KAMUT. This heirloom wheat is larger than common wheat. It is also higher in protein, iron, zinc, magnesium, potassium phosphorous, copper and vitamins B_1, B_2, and E. It's great in pilafs, stuffings, and salads.

MILLET. This small yellow grain has a slightly sweet taste and is high in phosphorous, magnesium, and B vitamins. When cooked millet cools, it can be cut like a brownie, making it suitable for grain loaves. It is also a good addition to croquettes, stuffings, and pilafs.

OATS, ROLLED (OATMEAL). In addition to making wonderful breakfast porridge, fiber-rich rolled oats are popular in soups, sauces, cookies, granolas, and fruit crisps. They are high in calcium, potassium, phosphorous, magnesium, iron, and B vitamins.

QUINOA. Quick-cooking sesame-flavored quinoa is high in calcium, iron, zinc, potassium, phosphorous, magnesium, manganese, vitamin E, and B vitamins. It is the only grain that is a complete protein. Served alone or in combination with other grains and vegetables, quinoa is delicious in salads, pilafs, and soups.

SORGHUM (MILO). A small round grain that has the texture of pearled barley, bland-flavored sorghum, like tofu, takes on the flavor of its surrounding ingredients. High in protein, sorghum is wonderful in pilafs, porridges, soups, casseroles, and marinated salads.

SPELT (FARRO). This heirloom wheat is easier to digest than common wheat. It is also higher in protein, fiber, copper, iron, zinc, and vitamins E, B_1, and B_2. Spelt is a good choice in pilafs, soups, and marinated salads.

TEFF. Tiny, sweet-tasting teff grains are moist in texture and have a subtle chocolate taste. Enjoy teff on its own or in porridge, stuffings, or grain loaves.

BEANS & SOYFOODS

Protein-rich beans (legumes) and soyfoods are the mainstays of a vegetarian diet. The following varieties are called for in many of the recipes in this book. The inset beginning on page 14 offers helpful tips and guidelines for preparing dried beans, while the table on page 13 provides cooking instructions.

ADUKI BEANS. Lowest in fat of all beans, small reddish-brown adukis have a mild sweet flavor and soften like split peas when cooked. They are popular in the cuisines of Japan and China.

ANASAZI BEANS. Similar to pinto beans, maroon and white speckled anasazi beans are sweeter in flavor. They are great additions to Southwestern-style foods like chili and burritos.

BLACK BEANS. Also called *turtle beans,* kidney-shaped black beans are characteristically found in Caribbean and Latin American dishes. Their slightly mealy texture and distinctive flavor make them delicious additions to soups and stews. They are also commonly served over rice.

CHICKPEAS. Also known as *garbanzo beans,* nutty, sweet-tasting chickpeas are popular in the cuisines of the Middle East, India, Italy, France, and Africa. They are often tossed into soups, stews, and salads, or ground into paste and used in sauces and dips.

KIDNEY BEANS. These medium-sized red beans are popular in Caribbean, Mediterranean, and Latin American cooking. Their meaty texture makes them a perfect addition to salads, wraps, soups, and stews.

LENTILS. Ideal in tomato-based soups and stews, brown and red lentil varieties do not require presoaking and are ready in about thirty minutes. Red lentils are classic in Indian cooking.

LIMA BEANS. Creamy lima beans become soft and nearly melt in your mouth when cooked. They are delicious on their own or added to soups or stews.

NAVY BEANS. Also called *cannellini beans,* navy beans are small, white, and a popular addition to soups, stews, salads, and pasta dishes.

PINTO BEANS. The medium-sized brown pinto bean is popular in Latin American, Caribbean, and Mediterranean dishes, including soups, salads, stews, and wraps.

Cooking Beans

When cooking dried beans, use the following table as a guideline. It provides the amount of water needed to cook a variety of different beans, along with their cooking times and approximate yields. For additional information, see "Preparing Dried Beans" on pages 14 and 15.

Bean Type (1 Cup)	Water	Cooking Time	Yield
Aduki	4 cups	1½ hours	2 cups
Anasazi	3 cups	1½ hours	2 cups
Black	4 cups	1½ hours	2 cups
Chickpeas (garbanzo)	4 cups	3 hours	2 cups
Kidney	3 cups	1½ hours	2 cups
Lentils	3 cups	20 minutes	2¼ cups
Lima	2 cups	1½ hours	1¼ cups
Navy (cannellini)	3 cups	1½ hours	2 cups
Pinto	3 cups	1½ hours	2 cups
Soybeans	4 cups	3 hours or more	2 cups
Split peas	3 cups	45 minutes	2¼ cups

SOYBEANS. An excellent source of protein, essential fatty acids, vitamins, and minerals, the simple soybean has been a main crop of Eastern Asia for thousands of years. A number of traditional natural foods, including tofu, tempeh, and soymilk, are derived from soybeans.

SPLIT PEAS. This classic soup ingredient does not require presoaking. Split peas soften and even dissolve when cooked, resulting in creamy-textured soups and sauces.

TEMPEH. Made from cooked and fermented soybeans, tempeh is high in protein, easy to digest, and cholesterol free. It has a meaty texture that lends itself to sautéing, baking, broiling, and steaming. Tempeh is a great addition to sushi, sandwiches, and stews.

TOFU. Also called *bean curd*, tofu is made from soybeans and *nigari* (a sea salt extract). Cholesterol-free, low calorie, high in protein and calcium, tofu is available in extra-firm, firm, soft, and silky tex-

PREPARING DRIED BEANS

Fresh beans or legumes vary in size, appearance, and flavor. They contain moisture, which means they have a shorter shelf life than dried varieties. Dried beans are categorized as hard, medium-soft, and soft. Soft varieties include lentils and split peas. Aduki, black, lima, navy, and pinto beans are considered medium-soft types. Beans such as chickpeas and soybeans fall under the hard-bean category. Depending on the type of bean and amount of cooking water, the cooking time will vary (see the table on page 13); however, the following preparation and cooking guidelines are universal.

CLEANING

Packages of dried beans sometimes contain shriveled or discolored beans, or empty shells. Always sort through the dried beans, picking out and discarding those that are blemished. Place the beans in a bowl, cover with water, and swish them around. Discard any beans or shells that float to the top, then transfer the beans to a colander and rinse well.

PRESOAKING

With the exception of certain legumes, such as lentils and split peas, most dried bean varieties benefit from presoaking before they are cooked. Soaking reduces a bean's cooking time, and decreases gas-producing *oligosaccharides*. For this reason, never cook beans in their soaking water. Always rinse and drain them before cooking in a pot of fresh water.

Basically, there are two presoaking methods—slow and quick. Although both are effective, the slow method is preferred because it is better for reducing oligosaccharides.

☑ SLOW-SOAKING METHOD

After the beans are cleaned and rinsed, place them in a large pot or bowl. For every cup of beans, add four cups of cold water. Let the

tures. You can grill, sauté, bake, steam, simmer, and purée the firm and extra-firm varieties. Blend soft and silky tofu into creamy sauces, dressings, pie fillings, and puddings. Tofu's mildly sweet, almost bland taste takes on the flavor of its surrounding ingredients.

MUSHROOMS ——————

Mushrooms, both cultivated and wild, have a distinctive fresh, earthy flavor that adds depth to many dishes, particularly those without meat. When properly stored, fresh mushrooms will keep up to two weeks, depending on the variety. Either refrigerate them in a cloth bag (avoid plastic, which speeds deterioration), or arrange them in a shallow basket lined with paper towels. Be aware that some wild mushrooms may look similar to edible types, but they are actually poisonous. Unless you know the difference, *never* forage for wild mushrooms.

BLACK TRUMPET. Named for its trumpet-like shape, the wild black trumpet is a member of the chanterelle family and tastes like bacon. Available fresh from fall to spring, and dried all year round,

beans soak a minimum of four hours and a maximum of twelve. If you are soaking for four hours, you can do so at room temperature. However, if you are soaking for a longer period, the beans may begin to ferment, so place them in the refrigerator. Generally, hard-bean varieties require about six to eight hours soaking time, while medium-soft varieties need four to six. Soft beans do not require any soaking.

☑ QUICK-SOAKING METHOD

Once the beans are cleaned and rinsed, place them in a large pot. For every cup of beans, add four cups of water. Bring to a boil over high heat, then reduce the heat to low and simmer seven to ten minutes. Cover the pot, turn off the heat, and let soak at least one hour, or approximately half the time required for that particular bean when slow soaked (see above).

COOKING

Rinse the soaked beans and place them in a pot along with fresh water (see the Cooking Beans table on page 13 for the proper water amount). Bring to a boil, reduce the heat to medium-low, and cover. Simmer gently until the beans are plump and tender. Avoid boiling, as this will cause the skins to burst and result in a mushy bean. The beans are ready when you can easily mash them with a fork. Also keep in mind that old beans may take longer to cook.

Generally, one cup of dried beans yields three cups when cooked. To allow for this expansion, always use a large pot or kettle. Do not add salt or acidic ingredients (tomatoes, lemon juice) to the pot until the beans are tender and nearly cooked. Acidic foods cause the beans to become tough, resulting in longer cooking time. When cooking at high altitudes, water boils at a lower temperature, which causes the beans to cook slower. To hasten cooking time, add a little baking soda to the cooking water (about one-quarter teaspoon baking soda per cup of water). This will also help soften the outer skin of the beans. Pressure-cooking is another option.

black trumpets are delicious additions to eggs, pasta, and risotto.

BLEWITT. A wild fall mushroom that is white with streaks of blue, the blewitt is similar in flavor to the oyster mushroom only stronger. Blewitts are a good choice for sautés; they are also delicious when marinated and grilled.

BLUEFOOT. This cultivated mushroom is a larger, denser version of the blewitt, and a good choice for grilling or adding to sauces or ragouts.

CHANTERELLE. An apricot-colored wild mushroom variety, the chanterelle has a light and slightly delicate, fruity flavor. It is available fresh from summer to winter, and dried all year round. Chanterelles are often sautéed and then added to pasta dishes and omelets; simmered in sauces, soups, and stews; and roasted with vegetables and grains.

CRIMINI. Also known as *baby portabellas*, cultivated crimini mushrooms are similar to white button mushrooms in size, but denser with a deeper, earthier flavor. They are delicious in soups, sauces, stews, and grain dishes.

LOBSTER. Sometimes called *chicken of the woods,* this wild summer mushroom is available dried all year round. Reddish orange in color, the lobster mushroom has a flavor and texture similar to chicken. Very versatile, it can be sautéed, grilled, and stir-fried; a delicious addition to sauces, soups, and stews.

MAITAKE. This firm, fleshy wild fall mushroom has a delicate earthy flavor and is available dried all year long. It is also known as *hen of the woods* because one maitake stem sprouts several caps, giving it the appearance of a fluffed-up feathered hen. Maitake are used in soups, stews, and sautés.

MATSUTAKE. A wild, slightly peppery flavored mushroom, the matsutake is harvested in summer and fall and available dried all year long. It is a great addition to soups, stews, pilafs, grain dishes, and sautés.

MOREL. Harvested in the spring and summer, wild morels are available dried all year round. Their meaty texture and nutty, earthy taste make them perfect additions to pasta dishes, sautés, pilafs, stews, and sauces. Stems of morel mushrooms are also edible.

MOUSSERON. This wild mushroom is small and delicate with an earthy flavor. Also known as *fairy rings* or *Scotch bonnets,* mousserons are available fresh in the spring and fall, and dried all year round. Add them to stews and casseroles, as well as pasta, grain, and egg dishes.

OYSTER. These mild flavored, velvety textured mushrooms have ear-shaped fluted caps and range in color from light beige to gray to oyster white. Cultivated fresh varieties are available all year round; wild varieties are harvested in the summer. Oyster mushrooms are best sautéed and then added to soups, sauces, or casseroles.

PORCINI. Considered "King of the Wild Mushrooms," porcini, also called *cepes,* have a woodsy, nutty flavor and velvety texture, making them excellent in sauces, stuffings, rice dishes, casseroles, and stews. They are also good raw. Due to their strong flavor, a little goes a long way—two tablespoons of dried porcini is equivalent in flavor to three cups of fresh crimini or white button mushrooms.

PORTABELLA. These cultivated jumbo mushrooms are known for their deep woodsy taste and meaty texture. Portabellas are delicious grilled, roasted, and sautéed, or simmered in soups and stews.

SHIITAKE. Available fresh and dried throughout the year, cultivated shiitake have broad, spongy umbrella-shaped caps and range in color from tan to dark brown. Popular for their rich, nutty flavor and meaty texture, shiitake are great sautéed and grilled; added to stir-fries, eggs, and tofu dishes; and simmered in soups, sauces, and stews. They can also be added raw to salads. Shiitake are also called *oak, Chinese,* and *Black Forest* mushrooms.

WHITE BUTTON. The most widely cultivated mushroom in the United States, the all-purpose white button has a mild woodsy taste that intensifies when cooked. Enjoyed raw or cooked, button mushrooms can be added to just about any type of dish.

WOOD EARS. Fresh varieties of this wild ear-shaped mushroom, also called *tree ears,* are black and shiny; dried, they are dark brown and dull-textured. Used more for their crisp, chewy texture than their taste, wood ears are popular in Asian dishes, including soups, stir-fries, and egg rolls. Smaller varieties are known as *cloud ears.*

VEGETABLES ————————————

In addition to standard vegetables, the following not-as-common varieties add both visual and palatable interest to many of the recipes in this book. Most are available at major supermarkets, ethnic and farmer's markets, and gourmet food shops.

BOK CHOY. Also spelled *bok choi,* this sweet, crisp Chinese vegetable looks similar to celery. Its long smooth stalks are white in color and topped with dark green leaves. Use bok choy in soups, salads, and stir-fries.

BURDOCK. Called *gobo* in Japan, this wild root vegetable is carrot shaped and used in soups, sautés, stews, and sauces. It is also used to flavor vinegars.

CHINESE CABBAGE. Also known as *Napa cabbage,* Chinese cabbage resembles romaine lettuce. It has light green leaves that are slightly sweet. When young and tender, it is often chopped or shredded and used as a salad green. Quicker cooking than standard cabbage, Chinese cabbage is also sautéed and enjoyed as a side dish, or added to stir-fries, soups, and egg rolls.

COLLARDS. These hearty leafy greens, sometimes called *collard greens,* belong to the cabbage family. They have long stalks topped with dark oval leaves, and are high in calcium, iron, and vitamins A and C. Both the leaves and stems can be sautéed, steamed, or simmered in soup or stews.

DAIKON. This large, sharp-tasting, white Asian radish is fresh, crisp, and juicy. It is eaten raw in salads, shredded and used as a garnish, and cooked in dishes like soups, stews, and stir-fries.

JICAMA. Also called a *Mexican potato,* jicama (pronounced HEE·kah·mah) is a tuber from Central America and Mexico. It is low in sodium and high in vitamin C. Raw jicama is crunchy, sweet, and juicy—perfect to toss into a salad or enjoy with a dip. When lightly cooked, it becomes milder but stays crisp—a good choice for stir-fries and stews.

MACHE. A tender, mild-flavored green with a sweet nutty flavor, mache is a delicious addition to green salads.

MIZUNA. This Japanese green has dandelion-like jagged leaves with a mild mustard flavor. An excellent addition to salads, mizuna also cooks quickly and is good in soup and stir-fries.

MUSTARD GREENS. High in calcium, iron, and vitamins A and C, the peppery leaves of the mustard plant are delicious in salads, soups, sushi, and stir-fries.

TAT SOI. Also known as *Chinese flat cabbage,* tat soi looks like baby spinach; it has dark green spoon-shaped leaves and sweet crunchy stalks. Tat soi is often mixed with other greens in a salad, and can be added to soups and stir-fries.

SEA VEGETABLES ————————————

Edible plants that are harvested from the sea are fat-free, low in calories, and rich in vitamins and minerals. They are available in most natural foods stores and Asian markets.

AGAR-AGAR. Derived from various species of red algae, flavorless agar-agar (also called simply *agar*) is used primarily as a thickener for jams, pie fillings, puddings, gelatins (kanten), fruit molds, candies, and aspics. High in calcium, iodine, fiber, and trace minerals, agar is available in powder, flakes, and bars. Add one tablespoon of flakes or a half-teaspoon of powder per cup of liquid.

ALARIA. Similar to Japanese wakame, alaria is a leafy, mild-flavored seaweed that is harvested off the coast of Maine. It is high in calcium, potassium, vitamin A, and some B vitamins, including B_{12}. Alaria must be simmered at least forty-five minutes, and is a delicious addition to soups and bean stews.

ARAME. After this black, mildly sweet Japanese sea vegetable is harvested, it is shredded into thin strips (similar to angel hair pasta) and dried. Sodium-free, arame is rich in calcium, iodine, and potassium. To rehydrate, soak in water or broth for five minutes. For added color, flavor, and nutrition, toss arame into salads, soups, stir-fries, stews, or vegetable dishes.

DULSE. A soft, leafy, maroon-colored Maine sea vegetable, mild-flavored dulse is similar in taste to potato chips. It contains vitamin B_{12} and is high in potassium, phosphorus, iron, protein, and vitamin C. Dulse can be eaten raw as a snack or tossed into salads; it can also be simmered (five minutes is all it needs) in soups and stews, or added to bean, vegetable, or grain dishes. Use dulse in any recipe that calls for wakame.

HIZIKI. A spaghetti-like black Japanese sea vegetable, hiziki is sodium-free, rich in vitamin A and iron, and highest in calcium of all the sea vegetables. To rehydrate, simply soak hiziki for five minutes before adding it to salads, egg rolls, stir-fries, and stews.

KELP. Thin and delicate, kelp is a leafy variety of kombu that is high in iron, iodine, fiber, and calcium; it also helps reduce high blood pressure. Kelp that is harvested in Washington State is crisp like a potato chip and great for snacking. It can be ground into a powder, combined with toasted sesame seeds, and used instead of table salt or as a condiment to sprinkle on soups, rice, popcorn, and other foods. Kelp that is harvested from Maine melts into soups, beans, and stews with long cooking.

KOMBU. A versatile sea vegetable, kombu is sold dried in flat sheets or strips, and is most commonly used as a flavoring agent. It is a good source of calcium, sugar, potassium, iodine, vitamin A, glutamic acid, and B-complex vitamins. Kombu adds flavor to soups and stews. Small pieces may be added to a pot of cooking beans for improved flavor and digestibility. Once cooked, kombu can either be removed from the pot or allowed to cook further and dissolve. Ocean ribbons kombu, which is harvested off the coast of California, is the most tender and quick-cooking variety.

NORI. Dried and pressed into thin sheets, nori ranges in color from dark green to purplish black. The toasted sheets are ready to eat as a snack, garnish, or condiment. They are also ideal wrappers for various rice and vegetable rolls. Nori is sodium-free and rich in protein, iron, and vitamins A, B_2, and B_{12}.

SEA PALM. The "fettuccine" of sea vegetables, sea palm—the dark-green fronds of miniature marine palm trees—hails from the California coast. It is succulent and mildly sweet, making it a delicious addition to salads, sautés, stews, and noodle dishes. Rich in trace minerals, sea palm can also be pickled, or toasted and enjoyed as a condiment or snack.

WAKAME. This dark-green sea leaf, harvested in California and Japan, is high in calcium, vitamin B_{12}, and alginic acid, which cleanses heavy metals like lead and mercury from the digestive tract. Wakame's sweet taste and delicate texture make it a welcome ingredient in soups, particularly miso soup. It is also a wonderful complement to beans, noodles, marinated salads, and stir-fries.

COOKING OILS

Oil enhances the flavor of food, promotes browning, and prevents sticking. The following oils are used throughout this book.

CANOLA OIL. Mild in flavor, neutral-tasting canola oil is a good choice for baking and deep-frying. It has approximately 6-percent less saturated fat than other oils.

OLIVE OIL. The foundation of the Mediterranean diet for thousands of years, olive oil lends incomparable flavor to sautés, dressings, soups, stews, and sauces. Extra-virgin olive oil, which comes from the first pressing of the olives, is the finest. It is the most flavorful, aromatic, and least acidic of all the olive oils. Extra-virgin olive oil is my favorite choice for making flavored oils. (See Chapter 5 for recipes.)

SESAME OIL. Made from pressed sesame seeds, this oil lends an Asian/Middle Eastern accent to marinades, sauces, and salad dressings. Low in saturated fat, sesame oil is also ideal for light sautéing. Toasted sesame oil, pressed from toasted seeds, has a very strong sesame flavor and aroma. Just a little gives dressings, stir-fries, marinades, sauces, tofu, and noodle and grain dishes a decidedly Asian taste. When used in cooked foods, toasted sesame oil should be added at the end of the cooking process.

NOODLES

The following noodle varieties, which are used in many of the recipes in this book, are staples in the Asian cuisine.

BIFUN. Transparent and quick cooking, these vermicelli-like noodles are made from rice flour and potato starch. They are commonly added to soups, salads, and stir-fries.

SOBA. Thick and spaghetti-like, quick-cooking soba noodles are made from buckwheat flour or a combination of buckwheat and wheat flour. Some varieties contain other ingredients such as dried mugwort powder, wild yam flour, powdered green tea, or kamut. Soba noodles are typically enjoyed with dipping sauce, or added to various hot and cold dishes.

UDON. Flat in shape and quick cooking, udon noodles are made of wheat flour or a combination of wheat and brown rice (genmai) flours. Some may contain flour made from kamut or spelt. Traditionally, udon noodles are served in a broth with shiitake mushrooms, but they can be added to other hot and cold dishes as well.

SWEETENERS

In addition to granulated sugar and honey, the following "sweet" options are available.

BARLEY MALT SYRUP. A liquid sweetener made from roasted sprouted barley, barley malt syrup tastes like caramel and is about half as sweet as sugar or honey.

DATE SUGAR. More a food than a sweetener, date sugar is made from ground dehydrated dates. It is high in fiber, B vitamins, and iron. Date sugar is useful in baked goods, but does not dissolve well in liquids.

MAPLE SUGAR. Flavorful maple sugar is a crystallized form of maple syrup, and commonly used in baking.

MAPLE SYRUP. Made from the boiled down sap

of the sugar maple tree, maple syrup is a popular choice for drizzling over pancakes and waffles. It is also a commonly used sweetener in many baked goods.

MIRIN. This sweetened rice wine is a high-quality, low-alcohol sweetener for sauces, glazes, and a number of dishes. Mirin varieties that contain salt add savory flavor to dishes.

RICE SYRUP. Light, delicate, and half as sweet as sugar, rice syrup is made by converting the starch that is found in rice into sugar. Some are flavored with ingredients such as fruit, maple, and chocolate. Syrups made with brown rice are darker in color but similar in taste. This sweetener is also available in powdered form.

SUCANAT. A granulated, dark organic sweetener obtained from evaporated sugar cane juice, Sucanat contains small amounts of calcium, iron, and vitamins A and C.

VINEGARS

Since ancient times, the versatility of vinegar has been noted. In addition to its role as an antiseptic, a cleaning solution, and a medicine, vinegar has played a vital role as a flavoring agent and food preservative. Made primarily from fruits and grains, vinegars possess distinctive flavors, colors, and aromas, depending on their origin.

BALSAMIC VINEGAR. Aromatic, strong flavored, and sweet tasting, balsamic vinegar is produced in the Modena and Reggio regions of Italy, where it is aged in fragrant wooden casks for a minimum of six years—although most varieties age for decades.

RICE VINEGAR. Made from rice wine, mellow-tasting rice vinegar is light in color and has a low

acid level. Varieties derived from brown rice (labeled "brown rice vinegar") have greater nutritional value than those made from white rice, which often contain additives. Rice vinegar is a great substitute for lime juice.

UMEBOSHI PLUM VINEGAR. This salty lemony seasoning, also called *ume su*, is technically not a vinegar, but rather the ruby red juice that comes from pickled umeboshi plums. Ume has an alkalizing effect on digestion, and is a good alternative to soy sauce, lemon juice, and salt.

WINE VINEGAR. Red and white are the two main types of wine vinegar. Each comes from grapes of the same color. Red wine vinegar is full bodied, while the white is more delicate in flavor.

OTHER INGREDIENTS

A number of additional ingredients that are called for in this book are described below.

ARROWROOT. Used like cornstarch, this thickening agent comes from the roots of the tropical arrowroot plant. A good binder for meatless loaves that do not contain eggs, arrowroot is also used to thicken stews, sauces, and puddings.

BRAGG LIQUID AMINOS. Similar to soy sauce, this unfermented liquid protein contains essential and nonessential amino acids.

CAPERS. The pickled tiny green flower buds of a prickly Mediterranean bush, capers are used to add a distinctively Mediterranean flavor to salads, sauces, stews, and roasted vegetables.

CHESTNUTS, DRIED. After hydrating dried chestnuts by presoaking them overnight, cook them and their soaking water along with grains, beans, or vegetable for an incomparable smoky flavor.

FLAXSEEDS. Tiny, nutty-flavored flaxseeds are a rich source of beneficial omega-3 fatty acids and vitamin E. They also aid in the digestion of fiber-rich whole grains. You can purchase the seeds whole or ground (you can grind them yourself in a spice or coffee grinder) and sprinkle them on cereal and salads. The ground meal can take the place of eggs in pancake batters, pie crusts, and quick breads. Flax flour, made from defatted flax-seeds, boosts the nutritional content of baked goods. Flaxseed oil is good in salads and drizzled over cooked foods.

KUDZU. Also spelled *kuzu*, this powdery white starch comes from the root of the wild kudzu plant. It is used as a thickener in soups, stews, sauces, jellies, and jams.

MISO. A fermented paste made from beans, grains, and salt, miso has been a staple seasoning in Japan for thousands of years. It is used primarily as a flavoring agent for soups, stews, and marinades, and comes in a variety of flavors, depending on the bean or grain from which it is made. Light-colored white or yellow misos, which are aged from three to six months, are delicate flavored and typically used in cream sauces, light soups, and salad dressings. Dark-colored misos, which are aged from one to three years, are strong flavored and added to hearty winter soups and stews. In addition to its role as flavoring agent and salt substitute, miso has been shown to aid digestion. It has also been effective in the prevention and treatment of certain cancers, heart disease, and hypertension.

NUT BUTTERS. Unsweetened and free of hydro-genated oils, natural nut and seed butters and spreads are readily available in most grocery and health food stores. Made from almonds, cashews, hazelnuts, peanuts, pecans, and sunflower seeds, they are cholesterol free and a rich source of protein and calcium. Although they are high in fat, the fat is primarily unsaturated. When baking and cooking, use nut and seed spreads in place of butter.

SEITAN. Made by slow-simmering the gluten found in whole wheat flour, seitan (sometimes called *wheat meat*) is a high-protein meat substitute. Like tofu, it picks up the flavors of surrounding foods or liquids, and can be substituted for meat in just about any recipe.

TAHINI. A nondairy butter made from sesame seeds, tahini is high in calcium and iron. Use it in dressings, sauces, spreads, and stews for a rich, creamy texture and Middle Eastern flavor.

TAMARI. This traditional Japanese wheat-free soy sauce is the rich dark liquid that pools on the surface of fermenting miso. Tamari's flavor stands up under high heat, making it a good choice for a wide range of dishes—from soups and sauces to stir-fries and stews.

UMEBOSHI PASTE. This sour, salty-tasting purée is made from pickled umeboshi plums. It is a lively seasoning that is typically used to flavor salad dressings, dips, cooked vegetables, and sauces. It is also spread on toasted nori when making sushi.

FOOD PREPARATION AND COOKING METHODS

Proper food preparation and cooking methods are important components of good cuisine as they help develop a food's flavor and enhance its texture and appearance. When preparing the recipes found in the book, you will come across the following terms:

AL DENTE. Literally translated as "to the bite," al dente describes grains, pasta, or vegetables that are cooked until tender, yet still firm "to the bite."

BAKE. To cook in an oven with dry heat, usually set a temperature between 250°F and 375°F.

BOIL. To heat liquid until bubbles appear on the surface.

BROIL. To cook food by placing it beneath the direct heat of an oven broiler or over an open fire.

CHOP. To cut food into irregular-shaped pieces.

DEEP-FRY. To cook food by submerging it completely in hot fat, resulting in a crisp browned crust and thoroughly cooked interior. The high heat of the fat prevents it from being absorbed into the food.

DICE. To cut food into small ($\frac{1}{8}$ to 1-inch) cubes.

DRY ROAST. To brown grains, nuts, or seeds in an unoiled skillet on top of the stove, or on a cookie sheet in the oven.

FRY. A general term for cooking food in fat.

GRATE. To grind or shred foods using a hand grater or food processor.

GRILL. To cook foods quickly over high heat on either an indoor or outdoor grill.

JULIENNE. To slice food into thin strips resembling wooden matchsticks.

MARINATE. To steep food in a seasoned liquid before cooking.

MINCE. To chop food very finely.

PAN-FRY. To cook food in a small amount of fat.

ROAST. To cook with dry heat, usually in an oven, at a temperature between 400°F and 500°F.

SAUTÉ. To brown or cook food lightly in an open pan over direct heat.

SIMMER. To slowly and gently cook liquid just at or below the boiling point.

STEAM. To cook food in a vented container over boiling water.

STIR-FRY. To cook food over high heat while lightly tossing and stirring constantly.

LET'S GET STARTED

There isn't a recipe I prepare that's etched in stone, and I don't encourage yours to be either. Improvise. The more you cook, the easier it becomes to experiment. Calm and confident, you can focus, choose ingredients, rinse and chop, mix and taste. Let your inner wisdom act as your guide.

Like jazz, good cooking balances skill and intuition. Feel free to prepare the recipes in the following chapters exactly as written, or use them as springboards for your own culinary improvisations. Rely on your instincts and creative whims to make use of whatever ingredients are in season or on hand. Anyone can do it. Come on, it's time to get started. Let's go wild in the kitchen!

2

Morning Bliss

I love breakfast! Whether it's warm from the oven, hot off the stove, or straight from the blender, I find it hard to start the day without the pleasure of a good meal.

Depending on my mood (and what's on hand in the pantry), breakfast choices can be hot, cold, savory, or sweet. Some days, a hearty dish of eggs with veggie bacon, a goat cheese omelet, or a tofu scramble is perfect for satisfying the lumberjack in me. On hot days, for a quick no-fuss breakfast, refreshing fruit smoothies are a natural choice. When the weather turns brisk, nothing warms me like a bowl of hot porridge. On some winter mornings, I bake up some fresh granola, sweet scones, or quick breakfast cakes that taste like muffins. I must confess—I have always loved sweet treats and I enjoy them for breakfast. If there is some leftover pie or apple crisp from the day before,

there's a good chance that I will have it in the morning along with a cup of piping hot tea. And when time is not an issue, I make a stack of delicious waffles or pancakes, especially those made with teff flour. I do not know what it is about teff pancakes, but I never grow tired of them.

The following collection of breakfast recipes includes a number of my favorites. Prepare them as presented or try your own unique variations. To encourage your culinary creativity, the "Mix and Match" chart on page 24, provides alternative ingredient ideas for juices, milks, oils, yogurts, sweeteners, and salty seasonings.

No matter what your breakfast preference—whether you are an occasional or traditional vegetarian, a vegan, or someone who requires a wheat-free diet—you'll find plenty of healthy and delicious choices to start your day on the following pages.

MIX AND MATCH

Creating various tastes, textures, and eye-appealing colors for the breakfast recipes in this chapter can be achieved by substituting one ingredient for another. The chart below provides some wonderful ingredient alternatives.

Go Wild for Breakfast

MILKS	Almond milk, cow's milk, goat's milk, oat milk, plain or vanilla rice milk, plain or vanilla soymilk, and juice.*
JUICES	Apple juice, apricot juice, cherry juice, cranberry nectar, pear juice, raspberry juice, and milk.*
YOGURTS	Varieties made with cow's milk, goat's milk, sheep's milk, soymilk.
SWEETENERS**	DRY: Granulated sugar, date sugar, maple sugar, and Sucanat.
	LIQUID: Honey, maple syrup, molasses, rice syrup, and barley malt.
OILS	Almond oil, canola oil, coconut oil, corn oil, hazelnut oil, light olive oil, safflower oil, sunflower oil, and unsalted butter.
SALTY SEASONINGS	Shoyu, tamari, umeboshi vinegar, and Bragg Liquid Aminos.

* For baked goods, substituting juice for milk will offer sweeter results. You can also use a combination of milk and juice.

** For pancakes and waffles, small amounts of dry and liquid sweeteners (up to 1 tablespoon) may be interchanged. When using liquid sweeteners in larger quantities (for cakes that need to rise) you can swap $\frac{1}{2}$ cup maple syrup with $\frac{1}{2}$ cup honey or $\frac{1}{3}$ cup molasses. Do not use barley malt or rice syrup in my cake recipes.

Raspberry-Almond Smoothie

Almond milk is a delicious low-fat vegan alternative to cow's milk. Using frozen berries in this smoothie creates a cold, refreshing drink—perfect for the start of a hot summer day.

1. Place all the ingredients in a blender and purée until smooth.

2. Pour into glasses and serve.

FOR A CHANGE . . .

• Substitute pitted cherries, peaches, or blueberries for the raspberries.

Yield: About 4$\frac{1}{2}$ cups
. . . .
2$\frac{1}{2}$ cups fresh or frozen raspberries

2 cups almond milk

1 cup plain yogurt

$\frac{1}{4}$ cup maple syrup

$\frac{1}{2}$ teaspoon almond extract

$\frac{1}{4}$ teaspoon nutmeg

Cranberry-Banana Smoothie

Bananas and peach juice naturally sweeten the beautiful tart red cranberries in this luscious smoothie.

1. Place all the ingredients in a blender and purée until smooth.

2. Pour into glasses and serve.

FOR A CHANGE . . .

• Substitute strawberries, peaches, or blackberries for the cranberries.

Yield: About 6 cups
. . . .
3 small bananas or 2 large

1 cup fresh or frozen cranberries

2 cups vanilla soymilk

1 cup peach juice

$\frac{1}{2}$ cup plain cow, goat, sheep, or soy yogurt

Vanilla-Scented Bulgur with Dried Cherries and Toasted Walnuts

Thanks goes to noted natural foods chef and restaurant owner Jesse Cool Ziff for inspiring this sweet breakfast—a fortified meal of grains, nuts, yogurt, and fruit.

Yield: 4 servings

2 cups water

1/3 cup dried pitted cherries

2-inch-piece vanilla bean, halved lengthwise

1 cup bulgur wheat

1/4 teaspoon sea salt

1/2 cup walnuts

2 cups plain yogurt

1. Place the water, cherries, and vanilla bean in a 1-quart saucepan, and bring to a boil over medium heat.

2. Add the bulgur and salt, reduce the heat to low, and simmer 10 minutes or until the water is absorbed and the bulgur is tender. Remove the vanilla bean.

3. While the bulgur simmers, place the walnuts in a small unoiled skillet over medium-low heat. Stirring occasionally, dry-roast the walnuts for 5 minutes, or until they darken and become fragrant.

4. Spoon the hot bulgur into bowls, top with yogurt and walnuts, and serve.

FOR A CHANGE . . .

• Instead of vanilla bean, use 1 teaspoon vanilla extract. Stir it into the mixture once the bulgur is cooked.

Coconut Pecan Granola

Shredded coconut and cinnamon make this granola taste like a sweet cookie. Ground flaxseeds, rich in omega-3 fatty acids and vitamin E, easily replace flour—a common ingredient in most granolas. Feel free to go wild with substitutions, too. Use different oils, flakes, flours, sweeteners, extracts, and nuts. Just about every ingredient can change and still offer the same delicious results.

1. Preheat the oven to 325°F. Lightly oil a large baking sheet and set aside.

2. Place all of the ingredients in a large bowl and mix well. Spread the mixture onto the baking sheet.

3. Bake for 50 to 60 minutes, stirring occasionally, until the mixture is browned and crisp. Remove from the oven and let cool.

4. Enjoy as a cereal with milk, soymilk, or rice drink. Store any leftovers in an airtight container.

FOR A CHANGE . . .

• Replace ground flaxseeds with teff flour, almond meal (flour), or hazelnut flour.

• Substitute 1 cup of the rolled oats with wheat or barley flakes.

• Omit the coconut.

• Add dates, raisins, or dried apples to the granola after it has cooled.

• Instead of (or in combination with) the pecans or cashews, use other nuts and seeds, such as walnuts, almonds, hazelnuts, and sunflower seeds.

Yield: About 5 cups

• • • • • • •

3 cups rolled oats

$2/_3$ cup raw pecans halves or whole cashews

$1/_2$ cup shredded coconut

$1/_2$ cup ground flaxseeds

$1/_2$ cup maple syrup

$1/_3$ cup canola oil

2 tablespoons vanilla

I teaspoon cinnamon

Pinch sea salt

Super Breakfast Porridge

Get your day off to an energized start with this nutritious porridge made of quinoa and amaranth.

Yield: 4 servings

. . . .

$^1/_2$ cup quinoa, rinsed

$^1/_2$ cup amaranth

$2^1/_2$ cups boiling water

Pinch sea salt or nori flakes

1. Place all the ingredients in a 2-quart saucepan. Cover and bring to a boil over medium-high heat. Reduce the heat to low and simmer 20 minutes, or until the water is absorbed and the grains are tender.

2. Serve hot, either as is or topped with your favorite milk, yogurt, or maple syrup.

FOR A CHANGE . . .

• Add $^1/_2$ cup shredded coconut, toasted nuts, or seeds to the mixture before boiling.

Porridge With Coconut and Dates

This porridge, made with teff and rolled oats, is one of my winter morning favorites. Although this recipe is for one serving, it can be easily multiplied.

Yield: 1 serving

. . . .

$^1/_2$ cup rolled oats

$^1/_2$ cup pitted chopped dates

2 tablespoons teff

2 tablespoons shredded coconut

1 teaspoon cinnamon

Pinch sea salt

$1^2/_3$ cups water

1. Place all the ingredients in a 1-quart saucepan, adding the water last. Cover and bring to a boil over medium heat. Reduce the heat to low and simmer 10 minutes, or until the teff is tender and the mixture begins to thicken.

2. Turn off the heat and let sit for 5 minutes to absorb the remaining liquid.

3. Serve hot, either as is or topped with your favorite milk, yogurt, or maple syrup.

Goat Cheese Omelet with Chanterelle Mushrooms and Ramps

While it is certainly exotic to use wild mushrooms like chanterelles, common white button mushrooms are perfectly acceptable alternatives. Ramps, also called wild leeks, can be replaced with chives or scallions.

1. In a large mixing bowl, beat the eggs with a whisk or fork. Add the mushrooms, ramps, and salt and pepper, if using. Set aside.

2. Heat the oil in a medium-sized skillet over medium-low heat. Add the egg mixture and cook 2 to 3 minutes, stirring gently until the mixture begins to set. Crumble the chèvre over half the eggs. Using a spatula, gently fold the other half over the cheese.

3. Continue to cook the omelet until the cheese melts. Serve immediately.

FOR A CHANGE . . .

• Use ½ cup grated cheddar or mozzarella instead of chèvre.

Yield: 2 servings

• • • • • • • •

4 eggs

³/₄ cups coarsely chopped chanterelle caps

¹/₄ cup coarsely chopped ramps

¹/₄ teaspoon sea salt, optional

Pinch fresh black pepper, optional

1 tablespoon extra virgin olive oil

3 ounces chèvre

Scrambled Tofu With Garlic Scapes

Yield: 2 to 4 servings

• • • • • • • •

1 tablespoon basil oil or extra virgin olive oil

5 garlic scapes or thickly sliced garlic cloves

1 cup green beans, cut into 1-inch slices

$2/3$ cup diced red bell pepper

$1/2$ cup coarsely chopped red onion

1 teaspoon turmeric

1 pound soft tofu, cut into $1/2$-inch cubes

2 cups coarsely chopped tat soi or spinach

$1/2$ cup coarsely chopped basil

4 tablespoons nutritional yeast

1 tablespoon tamari

Available fresh in summer, scapes are the tender curly green stems with white flowers that rise from the garlic plant. They impart incredible garlicky flavor to this breakfast scramble, in which tofu takes on a yellow color (thanks to the turmeric) and resembles eggs.

1. Heat the oil in a medium-sized skillet over medium heat. Add the garlic scapes, beans, bell pepper, onion, and turmeric, and sauté, stirring occasionally for 3 to 5 minutes, or until the vegetables brighten in color and become fragrant.

2. Add the tofu and combine with the ingredients. Continue to cook 3 minutes, or until the tofu is yellow in color.

3. Stir in the tat soi, and cook about 1 minute or until it begins to wilt. Add the basil to the mixture, cook a minute, then turn off the heat. Stir in the yeast and tamari.

4. Adjust the seasonings, if desired, then serve immediately.

FOR A CHANGE . . .

• Change the flavors of this scramble by substituting cilantro for the basil, collards for the tat soi, corn for the bell pepper, and/or scallions for the red onion.

• Use firm or extra-firm tofu for different textures.

Scrambled Tofu with Tomatoes and Fresh Basil

For a spectacularly simple scrambled tofu dish, combine turmeric, nutritional yeast, and tamari with just about any vegetable and herb of the season. This variation, which I serve for breakfast along with sourdough bread, is a summer staple in my home.

1. Heat the oil in a medium-sized skillet over medium heat. Add the zucchini, carrots, and celery, and sauté, stirring occasionally for 3 to 5 minutes, or until the vegetables brighten in color.

2. Add the turmeric, tomatoes, and bell pepper. Continue to sauté 2 to 3 minutes, add the tofu, and mix the ingredients well. Sauté another 3 to 5 minutes, then stir in the basil, yeast, and tamari.

3. Adjust the seasonings, if desired, and serve immediately.

FOR A CHANGE . . .

• Use soft or extra-firm tofu for different textures.

• To add color to the dish, use various types of bell peppers—red, orange, and/or yellow.

• During fall and winter seasons, use vegetables such as collards and scallions, and herbs like cilantro.

• Instead of carrots and celery, use more tomatoes and bell peppers.

Yield: 4 to 6 servings

• • • • • • •

1 tablespoon sesame or extra virgin olive oil

1 cup coarsely chopped zucchini

$1/2$ cup julienned carrots

$1/2$ cup coarsely chopped celery

$1/2$ teaspoon turmeric

$1 1/2$ cups coarsely chopped plum tomatoes

1 cup coarsely chopped green bell pepper

1 pound firm tofu, cut into $1/2$-inch cubes

$1/2$ cup tightly packed, coarsely chopped basil

2 tablespoons nutritional yeast

1 tablespoon tamari

Berry Good Waffles

With berries or without, these waffles are easy to make and simply delicious. Serve with maple syrup or hot Strawberry Sauce (page 73) for a divine breakfast.

Yield: 4 waffles (about 4-inches)

• • • • • • •

2 eggs

2 cups whole wheat pastry flour

2 tablespoons baking powder

1 teaspoon sea salt

1 1/2 cups apple juice

1/3 cup canola oil

4 tablespoons vanilla

1 cup blueberries or thinly sliced strawberries

1 tablespoon honey, optional

1. Preheat the waffle iron.

2. In a large mixing bowl, beat or whisk the eggs until smooth. Stir in the flour, baking powder, salt, apple juice, oil, vanilla, berries, and honey (if using).

3. If the waffle iron does not have a nonstick surface, brush it with oil. Ladle enough batter to cover the bottom surface of the iron and cook until golden brown.

4. Serve hot with maple syrup, yogurt, or fruit sauce.

FOR A CHANGE . . .

• For chocolate chip waffles, substitute 1 cup dark, milk, or white chocolate chips for the berries.

• For carob waffles, use 1 cup carob chips instead of berries.

• Substitute milk for the apple juice.

TIP . . .

Substituting juice for milk when preparing pancakes, waffles, and other breakfast cakes will offer sweeter pastries.

Applesauce Pancakes

Sweet brown teff flour makes great pancakes that look like they are made of chocolate. This recipe calls for applesauce instead of eggs, which makes a thicker batter. Sometimes, I pick up these pancakes with my hands and eat them like scones. Try them topped with Cinnamon-Vanilla Applesauce (page 74).

1. Place all the ingredients in a large mixing bowl, and stir until well combined.

2. Heat a griddle, cast iron skillet, or large frying pan over medium heat. If it does not have a nonstick surface, brush with oil.

3. Drop heaping tablespoons of batter onto the hot griddle and cook $1\frac{1}{2}$ minutes, or until the tops are bubbly and the edges are dry. Using a spatula, turn the pancakes over and cook another minute, or until the bottoms are brown.

4. Serve immediately with your favorite topping.

FOR A CHANGE . . .

• Try other flavors of applesauce, such as apple-strawberry, apple-apricot, or apple-blackberry.

• Increase the vanilla to 1 tablespoon for stronger flavor.

• Instead of applesauce, use 1 egg, or 2 tablespoons ground flaxseeds and 1 tablespoon honey.

Yield: About 16 pancakes (3 inches)

• • • • • • • •

1 cup teff flour

1 teaspoon baking powder

$\frac{1}{8}$ teaspoon sea salt

$1\frac{1}{4}$ cups apple juice

2 tablespoons applesauce

$1\frac{1}{4}$ teaspoons vanilla

1 teaspoon almond or canola oil

Teff Banana Pancakes

You'll flip for these delicious pancakes, made with naturally sweet teff and bananas. Although my family enjoys them plain or topped with applesauce, they also like dipping them in yogurt and Strawberry Sauce (page 73).

Yield: About 25 pancakes (3 inches)

• • • • • • • •

2 tablespoons flaxseeds

2 ripe bananas

1 1/2 cups vanilla soymilk

1 tablespoon vanilla

1 tablespoon honey

2 teaspoons safflower, almond, or canola oil

1 1/2 cups teff flour

1 tablespoon baking powder

1/2 teaspoon cinnamon

1/4 teaspoon sea salt

1. Place the flaxseeds in a blender and grind until powdery. Add the bananas, soymilk, vanilla, honey, and 1 teaspoon of the oil. Blend well.

2. Combine the flour, baking powder, cinnamon, and salt in a large mixing bowl. Add the banana mixture and stir until well combined.

3. Heat a griddle, cast iron skillet, or large frying pan over medium heat. If it does not have a nonstick surface, brush with the remaining oil.

4. Drop heaping tablespoons of batter onto the hot griddle and cook 1 1/2 minutes, or until the tops are bubbly and the edges are dry. Using a spatula, turn the pancakes over and cook another minute, or until the bottoms are brown.

5. Serve immediately with your favorite topping.

FOR A CHANGE . . .

• Add 1/4 cup coarsely chopped pecans or walnuts to the batter.

• Use maple sugar or rice syrup instead of honey.

• Replace the soymilk with juice.

• Add 2 eggs to the blender along with the bananas for added protein.

Banana-Blueberry Pancakes

Hot off the griddle, these delectable vegan banana-flavored pancakes—bursting with fresh blueberries— are sure to please kids of all ages.

1. Place the banana, rice milk, and apple juice in a blender, and purée until smooth.

2. Combine the flour, baking powder, and salt in a large mixing bowl. Add the banana mixture and blueberries, and stir until well combined.

3. Heat a griddle, cast iron skillet, or large frying pan over medium heat. If it does not have a nonstick surface, brush it with oil.

4. Drop heaping tablespoons of batter onto the hot griddle and cook $1\frac{1}{2}$ minutes, or until the tops are bubbly and the edges are dry. Using a spatula, turn the pancakes over and cook another minute, or until the bottoms are brown.

5. Serve immediately with your favorite topping.

FOR A CHANGE . . .

• Instead of whole wheat pastry flour, use $1\frac{3}{4}$ cups spelt flour, which will give the pancakes a nutty taste.

Yield: About 25 pancakes (3 inches)

• • • • • • •

I ripe banana

I cup rice milk

I cup apple juice

$2\frac{1}{3}$ cups whole wheat pastry flour

5 teaspoons baking powder

$\frac{1}{2}$ teaspoon sea salt

I cup blueberries

Cranberry Scones

If you love cranberries, you will go nuts for these scones,
which you can whip up in just twenty-five minutes.

Yield: 18 scones

• • • • • • • •

3 cups whole wheat
pastry flour

1 tablespoon baking
powder

$\frac{1}{2}$ teaspoon baking
soda

$\frac{1}{4}$ teaspoon
sea salt

$\frac{1}{2}$ cup apple juice

$\frac{1}{2}$ cup honey

$\frac{1}{3}$ cup canola oil

$\frac{3}{4}$ cup fresh or frozen
cranberries

$\frac{1}{4}$ cup raisins

1. Preheat the oven to 350°F. Lightly oil a cookie sheet and set aside.

2. Combine the flour, baking powder, baking soda, and salt in a large mixing bowl. Add the apple juice, honey, oil, cranberries, and raisins, and stir to form a moist dough.

3. Shape the dough into 2$\frac{1}{2}$-inch rounds about $\frac{3}{4}$ inch high. Place them on the cookie sheet about 1 inch apart.

4. Bake for 15 minutes or until lightly browned.

5. Transfer to a cooling rack for 15 minutes, then serve.

FOR A CHANGE . . .

• Instead of apple juice, use vanilla soymilk.

• For an exotic variation, replace the whole wheat pastry flour with a combination of 2$\frac{1}{2}$ cups spelt flour and $\frac{1}{2}$ cup teff flour.

FYI . . .

Cranberries are a rich source of fiber and vitamin C.
They also contain a significant amount of
vitamin A and potassium.

Lemon-Poppy Seed Cake

*Teff, quinoa, and whole wheat pastry flour team up
to lend a delicious twist to this fiber-rich luscious classic.*

1. Preheat the oven to 350°F. Lightly oil an 8-inch loaf pan and set aside.

2. Place the teff in a small bowl. Bring the water to a boil and pour it over the teff. Let stand 10 minutes.

3. Place the apple juice, maple syrup, oil, lemon juice, soymilk, and vanilla in a blender and blend until smooth.

4. Combine the whole wheat flour, teff flour, quinoa flour, poppy seeds, baking powder, and salt in a large mixing bowl. Add the apple juice mixture, teff grain, and zest, and stir until well combined.

5. Spoon the batter into the loaf pan and bake for 45 minutes, or until a toothpick inserted into the center of the cake comes out clean.

6. Allow to cool 30 minutes before serving.

FOR A CHANGE . . .

• Use nutty, earthy-flavored Bhutanese red rice flour instead of quinoa flour.

• For an orange-flavored poppy seed cake, do the following: use orange juice instead of apple juice, omit the lemon juice, and increase the soymilk to $\frac{1}{2}$ cup. Use a combination of $1\frac{1}{2}$ cups whole wheat pastry flour and $\frac{1}{2}$ cup teff flour.

Yield: 8 servings

$\frac{1}{4}$ cup brown teff grain

$\frac{1}{8}$ cup water

$\frac{3}{4}$ cups apple juice

$\frac{1}{2}$ cup maple syrup

$\frac{1}{4}$ cup canola oil

$\frac{1}{4}$ cup lemon juice

$\frac{1}{4}$ cup vanilla soymilk

$\frac{1}{2}$ tablespoon vanilla

I cup whole wheat pastry flour

$\frac{1}{2}$ cup teff flour

$\frac{1}{2}$ cup quinoa flour

$\frac{1}{4}$ cup poppy seeds

I tablespoon baking powder

$\frac{1}{4}$ teaspoon sea salt

$\frac{1}{4}$ teaspoon lemon zest

Blueberry Muffin Cake

Yield: 8 servings

1 1/2 cups whole wheat pastry flour

1/2 cup teff flour

1 tablespoon baking powder

1/4 teaspoon sea salt, optional

3/4 cup apple juice

1/2 cup maple syrup

1/4 cup canola or corn oil

1 tablespoon vanilla

1 cup fresh or frozen blueberries

Although this delectable blueberry cake is good any time of the day, I usually serve it warm as a sweet morning pastry. The teff flour provides extra calcium and iron.

1. Preheat the oven to 350°F. Lightly oil an 8-inch loaf pan and set aside.

2. Place all the ingredients in a large mixing bowl and mix until smooth.

3. Spoon the batter into the loaf pan and bake for 45 minutes, or until a toothpick inserted into the center of the cake comes out clean.

4. Allow to cool 30 minutes before serving.

Blueberry Cornbread

Yield: 8 servings

1 cup cornmeal

3/4 cup whole wheat pastry flour

1/4 cup quinoa flour

2 teaspoons baking powder

1/4 teaspoon sea salt

1 cup apple juice

3/4 cup blueberries

1/4 cup canola oil

1/4 cup maple syrup

1/2 tablespoon vanilla

Quinoa flour adds protein and nutrients to this tasty cornbread.

1. Preheat the oven to 350°F. Lightly oil an 8-inch loaf pan and set aside.

2. Place all the ingredients in a large mixing bowl and mix until smooth.

3. Spoon the batter into the loaf pan and bake for 45 minutes, or until a toothpick inserted into the center of the cake comes out clean.

4. Allow to cool 30 minutes before serving.

3

LoVing Spoonfuls

Throughout the world, soup making is a common ritual. A symphony for the senses, soup magically seems to nourish the body as well as the soul. Sitting down to a steaming hot, fragrant bowl of soup is pure bliss.

Making soup is fun and easy—a large pot, a sharp knife, and a handful of ingredients are all you need for most recipes. This chapter offers a wide variety of my favorite soup sensations, ranging from the light and simple to thick and hearty blends. I've also included important soup-making basics and helpful tips and suggestions for successful results. You'll find full-bodied vegetable soups, such as Asparagus with Fresh Fennel and Golden Split Pea, that are perfumed with herbs and spices, and make wonderful first courses or light meals. For more substantial main-course offerings, soups like Curried Split Pea with Chard and the very filling Minestrone with Oyster Mushrooms, Nettles, and Calendula Flowers are sure to fill the bill. Such palate-pleasing choices need only some whole grain bread and a fresh salad to round out the meal and satisfy the heartiest of appetites.

Although cheese is offered as an optional garnish, all of the recipes presented are rich, robust, and vegan (eggless and dairy-free). This doesn't mean that the chapter is without "cream" soup varieties. Creamy textures are made possible by using ingredients such as coconut milk, and by puréeing vegetable and/or bean soups. Some bean varieties, such as lentils and split peas, and flaked grains, like rolled oats and spelt flakes, dissolve with long cooking to create velvety textured soups, as well.

Soup making lends itself to creativity. It is a game of mix and match between the seasons, your mood, available ingredients, and time. As the seasons change and the availability of local produce varies, you might find yourself making the same basic soup with dandelion greens in early spring, spinach in the summer, and kale in the fall. If you live in a city, note the comings and goings of fresh asparagus, green beans, and butternut squash at your grocery store or produce market. Although some vegetables may be stocked there all year round, at certain times of the year, they taste particularly fresh. The earth's journey around the sun inspires the savvy cook to reinvent favorite recipes over and over.

The "Mix and Match" chart on page 41 presents a number of ingredients that can be successfully interchanged to create new and enjoyable soup variations. Furthermore, if you don't have an ingredient that is called for in a recipe, this chart provides alternative choices. Be aware, however, when making substitutions, you may need to adjust cooking times and the order in which you add ingredients to the pot. The information presented in "First Things First" on page 46 offers helpful guidelines for determining what goes into the soup pot first.

None of my recipes requires soup stock. Instead, each one begins with plain fresh water that transforms into flavorful broth through the addition of spices and/or ingredients such as sea vegetables, dried mushrooms, and dried vegetables. I have also found that cooking dried beans

and grains right in the soup pot enriches the flavor of the broth.

To make soups as delicious and nutritious as possible, I always use organic ingredients, and I encourage you to, as well. To preserve the nutrients contained in the skin of organic fruits and vegetables, never peel them (this also saves time). Simply scrub the dirt from root vegetables under running water with a vegetable brush, and give leafy vegetables like collards and kale a quick rinse. Most other vegetables need only a quick rinse as well. Leeks are the exception. They need to be sliced lengthwise and rinsed thoroughly between the layers, where dirt typically hides.

Keep in mind the importance of presentation for maximizing every loving spoonful. I always serve main-course soups in deep earthy ceramic bowls, which help retain heat. White or brightly colored shallow bowls house my first-course soups beautifully and get everyone ready for the main meal. Before serving, I usually add a sprinkling of chopped herbs, a swirl of flavored oil, or a dollop of pesto to make the soup come alive. "Great Garnishes" on page 55 offers lots of ideas for crowning your soup with added flavor, texture, and color.

Ready? Let's get the soup pot simmering!

MIX AND MATCH

Personalize your soups! Improvise! Substitute ingredients by colors, seasons, flavors, and textures. Use the chart below to help create your own variations to the soups in this chapter. Feel free to swap, mix, substitute, and exchange the following ingredient choices. Be sure to check out "More Soup Ideas" on page 42 for additional suggestions.

Go Wild With Soups

FALL/WINTER VEGETABLES	Carrots, butternut squash, delicata squash, Jerusalem artichokes, sweet potatoes, and yams.
SPRING/SUMMER VEGETABLES	Asparagus, broccoli, green beans, patty pan squash, yellow summer squash, and zucchini
DOMESTIC/ WILD GREENS	Bok choy, chard, collards, dandelion greens, fiddleheads, kale, lamb's quarters, mizuna, mustard greens, napa cabbage, nettles, purslane, spinach, tat soi, and watercress.
BEANS	FOR CURRIED SOUPS: Chickpeas, lentils, lima beans, mung beans, navy beans (cannellini), and split peas.
	FOR TOMATO-BASED SOUPS: Anasazi beans, black beans, chickpeas, fava beans, kidney beans, lentils, lima beans, navy beans (cannellini), and pinto beans.
	FOR "CREAMY" SOUPS: Aduki beans, mung beans, red lentils, and split peas.
MUSHROOMS	DOMESTIC VARIETIES: Crimini, portabella, shiitake, and white button.
	WILD VARIETIES: Black trumpet, chanterelles, lobster, maitake, matsutake, morels, mousseron, porcini,* and wood ears.
ONION VARIETIES	Chives, leeks, onions, ramps (wild leeks), scallions, and shallots.**
SEA VEGETABLES	LEAFY VARIETIES: Alaria, digitata kelp, dulse, kelp, ocean ribbons kombu, and wakame.
	NOODLE-LIKE VARIETIES: Arame, hiziki, and sea palm.
TOFU	Soft, firm, and extra-firm varieties.
CHILI PEPPERS	VERY HOT: Cayenne peppers, habañero chilies, and Scotch bonnets.
	MODERATELY HOT: Serrano chilies.
	MILDLY HOT: Anaheim chilies, ancho chilies, jalapeño peppers, and poblano chilies.
HERBS AND SPICES	See "Spice It Up!" (page 8) for substitutions.
OILS	Extra virgin olive, sesame, hi-oleic sunflower, and flavored oils; ghee; and coconut butter.
SALTY SEASONINGS	Dulse flakes, kelp granules, miso, nori flakes, sea salt, shoyu, tamari, umeboshi vinegar, and Bragg Liquid Aminos.

* Only 2 tablespoons dried porcini are equivalent to 2 cups fresh, milder-flavored mushrooms like white button.
** Approximately $1/3$ cup coarsely chopped shallots is equivalent to 1 cup onions or leeks.

MORE
SOUP IDEAS

Along with the ideas presented in the "Mix and Match" chart on page 41, keep the following recommended ingredient substitutions and cooking suggestions in mind when creating your own unique soup variations.

☐ Cauliflower is a good substitute for potatoes or cabbage; celeriac can replace celery; and daikon radish is a good alternative for turnips. Their flavors are similar and cooking times about the same.

☐ Change the appearance of your soup by choosing different colored varieties of the same vegetable. For instance, choose among orange, red, green, and yellow bell pepper varieties; or white, yellow, purple, and red potatoes.

☐ To sweeten the flavor of soups that call for potatoes, try using yams or sweet potatoes instead.

☐ When replacing leeks with ramps, keep in mind that ramps are quicker cooking and should be added to the soup along with the quicker-cooking vegetables.

☐ When mild garlic flavor is desired, use cloves of elephant garlic or garlic scapes. They are milder-flavored than regular garlic.

☐ When strong garlic flavor is desired, press the cloves into the cooked soup before serving.

☐ Scallions and chives, which are good raw, should be added to the soup at the end of the cooking time.

☐ For a faster version of any recipe that calls for dried beans, use twice the amount of cooked varieties.

☐ Fresh and dried herbs and spices are interchangeable, but require about three times more fresh than dried. One cinnamon stick is equivalent to 1 teaspoon ground.

☐ Vary the types of pasta you add to soups. For diverse color, taste, and texture, try pastas made from assorted grains (whole wheat, spelt, kamut, rice), vegetables (spinach, bell peppers, tomatoes), and herbs (garlic, basil, and parsley). Also use different shaped pastas.

☐ Instead of adding noodles to soup, try a "noodle-like" sea vegetable like hiziki, sea palm, or arame.

☐ If you prefer your soup chunky style, use less water than is called for in the recipe. Conversely, for a lighter soup, add more liquid.

Creamy Asparagus Soup

Sautéed garlic and dill enhance the flavor of this light and luscious asparagus soup. Although blending gives it creamy texture, you can omit this step and enjoy the soup "chunky-style."

1. Bring the water to boil in a teakettle or small pot.

2. Heat the oil in a 4-quart stockpot over medium heat. Add the garlic, onions, dill seeds, and salt, and sauté, stirring occasionally for 5 minutes, or until the onions begin to soften and the ingredients are fragrant.

3. Add the cauliflower and celery, and continue to sauté for about 5 minutes, or until the celery turns bright green and the cauliflower begins to soften.

4. Pour the boiling water into the pot, along with the asparagus, basil, thyme, and bay leaf. Bring the ingredients to a boil, then reduce the heat to medium-low. Simmer the soup about 10 minutes, or until the cauliflower is tender. Remove and discard the bay leaf.

5. Carefully ladle some of the soup into the blender until it is half full, and purée until smooth. Pour the purée into a large bowl and continue to blend the remaining soup.*

6. Return the puréed soup to the pot and simmer over medium heat until heated through. Adjust the seasonings and serve piping hot.

* If you have a hand blender, you can purée the cooked soup right in the pot.

Yield: 4 to 6 servings

• • • • • • •

6 cups water

1 tablespoon extra virgin olive oil

8 cloves garlic, thickly sliced

1 cup coarsely chopped onions

$\frac{1}{2}$ teaspoon dill seeds

1 teaspoon sea salt, or to taste

2 cups bite-sized cauliflower florets

1 cup coarsely chopped celery

4 cups asparagus, cut into 1-inch pieces

2 tablespoons dried basil

2 teaspoons dried thyme

1 bay leaf

Asparagus Soup With Fresh Fennel

*Fennel, with its subtle anise flavor, goes well with potatoes
and asparagus in this simple puréed soup.
A great first course.*

Yield: 4 to 6 servings

• • • • • • •

6 cups water

1 tablespoon extra virgin
olive oil

3 cloves garlic,
thickly sliced

$^3/_4$ cup coarsely chopped
fennel

1 cup coarsely chopped
unpeeled red potatoes

$^1/_2$ teaspoon sea salt,
or to taste

$3^1/_2$ cups asparagus,
cut into 1-inch pieces

$^1/_2$ cup coarsely chopped
parsley

6 thin orange slices

1. Bring the water to boil in a teakettle or small pot.

2. Heat the oil in a 4-quart stockpot over medium heat. Add the garlic, fennel, potatoes, and salt, and sauté, stirring occasionally for 3 minutes, or until the fennel begins to soften.

3. Carefully pour the boiling water into the pot along with the asparagus. Simmer for 5 minutes or until the asparagus is bright green and tender. Stir in the parsley and remove the pot from the stove.

4. Carefully ladle some of the soup into the blender until it is half full, and purée until smooth. Pour the purée into a large bowl and continue to blend the remaining soup.*

5. Return the puréed soup to the pot and simmer over medium heat until heated through. Adjust the seasonings, if desired.

6. Ladle the soup into bowls, garnish with an orange slice, and serve.

* If you have a hand blender, you can purée the cooked soup right in the pot.

TIP . . .

For flavor variety,
roast or sauté the vegetables
before adding them to the soup pot.

Curried Potato Soup

*Brothy and light, this colorful soup is
a flavorful start to most any meal.*

1. Heat the oil in a 6-quart stockpot over medium heat. Add the onions and cumin, and sauté, stirring occasionally for 5 minutes, or until the onions begin to soften and the ingredients are fragrant.

2. Add the water, potatoes, cauliflower, carrots, cinnamon, nettles (if using), and turmeric. Bring the ingredients to a boil, then reduce the heat to medium-low. Simmer covered for about 30 minutes, or until the vegetables are soft.

3. Add the beans, cardamom, curry powder, and salt to the pot. Simmer covered for another 5 minutes, or until the beans are tender. Adjust the seasonings, if desired.

4. Ladle the hot soup into bowls, garnish with scallions, and serve.

TIP . . .

To beat the heat of summer, cook soups in the early morning or at night when the house is cool. Cold days are ideal for long-simmering soups made with vegetables of the season, such as potatoes, onions, carrots, yams, and winter squash.

Yield: 6 to 8 servings

• • • • • • • • • •

1 tablespoon extra virgin olive oil

1 cup coarsely chopped onions

1 teaspoon cumin seeds

8 cups water

4$\frac{1}{2}$ cups unpeeled red potatoes, cut into $\frac{1}{2}$-inch cubes

4 cups bite-sized cauliflower florets

1 cup coarsely chopped carrots

1 cinnamon stick

1 tablespoon dried nettles, optional

1 teaspoon turmeric

1 cup green beans, cut into 1-inch pieces

$\frac{1}{4}$ teaspoon cardamom

2 teaspoons curry powder

2 teaspoons sea salt, or to taste

$\frac{1}{2}$ cup coarsely chopped scallions

FIRST THINGS FIRST

Understanding the order in which certain ingredients should be added to the soup pot will make it easier to create successful recipes. Basically, this is an exercise in logic—longer-cooking ingredients should begin simmering first, with the delicate, quicker-cooking additions added later. The following list will give you a general idea of the recommended ingredient order for the soup pot.

1. Dried and/or presoaked beans and long-cooking grains, need more time to cook than vegetables. It's best to begin simmering them first along with some spices, including dried nettles, dried mushrooms, burdock, and/or sea vegetables. When they are fully or nearly cooked (depending on the recipe), begin to add the remaining ingredients to the pot.

2. Strong-flavored and/or aromatic vegetables such as leeks, onions, and celery should be added next. For a richer broth, first sauté these vegetables in a little oil, ghee, or coconut butter. Adding a pinch of salt will draw out their juices and hasten sautéing time.

3. Add firm vegetables, such as carrots, potatoes, beets, cauliflower, and winter squash, to the pot next and simmer for ten to fifteen minutes, or until they begin to soften.

4. Quick-cooking grains, like kasha, amaranth, quinoa, and uncooked pasta should be added next. If this is the last ingredient, you can simply add it to the pot, turn off the heat, and cover. Let the heat of the soup do the cooking, which generally takes from twenty to thirty minutes.

5. Quick-cooking vegetables, such as summer squash, leafy greens, fresh mushrooms, green beans, snow peas, broccoli, wild leeks, bean sprouts, asparagus, and tomatoes should be added during the final minutes. For bright color and firm or crunchy texture, these ingredients need to simmer only two to three minutes. For a softer, melt-in-your-mouth texture, simmer a little longer.

6. During the final minutes, add ingredients that require little or no cooking, such as tofu, fresh or frozen corn, and precooked noodles, beans, or grains. Let simmer a minute or so until heated through, or add to the pot, turn off the heat, and warm in the cooked soup.

7. When the soup is just about ready, it's time to add fresh herbs, wine, mirin, lemon juice, or salty seasonings like miso, tamari, shoyu, or sea salt. Miso, which loses its beneficial digestion-aiding enzymes when simmered for long periods, should be dissolved in a little of the broth before it is whisked into the cooked soup.

Once the soup is cooked, taste it and adjust the seasonings. If it has enough salt, but still seems to be missing something, try adding a splash of lemon juice or vinegar. Add any garnishes just before serving.

Ginger Carrot Soup

Not only is this soup delicious, it is a nutritional powerhouse, rich in calcium, essential fatty acids, and vitamin A.

1. Bring the water, dulse, carrots, sweet potato, onions, and ginger to boil in a 6-quart stockpot. Reduce the heat to medium-low and simmer covered for 20 to 30 minutes, or until the sweet potatoes are soft.

2. Add the tofu and simmer 2 to 3 minutes. Turn off the heat.

3. Stir in the mustard greens, scallions, and watercress. Dissolve the miso in some of the hot broth, then return to the pot. Adjust the seasonings, if desired

4. Ladle the hot soup into bowls and serve.

FOR A CHANGE . . .

• Replace $\frac{1}{2}$ cup of the carrots with the same amount of thinly sliced burdock or Jerusalem artichoke.

Yield: 6 to 8 servings

• • • • • • •

8 cups water

3-inch piece dulse, or 1 tablespoon flakes

$3\frac{1}{2}$ cups coarsely chopped carrots

$3\frac{1}{2}$ cups coarsely chopped unpeeled sweet potato

$1\frac{1}{2}$ cups coarsely chopped onions

3 tablespoons grated ginger

1 pound firm tofu, cut into $\frac{1}{2}$-inch cubes

1 cup thinly sliced mustard greens

1 cup coarsely chopped scallions

$\frac{1}{2}$ cup coarsely chopped watercress

1 tablespoon dark miso or tamari, or to taste

Vegetable Soup with Quinoa and Cilantro

Yield: 6 to 8 servings

• • • • • • •

1 tablespoon extra virgin olive oil

1 tablespoon cumin seeds

6 cloves garlic, thickly sliced

1 cup coarsely chopped onions

1 cup quinoa, rinsed and drained

2½ cups coarsely chopped celery

2½ cups coarsely chopped unpeeled yams

2 cups coarsely chopped red bell pepper

8 cups water

1 teaspoon sea salt, or to taste

½ cup coarsely chopped cilantro

The New England fall foliage inspired this colorful and soothing soup, which is made with yams and quinoa.

1. Heat the oil in a 6-quart stockpot over medium heat. Add the cumin, garlic, and onions, and sauté, stirring occasionally for 5 minutes, or until the onions begin to soften and the ingredients are fragrant.

2. Add the quinoa, celery, yams, bell pepper, water, and salt. Bring the ingredients to a boil, then reduce the heat to medium-low. Simmer covered for 20 minutes, or until the quinoa is tender and the yams are soft. Stir in the cilantro. Adjust the seasonings, if desired.

3. Ladle the hot soup into bowls and serve.

TIP . . .

Whole grains, such as rice, barley, and quinoa, are perfect for adding texture, variety, and flavor to soups. They are also low in fat, cholesterol-free, fiber-rich, and loaded with vitamins and minerals. For a richer tasting soup, first sauté the grains a few minutes in a little extra virgin olive oil, butter, or ghee along with some aromatic spices or vegetables, like shallots or celery. For detailed guidelines on preparing grains, see page 10.

Spicy Tomato Quinoa Soup

Quinoa is a delicious addition to this chili-spiced soup that also benefits from a touch of cinnamon.

1. Heat the oil in a 6-quart stockpot over medium heat. Add the cumin and sauté, stirring constantly for about 1 minute, or until fragrant.

2. Add the cayenne, garlic, and onion, and continue to sauté for 3 minutes. Add the quinoa, mix well with the spices, and sauté another 3 minutes.

3. Add the cauliflower, tomatoes, jalapeño peppers, cinnamon, and water to the pot, and bring to a boil. Reduce the heat to medium-low, add the bell pepper, and simmer uncovered for 15 minutes, or until the cauliflower and quinoa are tender.

4. Stir in the thyme and salt. Adjust the seasonings, if desired.

5. Ladle the hot soup into bowls, garnish with cilantro, and serve.

FOR A CHANGE . . .

• Want a thicker variation? Once the soup is cooked, allow it to sit 15 to 20 minutes before serving.

Yield: 4 servings

3 tablespoons extra virgin olive oil

2 teaspoons cumin seeds

2 teaspoons seeded, coarsely chopped cayenne pepper

5 cloves garlic, thickly sliced

1 cup coarsely chopped red onion

$^3/_4$ cup quinoa, rinsed and drained

4 cups bite-sized cauliflower florets

$3^1/_2$ cups coarsely chopped plum tomatoes

5 tablespoons seeded, coarsely chopped jalapeño pepper

1 cinnamon stick

5 cups water

1 cup coarsely chopped red bell pepper

2 tablespoons fresh thyme leaves

$^1/_2$ teaspoon sea salt

$^1/_2$ cup coarsely chopped cilantro

Basmati Rice Soup with French Herbs

*Nutty flavored basmati rice seasoned with a bouquet
of fresh herbs makes for a delicious soup.
Grated cheese melted over the top completes the picture.*

Yield: 4 to 6 servings

• • • • • • • • • • •

7 cups water

1 tablespoon extra virgin olive oil

1 cup brown basmati rice,
rinsed and drained

10 cloves garlic, thickly sliced

2 cups coarsely chopped leeks

1 1/2 cups coarsely chopped celery

1 cup coarsely chopped carrots

1 cup coarsely chopped scallions

1/2 cup coarsely chopped parsley

1/2 cup coarsely chopped dill

1 tablespoon plus 3/4 teaspoon
coarsely chopped sage

1 tablespoon thyme

1 1/4 teaspoons sea salt, or to taste

1 cup grated Manchego or
Parmesan cheese, optional

1. Bring the water to boil in a teakettle or small pot.

2. Heat the oil in a 6-quart stockpot over medium heat. Add the rice, garlic, leeks, celery, and carrots. Sauté, stirring occasionally for 5 minutes, or until the carrots begin to soften and the ingredients are fragrant.

3. Add the scallions and continue to sauté for 2 minutes, or until they begin to wilt and turn bright green.

4. Carefully pour the boiling water into the pot. Bring the ingredients to a boil, then reduce the heat to medium-low. Simmer covered for 30 minutes, or until the rice is tender.

5. Add the parsley, dill, sage, thyme, and salt. Adjust the seasonings, if desired.

6. Ladle the hot soup into bowls. Serve plain or with a sprinkling of cheese.

Multiple Mushroom and Barley Soup With Wine

Wine gives this winter soup extra depth and warmth. Maitake mushrooms, meaty portabellas, sweet dried porcini, and white button mushrooms make every loving spoonful delicious.

1. Bring 4 cups of the water, the barley, and bay leaf to boil in a 6-quart stockpot. Reduce the heat to medium-low and simmer covered for 30 to 40 minutes, or until the barley begins to soften.

2. Place the dried porcini and maitake mushrooms in a large bowl and set aside. While the barley simmers, boil the remaining water and pour it over the dried mushrooms. Let stand 20 minutes or until the mushrooms are soft.

3. Reserving the soaking water, strain the softened mushrooms through a fine sieve or coffee filter. Add the soaking water to the pot of simmering barley. Slice the mushrooms, and add to them to the pot as well. Cover and continue to simmer until the barley is soft.

4. Heat the oil in a medium-sized skillet over medium heat. Add the onions, carrots, and celery. Sauté, stirring occasionally, for 5 minutes, or until the carrots begin to soften and the ingredients are fragrant.

5. Add the portabella mushrooms, and continue to sauté 3 to 5 minutes, or until they begin to soften. Toss in the button mushrooms, and continue to cook another 3 to 5 minutes.

6. Add the sautéed vegetable-mushroom mixture to the pot, along with the wine, thyme, sage, salt, and pepper. Cover and simmer 5 minutes to blend the flavors.

7. Ladle the soup into bowls, garnish with parsley, and serve.

Yield: 4 to 6 servings

• • • • • • • • • •

7 cups water

$1/2$ cup pearled barley, rinsed and drained

1 bay leaf

1 tablespoon dried porcini mushrooms

1 tablespoon dried maitake mushrooms

2 tablespoons extra virgin olive oil

1 cup coarsely chopped onions

$1/2$ cup coarsely chopped carrots

$1/4$ cup coarsely chopped celery

$2^{1}/_{2}$ cups coarsely chopped portabella mushrooms

$2^{1}/_{2}$ cups coarsely chopped white button mushrooms

$1/2$ cup white wine

1 teaspoon dried thyme

$1/4$ teaspoon dried sage

$3/4$ teaspoon sea salt, or to taste

Pinch black pepper, or to taste

1 cup coarsely chopped parsley

ABOUT BEAN SOUPS

Canned beans are certainly an option for making quick soups, but there is nothing like the taste of slow-simmered beans that have been cooked from scratch. And while it's true that most dried bean varieties take a long time to cook, for the most part, they can simmer unattended. If you have a pressure cooker, they can be ready in about 15 minutes without presoaking. When making bean soups, keep the following points in mind.

☐ Lentils are ideal for making quick soups on a whim. After simmering for only 15 minutes, red lentils melt, turn yellow, and result in a delicious, smooth soup. They are my favorite bean choice for curried soups, which I season with ginger, cinnamon, and hot spices like chilies. Earthy green and brown lentils also take only 15 to 20 minutes to cook. I find they work best when flavored with Italian and French herbs like garlic, thyme, and parsley, and combined with ingredients like tomatoes, mushrooms, and wine.

☐ Aduki beans and split peas require only 45 to 60 minutes to dissolve into a tasty, velvety soup.

☐ Cooking a number of common beans, such as chickpeas, navy beans, and pinto beans, directly in the soup results in a thick broth that is rich in flavor.

For detailed guidelines on the preparation and cooking of dried beans, see the inset beginning on page 14.

"SOUPER" TIME SAVERS

✔ To reduce the cooking time of root vegetables, such as beets, celeriac, and potatoes, cut them into thin slices or small chunks, rather than large pieces.

✔ When time is at a premium, keep in mind that fewer ingredients mean shorter preparation time.

✔ Presoak longer-cooking grains and beans.

✔ For spontaneous soup making, keep a ready supply of quick-cooking ingredients, such as noodles, tofu, and dulse on hand, as well as cooked beans and grains.

✔ Begin boiling the water while preparing (chopping, sautéing) other ingredients.

✔ Rinse grains in the morning, and set aside in a strainer to cook for lunch or dinner.

Curried Lentil Soup With Coconut Milk

Adapting this tasty main-course soup to the various seasons is easy. You can use fresh tomatoes, summer squash, spinach, and eggplant in the summer; canned tomatoes, carrots, yams, or delicata squash in the fall and winter.

1. Bring the water, lentils, cinnamon, ginger, cayenne pepper, garlic, and dulse (if using), to boil in a 6-quart stockpot. Reduce the heat to medium-low and simmer covered for 15 to 20 minutes, or until the lentils soften and begin to melt and turn yellow.

2. Add the onions, cauliflower, tomatoes, and coconut milk to the pot, and continue to simmer for 20 to 30 minutes, or until the cauliflower is soft.

3. Add the salt, and adjust the seasonings, if desired.

4. Ladle the hot soup into bowls. Serve plain or garnished with cilantro.

FOR A CHANGE . . .

• Substitute 7 to 8 cups of yams, sweet potatoes, delicata squash, and/or butternut squash for all of the cauliflower.

Yield: 6 to 8 servings

2 cups water

1 cup red lentils, rinsed and drained

1 cinnamon stick

2 tablespoons grated ginger

1 tablespoon seeded, coarsely chopped cayenne pepper

2 cloves garlic, finely minced

3-inch-piece dulse or 1 tablespoon dulse flakes, optional

1 cup coarsely chopped onions

10 cups bite-sized cauliflower florets

$3\frac{1}{2}$ cups coarsely chopped plum tomatoes

14-ounce can coconut milk

1 teaspoon sea salt, or to taste

1 cup coarsely chopped cilantro leaves, optional

Moroccan Lentil Soup with Saffron

A pinch of saffron deepens the flavor of this mildly spicy lentil soup.

Yield: 4 to 6 servings

6 cups water

1 cup brown lentils, rinsed and drained

3-inch piece dulse, optional

Pinch saffron

1 tablespoon extra virgin olive oil

2 cups bite-sized cauliflower florets

$1/2$ cup coarsely chopped carrots

$1/2$ cup coarsely chopped celery

4 cloves garlic, thickly sliced

$1/2$ tablespoon grated ginger

1 teaspoon ground cumin

3 pinches cayenne pepper

$1/4$ teaspoon turmeric

$1^3/4$ cups coarsely chopped plum tomatoes

$1/4$ cup coarsely chopped cilantro

$1/2$ teaspoon sea salt, or to taste

1. Bring the water, lentils, dulse (if using), and saffron to boil in a 6-quart stockpot. Reduce the heat to medium-low and simmer covered 15 to 20 minutes, or until the lentils soften.

2. While the lentils cook, heat the oil in a medium-sized skillet over medium heat. Add the cauliflower, carrots, celery, garlic, ginger, cumin, and cayenne. Sauté about 5 minutes, or until the cauliflower begins to soften and the vegetables are bright in color.

3. Add the sautéed vegetables and turmeric to the lentils. Simmer covered about 10 minutes, or until the lentils are soft.

4. Stir the tomatoes into the pot and simmer covered another 5 minutes. Add the cilantro and salt. Adjust the seasonings, if desired.

5. Ladle the hot soup into bowls and serve.

GREAT GARNISHES

The right garnish (or garnishes) can add the perfect touch to just about any soup. In addition to lending eye appeal, garnishes offer added flavor and texture. Before serving your next bowl of soup, consider dressing it up with one or more of the following:

- [ ] Sprig of rosemary, thyme, oregano, or fennel.

- [ ] Sprinkling of chopped parsley, chives, dill, or chervil.

- [ ] Basil, mint, or cilantro leaves.

- [ ] Fresh cracked black pepper.

- [ ] Plain or flavored croutons.

- [ ] Crisp toasted baguette slices.

- [ ] Toasted sesame seeds.

- [ ] Sensational Seasoning Blend (page 76).

- [ ] Fried or warmed tortilla strips.

- [ ] Orange slice, lemon wedge, or lime wedge—plain or sprinkled with vinegar.

- [ ] Thin strips of fresh greens like arugula, sorrel, spinach, tat soi, mizuna, and mustard greens.

- [ ] Finely chopped, sautéed spinach, kale, collards, chard, beet greens, or broccoli rabe. (These are particularly good choices for adding color and flavor to bean soups and potato soups.)

- [ ] Thinly sliced raw scallions, cucumber, or daikon radish.

- [ ] Dulse flakes, thin toasted nori strips, or kelp powder. In addition to salty flavor, these garnishes offer nutrient-rich minerals.

- [ ] Shredded carrots, jicama, or cabbage.

- [ ] Chopped fresh tomatoes.

- [ ] Heaping spoonful of yogurt, crème fraiche, or sour cream.

- [ ] Crumbled chèvre or feta cheese.

- [ ] Sprinkling of grated cheese.

- [ ] Drizzle of olive oil, sesame oil, or other flavored oil (see Chapter 5).

- [ ] Pat of butter.

- [ ] Spoonful of ghee.

- [ ] Dollop of pesto.

- [ ] Edible flowers such as calendula, chive flowers, or nasturtium.

- [ ] Plain or smoked tofu cubes—fresh or deep-fried.

- [ ] Thinly sliced fried tempeh.

- [ ] Soy bacon bits.

Tomato Lentil Soup with Red Wine

This simple yet robust soup is always a good choice, especially when entertaining guests. While the lentils simmer, pour yourself a glass of red wine to sip as the soup cooks.

Yield: 4 to 6 servings

5 cups water

1 1/2 cups brown lentils, rinsed and drained

3-inch piece wakame

1 tablespoon dried nettles, optional

2 1/2 cups coarsely chopped plum tomatoes

2 tablespoons extra virgin olive oil

1 cup coarsely chopped onions

5 cloves garlic, thickly sliced

1 cup coarsely chopped bell pepper

4 cups coarsely chopped chard

1/2 cup red wine

1 tablespoon coarsely chopped fresh oregano, or 1 teaspoon dried

1 tablespoon coarsely chopped fresh basil, or 1 teaspoon dried

1 teaspoon sea salt, or to taste

Pinch black pepper, or to taste

1. Bring the water, lentils, wakame, and nettles (if using) to boil in a 4-quart stockpot. Reduce the heat to medium-low and simmer covered for 15 to 20 minutes, or until the lentils are tender. Add the tomatoes, cover, and continue to cook for 10 minutes.

2. While the lentils simmer, heat the oil in a medium-sized skillet over medium heat. Add the onions and garlic, and sauté for 5 minutes or until onion begins to soften.

3. Add the bell pepper to the skillet, sauté for 1 to 2 minutes, then add the chard. Continue to cook another minute, or until the chard turns bright green and begins to wilt.

4. Transfer the sautéed vegetables to the soup pot along with the wine. Cover and continue to simmer 5 minutes. Add the oregano, basil, salt, and pepper. Adjust the seasonings, if desired.

5. Ladle the hot soup into bowls and serve.

FOR A CHANGE . . .

- Use dandelion greens or fresh nettles instead of chard.
- Substitute a bay leaf for the wakame.
- Try white or peach wine instead of red.

Curried Split Pea Soup with Chard

When the weather turns chilly, this mildly spicy soup is a welcome choice. Enjoy it along with some crusty bread and a mixed green salad.

1. Bring the water, split peas, ginger, serrano pepper, turmeric, kelp (if using), and nettles (if using) to boil in a 4-quart stockpot. Reduce the heat to medium-low and simmer covered for 1 to $1\frac{1}{2}$ hours, or until the peas are soft.

2. While the peas simmer, place the mustard seeds in a medium-sized unoiled skillet and dry roast over medium heat. Cover and toast about 2 minutes, or until they pop.

3. Add the sesame oil, cumin, onions, and cauliflower to the skillet, and sauté, stirring occasionally for 5 minutes, or until the onions and cauliflower begin to soften. Add the chard and sauté for a minute, or until it turns bright green and the leaves start to wilt.

4. Transfer the sautéed vegetables to the soup pot. Cover and continue to simmer 5 to 10 minutes, or until cauliflower is tender. Add the salt. Adjust the seasonings, if desired.

5. Ladle the hot soup into bowls and serve.

Yield: 4 to 6 servings

7 cups water

1 cup yellow split peas, rinsed and drained

1 tablespoon grated ginger

$\frac{1}{2}$ teaspoon seeded, coarsely chopped serrano pepper

$\frac{1}{2}$ teaspoon turmeric

3-inch-piece kelp, optional

1 tablespoon dried nettles, optional

1 teaspoon brown mustard seeds

2 tablespoons sesame oil

1 teaspoon cumin seeds

1 cup coarsely chopped onions

$1\frac{1}{2}$ cups bite-sized cauliflower florets

2 cups coarsely chopped chard

1 teaspoon sea salt, or to taste

Golden Split Pea Soup

Unlike most split pea soups, which are as thick as porridge, this lighter version is more like an elegant consommé.

Yield: 4 to 6 servings

• • • • • • • • • •

8 cups water

1 1/2 cups yellow split peas, rinsed and drained

2 bay leaves

I tablespoon dried nettles, optional

4 cups bite-sized cauliflower florets

2 tablespoons extra virgin olive oil

2 cups coarsely chopped carrots

I cup coarsely chopped onions

3 cloves garlic, thickly sliced

1/4 cup coarsely chopped parsley

2 tablespoons coarsely chopped dill

I teaspoon coarsely chopped rosemary

I teaspoon sea salt, or to taste

1. Bring the water, split peas, bay leaves, and nettles (if using) to boil in a 6-quart stockpot. Reduce the heat to medium-low and simmer covered for 30 minutes, or until peas are soft. Add the cauliflower florets and continue to simmer.

2. While the peas and cauliflower simmer, heat the oil in a medium-sized skillet over medium heat. Add the carrots, onions, and garlic, and sauté, stirring occasionally for 5 to 10 minutes, or until the carrots begin to soften.

3. Transfer the sautéed vegetables to the soup pot, and continue to simmer another 20 to 30 minutes, or until the peas melt.

4. Add the parsley, dill, rosemary, and salt. Adjust the seasonings, if desired. Remove and discard the bay leaves.

5. Ladle the hot soup into bowls and serve.

Mexican Bean Soup with Tomatillos

In this rich and colorful soup, tomatillos are simmered along with sweet and spicy peppers, garlic, carrots, tomatoes, and zucchini.

1. Bring the water to boil in a 2-quart pot.

2. Heat the oil in a 6-quart stockpot over medium heat. Add the garlic, onions, and bay leaves. Sauté while stirring occasionally about 5 minutes, or until the onions begin to soften.

3. Add the tomatillos, tomatoes, and carrots to the stockpot, and continue to sauté 5 minutes or until the carrots begin to soften. Add the beans, simmer 5 minutes, then add the bell pepper and zucchini. Simmer another minute.

4. Transfer the boiling water to the pot along with the habañero peppers. Cover and simmer 5 minutes to blend the flavors. Add the sea salt. Adjust the seasonings, if desired.

5. Ladle the hot soup into bowls and serve.

Yield: 4 to 6 servings

3 cups water

1 tablespoon extra virgin olive oil

10 cloves garlic, thickly sliced

$1\frac{1}{3}$ cups coarsely chopped onions

2 bay leaves

$3\frac{3}{4}$ cups coarsely chopped tomatillos, husks removed

$2\frac{1}{2}$ cups coarsely chopped plum tomatoes

$1\frac{1}{2}$ cups coarsely chopped carrots

4 cups cooked pinto beans

$1\frac{1}{2}$ cups coarsely chopped red bell pepper

$\frac{2}{3}$ cup coarsely chopped zucchini

$2\frac{1}{2}$ teaspoons seeded, coarsely chopped habañero peppers

1 teaspoon sea salt, or to taste

FYI . . .

Tart, lemony flavored tomatillos, which grow inside papery husks, are often used raw in salsas and chutneys. When added to soup, they dissolve, giving the broth a silky texture. Don't forget to remove the tomatillos from their husks and rinse well before using.

Black Bean Soup With Sun-Dried Tomatoes

Yield: 4 to 6 servings

4 cups water

1 cup dried black beans, presoaked (page 14), rinsed, and drained

4 bay leaves

3-inch-piece kelp, optional

1 tablespoon extra virgin olive oil

2 teaspoons cumin seeds

3 cloves garlic, thickly sliced

1 1/4 cups coarsely chopped onions

1 cup coarsely chopped carrots

1 1/3 cups bite-sized cauliflower florets

1 cup coarsely chopped red bell pepper

1/2 cup sun-dried tomatoes

1/3 cup coarsely chopped cilantro

1/2 teaspoon sea salt, or to taste

Enjoy this hearty country-style soup as a main course with warm corn tortillas and a green salad.

1. Bring the water, beans, bay leaves, and kelp (if using) to boil in a 4-quart stockpot. Reduce the heat to medium-low and simmer covered for 1 hour, or until beans are soft.

2. Heat the oil in a medium-sized skillet over medium heat. Add the cumin seeds, garlic, onions, and carrots, and sauté, stirring occasionally, for 5 minutes or until the onions and carrots begin to soften.

3. Transfer the sautéed vegetables to the simmering beans, along with the cauliflower, red bell pepper, and sun-dried tomatoes. Continue to simmer for 10 to 20 minutes, or until the cauliflower is soft. Stir in the cilantro and sea salt. Adjust the seasonings, if desired.

4. Ladle the hot soup into bowls and serve.

FOR A CHANGE . . .

• To make this a chili-flavored black bean soup, substitute 1/3 cup chopped basil for the cilantro and add 1 tablespoon chili powder.

Minestrone with Oyster Mushrooms, Nettles, and Calendula Flowers

Scented with rosemary, basil, and bay leaves, this "wild vegetable" version of classic minestrone is one the whole family will love.

1. Bring the water, beans, bay leaves, kelp, and nettles to boil in a 6-quart stockpot. Reduce the heat to medium-low, and simmer covered for 1 hour or until beans are soft.

2. Heat the oil in a medium-sized skillet over medium heat. Add the garlic, onions, and shallots. Sauté, stirring occasionally, for 5 minutes or until the onions begin to soften. Add the celery and continue to sauté for 3 minutes, or until the celery becomes bright green.

3. Transfer the sautéed vegetables, tomatoes, yams, potatoes, mushrooms, and saffron to the simmering beans. Continue to simmer 20 minutes, or until the potatoes and yams are tender. Stir in the basil, rosemary, and salt. Adjust the seasonings, if desired.

4. Ladle the hot soup into bowls, garnish with calendula petals, and serve.

FOR A CHANGE . . .

• Before serving the soup, drizzle with extra virgin olive oil or Garlic Basil Oil (page 103) as an additional garnish.

• Substitute 1 cup dried pasta, such as penne, elbows, or shells, for the mushrooms.

Yield: 4 to 6 servings

8 cups water

1 cup dried lima beans, presoaked (page 14), rinsed, and drained

2 bay leaves

3-inch-piece kelp

1 tablespoon dried nettles

1 tablespoon extra virgin olive oil

5 cloves garlic, thickly sliced

1 cup coarsely chopped onions

5 tablespoons coarsely chopped shallots

1 cup coarsely chopped celery

4 cups coarsely chopped plum tomatoes

$2\frac{1}{2}$ cups coarsely chopped unpeeled yams

$2\frac{1}{2}$ cups coarsely chopped unpeeled potatoes

1 cup coarsely chopped oyster mushrooms

Pinch saffron

5 tablespoons coarsely chopped fresh basil leaves

2 teaspoons coarsely chopped fresh rosemary

1 teaspoon sea salt, or to taste

1 heaping tablespoon fresh calendula petals

Spicy North African Vegetable Soup with chickpeas

Yield: 6 to 8 servings
. . . .

2 quarts water

2 cups cooked chickpeas

1 cinnamon stick

1 tablespoon extra virgin olive oil

6 cloves garlic, thickly sliced

$\frac{1}{2}$ teaspoon chili pepper flakes

1 cup coarsely chopped onions

$\frac{1}{2}$ cup coarsely chopped carrots

$2\frac{1}{2}$ cups coarsely chopped
unpeeled sweet potatoes

2 cups bite-sized
cauliflower florets

1 teaspoon turmeric

3 cups coarsely chopped
mustard greens

2 tablespoons dried sacred basil
or other basil variety

1 teaspoon sea salt, or to taste

There are dozens of different basil varieties from which to choose. The delicate sweet-flavored "sacred basil" called for in this soup is commonly used in the cuisines of Africa, India, and the Far East. Although sacred basil is recommended in this recipe, you can use any basil variety.

1. Bring the water, chickpeas, and cinnamon stick to boil in a 6-quart stockpot. Reduce the heat to medium-low, cover, and simmer 10 to 15 minutes, or until the cinnamon stick uncurls.

2. While the chickpeas simmer, heat the oil in a medium-sized skillet over medium heat. Add the garlic, chili flakes, onions, and carrots, and sauté, stirring occasionally for 5 minutes, or until the onions begin to soften.

3. When the cinnamon stick uncurls, transfer the sautéed vegetables to the stockpot along with the sweet potatoes, cauliflower, and turmeric. Simmer covered for 20 minutes, or until the sweet potatoes and cauliflower are tender.

4. Add the mustard greens and continue to simmer 2 to 3 minutes, or until bright green. Stir in the basil and salt. Adjust the seasonings, if desired.

5. Ladle the hot soup into bowls and serve.

Portabella Mushroom Soup

In addition to portabellas, this delicious soup—made creamy from the long-simmered navy beans—includes immune-enhancing maitake mushrooms. Dried nettles, which resemble and taste like parsley, provide extra calcium and iron.

1. Heat the oil in a 6-quart stockpot over medium heat. Add the garlic and onions, and sauté, stirring occasionally for 5 minutes, or until onions begin to soften.

2. Add the tomatoes, portabellas, beans, celery, maitake, nettles, and saffron to the pot. Increase the heat and bring to a boil, then reduce the heat to medium-low. Simmer covered for 15 minutes, or until maitake softens.

3. Add the dill and sea salt. Adjust the seasonings, if desired.

4. Ladle the hot soup into bowls and serve.

FOR A CHANGE . . .

• Interested in a fat-free option? Simply omit the oil. Add the garlic and onions to the pot along with the other ingredients in Step 2.

Yield: 4 to 6 servings

• • • • • • • • • •

1 tablespoon extra virgin olive oil

5 cloves garlic, thickly sliced

1½ cups coarsely chopped onions

3½ cups coarsely chopped plum tomatoes

2 cups coarsely chopped portabella mushrooms

2 cups cooked navy beans

1 cup coarsely chopped celery

1 teaspoon dried maitake mushrooms

1 tablespoon dried nettles or parsley

Pinch saffron

1 cup coarsely chopped dill

1 teaspoon sea salt, or to taste

Garlicky Potato Soup with Fresh Nettles

The rich flavor of fresh spring nettles can't be beat. This is a perfect first-course soup to rejuvenate the senses and wake up the palate after a winter of root vegetables. Because fresh nettles have stingers, don't forget to wear garden gloves when handling them. Fortunately, the stingers melt away when cooked in the soup.

Yield: 4 to 6 servings

• • • • • • • •

1 tablespoon extra virgin olive oil

1 cup coarsely chopped onions

10 cloves garlic, coarsely chopped

8 cups water

8 cups unpeeled potatoes, cut into $1/4$-inch cubes

2 cups fresh nettle tops

2 teaspoons sea salt

$1/2$ teaspoon black pepper

1. Heat the oil in a 6-quart stockpot over medium heat. Add the onions and garlic, and sauté, stirring occasionally for 5 minutes, or until the onions begin to soften and the ingredients are fragrant. Add the water, potatoes, nettles, salt, and pepper.

2. Bring the ingredients to a boil, then reduce the heat to medium-low. Simmer covered for about 20 minutes, or until the potatoes are soft.

3. Carefully ladle some of the soup into a blender until it is half full, and purée until smooth. Pour the purée into a large bowl and continue to blend the remaining soup.*

4. Return the puréed soup to the pot and simmer until heated through. Adjust the seasonings, if desired.

5. Ladle the hot soup into bowls and serve.

* If you have a hand blender, you can purée the cooked soup right in the pot.

FOR A CHANGE . . .

• Instead of extra virgin olive oil, use basil or garlic oil.

• Substitute 2 cups of peas, spinach, mizuna, tat soi, bok choy, watercress, or mustard greens for the nettles. Add to the pot after the potatoes are cooked.

Creamy Wild Leek and Potato Soup

In this recipe, wild leeks provide a delicious twist to classic potato leek soup. Puréeing the ingredients offers thick and creamy results without dairy or soymilk.

1. Heat the oil in a 6-quart stockpot over medium heat. Add the garlic and potatoes and sauté for 5 minutes, or until the garlic is fragrant.

2. Add the water, navy beans, and bay leaf to the pot. Increase the heat and bring to a boil. Reduce the heat to medium-low and simmer covered for 25 minutes, or until the potatoes are soft.

3. Add the leeks and oregano, and continue to simmer another 2 minutes, or until the leeks turn bright green. Stir in the sea salt.

4. Carefully ladle some of the soup into a blender until it is half full, and purée until smooth. Pour the purée into a large bowl and continue to blend the remaining soup.*

5. Return the puréed soup to the pot and simmer over medium heat until heated through. Adjust the seasonings, if desired.

6. Ladle the hot soup into bowls, garnish with parsley, and serve.

* If you have a hand blender, you can purée the cooked soup right in the pot.

Yield: 4 to 6 servings

• • • • • • •

2 tablespoons extra virgin olive oil

5 cloves garlic, thickly sliced

4 cups coarsely chopped potatoes

4 cups water

2 $\frac{1}{2}$ cups cooked navy beans

1 bay leaf

3 cups coarsely chopped wild leeks

1 $\frac{1}{2}$ teaspoons dried oregano

1 teaspoon sea salt, or to taste

$\frac{1}{2}$ cup coarsely chopped parsley

FYI . . .

Wild leeks, also called ramps, are quick cooking and garlicky good. They resemble young scallions with a small bulb and tender green leaves that fan out like tiny tulips.

4

Sauces, Dips, and Dressings

Virtually every culture has its favorite herb and spice blends that, when mixed with oil, vinegar, beans, cheeses, fruits, or vegetables, result in memorable sauces, dressings, dips, and spreads.

In this chapter, you will find a wide range of recipes that have been inspired by many cultures throughout the world. From the Middle East, there is my HummBaba, an incomparable blend of two of the region's classic dips—hummus and baba ghanoush. Flavorful Tomatillo Salsa and the Tomatillo and Lime Dressing are inspirations from the countries of Latin America, while the Asian Cilantro Dressing, Asian Ginger-Orange Dressing, and Sweet-and-Sour Dipping Sauce are characteristically Far Eastern. Representing the cuisine of Greece, the Roasted Red Pepper and Feta Cheese Dip provides an instant meal to enjoy with bread or crackers.

My love of fusion—mixing and matching the cuisines of various world cultures—is a constant source of inspiration for new and different ingredient blends (I hope you find yourself experiencing the same). Enjoy the flavors of Mexico and the Mediterranean with my Cilantro-Olive Spread—the perfect topper for whole grain bread and crackers.

Dip an egg roll or potato knish into the Mustard Sauce with Maple Syrup and Miso for an unusual yet wonderful blend of sweet, salty, and spicy flavors. In the mood to dress your salad with something that's notably Italian and a little bit French? The Parsley and Garlic Scape Dressing is sure to please. Its olive oil and vinegar base has a decidedly garlic flavor that is piqued with the zing of spicy mustard.

I have also included a number of my old favorites to which I have added interesting new accents. Easy to prepare, they can be used to embellish simple meals as well as festive holiday spreads. There is the Tomato Sauce with Lobster Mushrooms—a delicious savory topping for pasta and grain dishes—and my Cranberry-Orange Sauce, which is perfect for adding a spark of flavor to traditional Thanksgiving feasts and complementing vegetarian favorites like Goat Cheese Mushroom Strudel.

The versatile recipes in this chapter are rich in flavor without being loaded with fat. They are also easy to use as starting points for conjuring up your own repertoire of sauces, dips, and dressings.

Be sure to use the "Mix and Match" chart below for ingredient-swapping ideas. And don't forget about the wide selection of flavored oils and vinegars in Chapter 5. Bon Appetit!

MIX AND MATCH

When you're feeling inspired to come up with your own dressings, dips, and sauces, check out the chart below. It offers some good ideas for ingredient swapping. And don't forget about replacing oil and vinegars with the flavored varieties found in Chapter 5.

Go Wild with Sauces, Dips, and Dressings

ONION VARIETIES	Chives, leeks, onions, ramps (wild leeks), scallions, and shallots.*
GARLIC VARIETIES	Garlic, elephant garlic, and garlic scapes.
CHILI PEPPERS	VERY HOT: Cayenne peppers, habañero chilies, and Scotch bonnets.
	MODERATELY HOT: Serrano chilies.
	MILDLY HOT: Anaheim chilies, ancho chilies, jalapeño peppers, and poblano chilies.
HERBS AND SPICES	See "Spice It Up!" (page 8) for substitutions.
VINEGARS	Balsamic, red wine, rice wine,** and flavored vinegars (see the selections found in Chapter 5).
OILS	Canola, extra virgin olive, hazelnut, pistachio, pumpkin, high-oleic safflower and sunflower, sesame, toasted sesame, walnut, and other flavored oils (see the selections found in Chapter 5).
SALTY SEASONINGS	Dulse flakes, kelp granules, miso, nori flakes, sea salt, shoyu, tamari, umeboshi vinegar, and Bragg Liquid Aminos.

* Approximately $1/3$ cup coarsely chopped shallots is equivalent to 1 cup onions or leeks.
** Lime juice is a good substitute for rice wine vinegar.

DRESSINGS

Tomatillo and Lime Dressing

Smooth and thick, this dressing's wonderfully sharp flavor is tasty on green salads, stuffed avocados, and fried tempeh.

1. Place all the ingredients in a food processor or blender. Blend until smooth, scraping down the sides of the bowl as necessary. Adjust the seasonings, if desired.

2. Use immediately. Refrigerate any leftovers.

Yield: About 1 cup

. . . .

3/4 cup husked, rinsed, and halved tomatillos

1/2 cup fresh basil

1/3 cup fresh cilantro leaves

1/3 cup extra virgin olive oil

1/4 cup lime juice

1 teaspoon sea salt

1/4 teaspoon black pepper

Asian Cilantro Dressing

A great change of pace from pesto, this Asian-inspired dressing is great on pasta, especially Japanese udon noodles. It also works well drizzled over steamed vegetables and sliced ripe summer tomatoes.

1. Place all the ingredients in a food processor or blender. Blend until smooth, scraping down the sides of the bowl as necessary. Adjust the seasonings, if desired.

2. Use immediately. Refrigerate any leftovers.

FOR A CHANGE . . .

• Instead of sesame oil, use peanut or toasted sesame oil.

Yield: About 2/3 cup

. . . .

1 tablespoon fresh ginger juice*

1/2 cup tightly packed fresh cilantro leaves

1/4 cup tamari

3 tablespoons lime juice

1 tablespoon rice vinegar

1 tablespoon sesame oil

* Squeeze about 2 tablespoons grated fresh ginger to produce this amount.

Zesty Parsley and Scallion Dressing

Yield: About 1 1/4 cups

• • • • • • • •

2 tablespoons extra virgin olive oil

5 tablespoons water

1/4 cup lemon juice

1 teaspoon grated lemon zest

1/2 cup coarsely chopped green bell pepper

2 scallions cut into thirds

2 cloves garlic

2 cups parsley leaves and tender stems

1/2 teaspoon sea salt, or to taste

Nutritious and refreshing, this thick, delicious dressing has a wonderful sharp flavor. Spoon it on lettuce or mesclun, or try it on cabbage for a different kind of coleslaw.

1. Place all the ingredients in a food processor or blender in the order listed. Blend until thick and well combined, scraping down the sides of the bowl as necessary. Adjust the seasonings, if desired.

2. Use immediately. Refrigerate any leftovers.

FOR A CHANGE . . .

• Try grated carrot in place of the green pepper.

• For a richer dressing, omit the water and increase the total amount of olive oil to 7 tablespoons.

Sweet Basil Vinaigrette

Yield: About 1 cup

• • • • • • • •

1 1/2 cups fresh basil

1/2 cup balsamic vinegar

1/3 cup extra virgin olive oil

5 garlic scapes or garlic cloves, coarsely chopped

2 tablespoons honey

1/4 teaspoon sea salt

I love the combination of garlic scapes and basil. Of course, you can substitute garlic cloves for the scapes.

1. Place all the ingredients in a food processor or blender, and purée until creamy. Adjust the seasonings, if desired.

2. Use immediately. Refrigerate any leftovers.

Orange-Raspberry Vinaigrette

This light and fruity salt-free vinaigrette is a snap to prepare!

1. Place all the ingredients in a jar with a tightly closed lid and shake well. Adjust the seasonings, if desired.

2. Use immediately. Refrigerate any leftovers.

FOR A CHANGE . . .

• Substitute fresh tangelo juice for the orange juice.

• Use store-bought orange juice instead of fresh squeezed, and omit the orange zest.

• Substitute Cherry Vinegar (page 90) for the raspberry.

• Instead of walnut oil, try hazelnut oil, extra virgin olive oil, or one of the flavored oils in Chapter 5.

Yield: About $^3/_4$ cup

· · · · · · · ·

$^1/_3$ cup freshly squeezed orange juice

$^1/_3$ cup raspberry vinegar

3 tablespoons walnut oil

I teaspoon grated orange zest

Asian Ginger-Orange Dressing

This gingery aromatic dressing is an excellent choice for green salads, steamed vegetables, sea vegetable salads, and pasta. Be aware that it's full-flavored . . . a little goes a long way.

1. Place all the ingredients in a 1-quart measuring cup or small mixing bowl, and stir until well combined. Adjust the seasonings, if desired.

2. Use immediately. Refrigerate any leftovers.

Yield: About $^2/_3$ cup

· · · · · · · ·

$^1/_2$ cup freshly squeezed orange juice

2 tablespoons fresh ginger juice*

2 tablespoons umeboshi vinegar

I tablespoon toasted sesame oil

* Squeeze about 4 tablespoons grated fresh ginger to produce this amount.

Parsley and Garlic Scape Dressing

This rich dressing has a classic Italian-style olive oil and balsamic vinegar base along with the French influences of mustard and parsley. The mustard adds texture. The parsley adds calcium. I like the rich flavor they create with olive oil.

1. Place all the ingredients in a food processor or blender, and purée until creamy.

2. Adjust the seasonings, if desired.

3. Use immediately. Refrigerate any leftovers.

FOR A CHANGE . . .

• Substitute half the parsley with $1/4$ cup basil.

• Instead of olive oil, try one of the flavored oils in Chapter 5.

• For milder flavor, substitute 1 tablespoon of balsamic vinegar with red wine vinegar.

Yield: About $2/3$ cup

• • • • • • •

$1/2$ cup extra virgin olive oil

$1/2$ cup fresh parsley leaves

5 garlic scapes or garlic cloves, coarsely chopped

2 tablespoons balsamic vinegar

1 teaspoon prepared mustard

TIP . . .

Every garlic bulb shoots a curly green stem topped with a white blossom. Called garlic scapes, these blossoms are mild tasting compared to garlic cloves. Farmers and gardeners snap these mid-summer treats off garlic bulbs to encourage the bulbs to grow larger.

SAUCES

Strawberry Sauce

My kids love a bowl of strawberry sauce any time of day.
It is heavenly on pancakes, waffles, yogurt, and ice cream.

1. Place the strawberries and maple syrup in a 1-quart saucepan over medium-low heat. Simmer, stirring occasionally for 5 minutes, or until the strawberries are soft and juicy.

2. Dissolve the arrowroot in the cold water, then add to the strawberries. Stir for a minute, or until the sauce thickens.

3. Remove from the heat and enjoy hot. Refrigerate any leftovers.

FOR A CHANGE . . .

• Add more maple syrup for a sweeter sauce.

• Use blueberries instead of strawberries.

Yield: About 2¼ cups

• • • • • • •

1 quart (4 cups) coarsely chopped fresh or frozen strawberries*

2 tablespoons maple syrup

1 tablespoon arrowroot powder

1 tablespoon cold water

* If using frozen berries, add an additional teaspoon of arrowroot and cold water.

Sweet-and-Sour Dipping Sauce

In my home, this tasty sauce is a hands-down favorite
for dipping egg rolls and spring rolls.

1. Place all of the ingredients in a small mixing bowl, and stir until well combined. Adjust the ingredient amounts, if desired.

2. Use immediately.

Yield: About ½ cup

• • • • • • •

4 tablespoons honey

2 tablespoons plus 1 teaspoon tamari

1 tablespoon rice vinegar

Cinnamon-Vanilla Applesauce

Healthy and delicious, this applesauce is great on pancakes and waffles, mixed with yogurt, or enjoyed plain.

Yield: About 6 cups

• • • • • • •

4 quarts (16 cups) coarsely chopped MacIntosh apples

1 tablespoon cinnamon

1 tablespoon vanilla

2 tablespoons maple syrup or maple sugar

1. Place the apples and cinnamon in a 6-quart stockpot over medium heat. Stirring occasionally, simmer until the apples soften into a sauce. For a smooth sauce, simmer about 20 minutes; simmer less for chunky style.

2. Turn off the heat and stir the vanilla and maple syrup into the sauce.

3. Serve hot, warm, cold, or at room temperature. Refrigerate any leftovers.

FOR A CHANGE . . .

• Choose from among a wide variety of apples. Cortland, royal galas, and Rome are other good choices.

• Instead of using only apples, try a combination of apples, peaches, and/or pears.

• For a sweeter applesauce, add more maple syrup or maple sugar.

FYI . . .

When preparing applesauce, peeling the apples is optional. Leaving the peels on will turn the sauce a beautiful reddish-pink color. Peeling the apples will result in a very smooth golden-colored sauce.

Cranberry-Orange Sauce

Include this wonderful sweet yet tart cranberry-orange sauce at your next Thanksgiving feast. It is also great with Goat Cheese Mushroom Strudel on page 177.

1. Bring the cranberries, orange juice, and orange zest to boil in a 2-quart saucepan. Reduce the heat to a medium-low and simmer 5 to10 minutes, or until the cranberries are soft.

2. Turn off the heat and stir in the maple syrup.

3. Serve warm. Refrigerate any leftovers.

FOR A CHANGE . . .

- Add more maple syrup for a sweeter sauce.

Yield: About 2 cups
. . . .
2 cups fresh or frozen cranberries

$1/2$ cup orange juice

1 tablespoon orange zest

3 tablespoons maple syrup, or to taste

Blackberry-Pear Sauce

Try this luscious sauce over Baked Ginger-Arame Rolls (page 122).

1. Place the blackberries, pears, orange juice, maple syrup, and orange zest in a 2-quart saucepan over medium-low heat. Simmer 5 to 10 minutes, or until the berries are soft.

2. In a small bowl, dissolve the arrowroot in the cold water. Add the mixture to the simmering blackberry-pear mixture, and stir for a minute or two until the sauce thickens.

3. Remove from the heat and enjoy hot. Refrigerate any leftovers.

FOR A CHANGE . . .

- Add more maple syrup for a sweeter sauce.

Yield: About $2^1/2$ cups
. . . .
2 cups fresh or frozen blackberries

$1^1/3$ cups coarsely diced Anjou pears

$1^1/3$ cups orange juice

$1/3$ cup maple syrup

$1^1/2$ tablespoons orange zest

1 teaspoon arrowroot

1 tablespoon cold water

Mustard Sauce With Maple Syrup and Miso

Sweet, spicy, and salty flavors come together in this wonderful dipping sauce for knishes and egg rolls.

Yield: About 1 cup

1/2 cup prepared mustard

1/2 cup maple syrup

3 tablespoons dark miso*

*South River brand Three-Year Barley Miso is recommended.

1. Place all the ingredients in a food processor and blend until smooth. Adjust the ingredients, if desired.

2. Use immediately. Refrigerate any leftovers.

Sensational Seasoning Blend

This mineral-rich seasoning blend is a great salt replacement and one of my kitchen staples. I sprinkle it on most foods— soups, salads, even popcorn—for added flavor. I also enjoy it plain by the handful. And talk about a nutritional powerhouse! The sesame seeds contain essential amino acids; the nettles provide lots of vitamins and minerals; and the kelp is high in fiber, iron, calcium, and iodine. The following recipe yields about 2 cups.

1/2 cup kelp pieces or granules

1 1/3 cups dry-roasted sesame seeds

1/4 cup dried nettles

Place the kelp in a blender and grind to a powder. Add the nettles and sesame seeds, and pulse until coarsely ground. Transfer to an airtight jar and store in a pantry or other cool, dry place. (I leave mine right on the kitchen table.) For added nutrition, include a cup of nutritional yeast in the blend.

Tomato Sauce with Lobster Mushrooms

Plum tomatoes, eggplant, and chili pepper form the base of this lively chunky-style pasta sauce. It also includes fresh meaty lobster mushrooms (chicken of the woods), although dried varieties are equally fabulous. This recipe makes enough sauce for one pound of pasta.

1. Place the eggplant in a large bowl and sprinkle with umeboshi vinegar. Let sit for 45 minutes to release some of the eggplant's bitter juices. Drain and set aside.

2. Heat the oil in a 6-quart stockpot over medium heat. Add the onions, garlic, chili pepper, and eggplant. Sauté, stirring occasionally for 10 minutes, or until the eggplant begins to soften. Add the tomatoes and mushrooms. Simmer covered for 20 minutes, stirring occasionally until the mushrooms wilt and the tomatoes are soft.

3. Stir the red and green peppers into the sauce along with the remaining herbs and spices. Continue simmering 5 minutes to blend the flavors. Adjust seasonings, if desired.

4. Use immediately. Refrigerate any leftovers.

FOR A CHANGE . . .

• Instead of (or in addition to) lobster mushrooms, try white button, shiitake, morels, chanterelles, porcini, or crimini varieties.

• Instead of sea salt, simmer the sauce with a 5-inch strip of dulse or kelp.

• Increase the amount of chilies for a hotter sauce.

• Use any of the flavored oils in Chapter 5.

Yield: About 2 quarts
. . . .
3 1/2 cups eggplant, sliced and quartered

1 teaspoon umeboshi vinegar, or sea salt

2 tablespoons Garlic Flower Oil (page 99), or extra virgin olive oil

2 cups coarsely chopped onions

6 cloves garlic, thickly sliced

1 tablespoon seeded, coarsely chopped mild chili pepper

5 cups coarsely chopped plum tomatoes

2 1/2 cups coarsely chopped lobster mushrooms

1 1/2 cups coarsely chopped red bell pepper

1 cup coarsely chopped green bell pepper

1/2 cup coarsely chopped fresh basil

3 tablespoons fresh oregano, or 1 tablespoon dried

1 tablespoon fresh thyme, or 1 teaspoon dried

1/4 teaspoon fresh rosemary, or pinch dried

1/4 teaspoon fresh sage, or pinch dried

1/2 teaspoon sea salt, or to taste

Pinch black pepper, or to taste

DIPS AND SPREADS

Sunflower Seed and Mushroom Pâté with Oregano and Sage

Yield: About 2 cups

• • • • • • •

³/₄ cup shelled sunflower seeds

1 tablespoon extra virgin olive oil

3 cups coarsely chopped mushrooms

2 cups green beans, cut into 1-inch pieces

1 cup coarsely chopped scallions

3 tablespoons coarsely chopped oregano or marjoram

1 ¹/₂ teaspoons coarsely chopped fresh sage

1 tablespoon dark miso*

* South River brand Three-Year Barley Miso is recommended.

This delicious vegan pâté makes a wonderful dip for fresh vegetables and crackers, as well as a fabulous spread on bread, particularly sourdough.

1. Place the sunflower seeds in medium-sized unoiled skillet over medium heat. Stirring occasionally, dry-roast the seeds for 5 minutes, or until they pop and are fragrant. Transfer to a food processor and grind into a meal.

2. Heat the oil in the skillet over medium heat. Add the mushrooms and beans, and sauté, stirring occasionally for 5 minutes, or until the mushrooms begin to shrivel and the beans turn bright green.

3. Add the sautéed beans and mushrooms to the food processor, along with the scallions, oregano, sage, and miso, and blend until smooth. Adjust the seasonings, if desired.

4. Use immediately. Refrigerate any leftovers.

Cilantro-Olive Spread

*Marinated sun-dried tomatoes and kalamata olives
make this a delicious spread for bread or crackers.
It also makes a fabulous dip for corn chips and vegetables.*

1. Place the almonds in a food processor and grind into flour.

2. Add the remaining ingredients and purée until smooth. Adjust the seasonings, if desired.

3. Use immediately. Refrigerate any leftovers.

FOR A CHANGE . . .

• Instead of puréeing the ingredients, finely chop the garlic, cilantro, tomatoes, and olives, and stir them into the ground almonds for a chunky-style spread.

• Try Marinated Red Peppers with Lemon and Garlic (page 119) instead of Marinated Sun-Dried Tomatoes with Calendula Flowers.

Yield: 1¼ cups

• • • • • • • •

⅓ cup almonds

6 garlic scapes or garlic cloves

½ cup tightly packed cilantro leaves

¼ cup Marinated Sun-Dried Tomatoes with Calendula Flowers (page 117), or plain sun-dried tomatoes in oil

1 tablespoon dark miso*

¼ cup pitted kalamata olives

2 tablespoons orange oil or extra virgin olive oil

¼ cup water

*South River brand Three-Year Barley Miso is recommended.

Roasted Red Pepper and Feta Cheese Dip

*The beauty of this fabulous dip is that it calls for
only three ingredients. Serve it with raw or
steamed vegetables, bread, or corn chips.*

1. Place all the ingredients in a food processor or blender, and blend until smooth.

2. Use immediately. Refrigerate any leftovers.

Yield: About ¾ cup

• • • • • • • •

¾ cup feta cheese

⅓ cup Marinated Red Peppers with Lemon and Garlic (page 119), or plain roasted red peppers

1 tablespoon pitted kalamata olives

Tomatillo Salsa

Yield: About 4 cups

• • • • • • • •

2 cups cherry tomatoes, halved

I cup tomatillos, husked, rinsed, and halved

2 cloves garlic, pressed

I $\frac{1}{2}$ cups diced yellow bell peppers

I teaspoon brown rice vinegar or lime juice

$\frac{1}{2}$ teaspoon seeded, chopped cayenne pepper, or to taste

$\frac{1}{4}$ teaspoon sea salt

Even before you taste this sensational salsa, you will be tempted by its bright orange cherry tomatoes, yellow peppers, and stimulating garlic aroma. This easy-to-prepare salsa is one of my favorite ways to use tomatillos. It makes a great topper for rice and beans on tortillas with warm goat cheese.

1. Place all of the ingredients in a medium-sized mixing bowl, and stir until well combined. Adjust the seasonings, if desired.

2. Use immediately. Refrigerate any leftovers.

Creamy Curry Dip

Yield: About 2 $\frac{1}{3}$ cups

• • • • • • • •

I $\frac{1}{4}$ pounds silken tofu, drained

2 teaspoons chopped or thinly sliced fresh ginger

2 cloves garlic

2 teaspoons curry powder

2 teaspoons Dijon mustard

I teaspoon sea salt, or to taste

$\frac{1}{2}$ teaspoon chili powder

$\frac{1}{2}$ teaspoon turmeric

Great with raw vegetables, this Indian-inspired dip also makes a great dressing. Use it instead of sour cream or mayo in cold potato or pasta salads, or as a condiment on veggie burgers.

1. Place all the ingredients in a food processor or blender, and blend until smooth.

2. Use immediately. Refrigerate any leftovers.

HummBaba

*Serve this delicious blend of two Middle Eastern standards—
hummus and baba ghanoush—on a tray surrounded by pita bread,
olives, sliced tomatoes, cucumbers, carrots, and celery. For a festive
touch, spoon some of this savory spread into scooped-out tomatoes.*

1. Fire up the grill or preheat the broiler.

2. Brush the olive oil on both sides of the eggplant. Grill or broil
3 to 4 minutes on each side, or until soft.

3. Transfer the cooked eggplant and all the remaining ingredients
to a food processor and blend until smooth. Adjust the seasonings,
if desired.

4. Serve immediately as is, or garnished with nasturtium flowers,
chopped parsley, or chopped scallions. Refrigerate any leftovers.

FOR A CHANGE . . .

• Add 1 cup chopped parsley and/or scallions, red onions, or
chives to the mixture before blending.

• Replace the olive oil with Garlic Flower Oil (page 99) or Basil Oil
(page 100).

• Sauté the eggplant in olive oil and garlic before blending with
the other ingredients.

Yield: About 4 cups
. . . .
¹/₄ cup extra virgin olive oil

1 medium eggplant,
sliced lengthwise into
¹/₂-inch-thick strips

2 cups cooked chickpeas
with liquid

¹/₃ cup tahini

¹/₄ cup umeboshi vinegar,
or juice of 1 lemon mixed
with ¹/₂ teaspoon sea salt

5 or 6 cloves garlic

Flavored oils and Vinegars

The emergence of chives, sorrel, and dande- lions hints to me that spring is here. Violets, lemon balm, strawberries, mint, nettles, and morel mushrooms confirm its arrival. In turn, summer offers the early promise of basil, thyme, oregano, nasturtiums, raspberries, chilies, and calendula flowers. The considerable pleasures of these plants linger until fall's first frost. So, from April to October, I use them to make flavored oils and vine- gars. It is the easiest way I know to preserve the wonder- ful aromas, colors, and flavors of fruits, herbs, edible flowers, spices, mushrooms, and other wild foods.

Although I have a few favorite flavored oils and vinegars that I make every year, like Cherry Vinegar and Garlic Basil Oil, I am always experimenting and concocting new combinations. When my neighbor Terry invited me into her garden one spring to pick net- tles, a wild green I had never used fresh before, I immediately suggested we use it for flavoring oils and vinegars.

I ran home and returned with olive oil and cider vinegar, as well as some fresh pears, ginger, and orange zest. Terry and I gathered nettles, vio- lets, mint, and lemon balm, which were grow- ing side by side in her garden, and then went to work in her kitchen stuffing the jars. Using the fresh nettles straight, we made a basic vine- gar and a basic oil. After that, we had fun discussing the endless combinations of in- gredients we had on hand to make more flavored vinegars and oils. We decided to infuse some oil with the violets, mint, and lemon balm (see page 107), and add pears, nettles, ginger, and orange zest to vinegar (see page 93). Both combina- tions turned out great!

Wait until you start flavoring your own oils and vinegars. If you're anything like me, it will become an annual ritual. You'll find yourself experimenting and trying all kinds of different flavor infusions. This chapter, which is divided into two sections—one for oils, the other for vinegars—offers lots of helpful ideas and suggestions. In addition to the ingredient "Mix and Match" chart on page 96, "A Splash of Color" on page 91 will show you which ingredients will turn your vinegar lovely hues. Use the many recipes in this chapter to jump-start your own unique blends, which will add wonderful flavor to soups and salads, pasta, vegetable dishes, and cooked beans and grains.

I'm betting that once you see how easy it is to create these precious liquids and discover the many ways to enjoy them, you'll find yourself creating jar after jar after . . . And the nice thing about keeping a stock of tasty oils and vinegars is that they make great gifts, too (see page 98).

FLAVORED VINEGARS

I remember making my first herbal vinegar. . . . It was back in autumn of 1995. I was one of ten apprentices under the guidance of an herbalist named Kate. Through her, I learned about herbs, wild foods, and edible flowers for health and healing.

I felt at ease, at home in Kate's beautiful healing herb and flower garden. With empty cup-sized jar in hand, I felt the magic in the air. Kate instructed us to be profoundly present and let our intuition guide us. In a delicious dreamlike state, we looked at and listened to the plants to see which ones beckoned us. When we felt inspired, we snipped leaves of basil, mint, or sage, and filled our jars with one type of herb or several. I remember topping my jar off with a pansy after filling it with various wild greens, thyme, chives, and other fragrant herbs. Everyone's jar held different herbs and flowers, which we covered with apple cider vinegar. We screwed on the lids, labeled them with the ingredients and the date, smiled at each other, and took our prized creations home to steep in a dark, cool cabinet.

During that memorable apprenticeship, we did a lot of sharing. We took turns bringing lunch and enjoying each other breads, salads, soups, and, of course, our vinegar creations. Kate made burdock vinegar, which was quite exotic and earthy—delicious. Like many herbalists, she had a wonderful collection of culinary infused oils and vinegars. She inspired me to follow her path. Now, I hope that I inspire you to do the same.

FLAVORED VINEGAR-MAKING "BASICS"

To make flavored vinegar, you can start with just about any vinegar type: wine, apple cider, rice, balsamic, or sherry. Although I certainly encourage you to flavor one or all of these vinegars by adding your own creative blend of ingredients (experimenting can bring about unexpected and magnificent results), be aware that certain ingredients are natural flavor enhancers for specific vinegar types.

Red wine vinegar, for example, pairs well with herbs and spices like rosemary, basil, thyme, oregano, garlic, and bay leaf—alone or in combination. Delicately flavored rice and white wine vinegars take on a delightful taste with the addition of chives, tarragon, and mint. Apple cider vinegar blends well with strong spices like ginger and chilies, wild foods like mushrooms, and fruits and nuts such as cherries and almonds. Balsamic vinegar is wonderful when flavored with vanilla beans and fruits such as strawberries, cranberries, and blueberries. A number of herbs and spices, including basil, oregano, marjoram, thyme, and dill, are quite versatile and complementary to most types of vinegar.

With the exception of dried fruits and mushrooms, I recommend choosing fresh ingredients over dried for flavoring vinegar. They have a better taste and aroma. If you are unsure whether to use particular flowers or wild foods, simply follow your nose. If you like the aroma, use it.

For extra nutrition and flavor, add edible flowers, such as bee balm and red clover; wild greens, such as dandelion and nettles; and wild roots, like burdock and horseradish. And don't forget about flavorful shallots, hot peppers, and ginger. The "Mix and Match" chart on page 96 offers lots of other flavorful suggestions.

FOR THE BEST RESULTS . . .

When preparing flavored vinegar, it's important to keep the following tips in mind for the best results:

❏ Use a clean glass jar with a nonmetallic lid (vinegar will corrode metal). A plastic or enamel-coated lid (the type used on canning jars) or a cork is recommended. If a jar with a metal lid is all that's available, place a piece of wax paper or plastic wrap over the mouth of the jar before screwing on the lid.

❏ When using fresh ingredients—herbs, spices, edible flowers, fruits, mushrooms—fill the jar to the top, and then cover completely with vinegar.

❏ When using dried fruits or mushrooms, fill the jar only halfway with these ingredients, as they will absorb the vinegar and expand, eventually filling the jar. As the ingredients steep and expand, continue adding vinegar to keep the ingredients covered.

❏ When using strong herbs and spices like mint, tarragon, and chilies, fill one-third of the jar with these ingredients, and two-thirds with vinegar.

❏ Once you have finished preparing the jar, label it with the plant (or plants) used, the type of vinegar, and the date it was prepared. Also include the date it will be ready to use—five or six weeks later.

❏ Store the jar in a cool, dark spot out of the sunlight. I like to keep mine in my kitchen cabinet, where I can keep an eye on it to observe color changes and, if needed, to add more vinegar to keep the ingredients covered.

❏ When the vinegar is ready and has been strained into a clean bottle or jar, add a label with the type of vinegar and the date—for example: *Cherry Vinegar, June 2005*. Use immediately or store in a cool dry place, where it will keep for at least a year.

In addition to these guidelines, be sure to check out "A Splash of Color" on page 91. It will show you how to add colorful hues to flavored vinegar. And for some pointers on bottling this precious liquid for gift giving, see the informative inset on page 98.

Shiitake Vinegar

This vinegar is so tasty, it is good enough to drink.
When added to olive oil, it makes a fabulous salad dressing.

1. Loosely pack the shiitake stems in a clean pint jar, and add enough vinegar to cover. Put the cap on the jar, and add a label that includes the jar's contents, the date prepared, and approximate date the vinegar will be ready (5 or 6 weeks from the preparation date). Store in a kitchen cabinet or another cool, dark place.

Yield: About 1 1/3 cups
• • • • • • • •
2/3 cup dried shiitake stems

1 2/3 cups apple cider vinegar

2. Give the jar a daily shake for the first few days. If needed, add more vinegar to keep the shiitake covered.

3. After 5 or 6 weeks, taste the vinegar. If a stronger flavor is desired, let it steep another week.

4. When the vinegar is ready, pour it through a fine mesh strainer or cheesecloth into a bowl, wide-mouth jar, or measuring cup. Before discarding the strained shiitake stems, either squeeze them through the cheesecloth or press them against the strainer with the back of a spoon to get every last drop of vinegar.

5. Transfer the vinegar to a clear bottle or jar, and label it with the type of vinegar and date. Store in a cool, dark place, where it will keep for at least a year.

FOR A CHANGE . . .

• Substitute rice vinegar for the apple cider vinegar.

• Use the caps and/or stems of one or more mushroom varieties, such as porcini, morels, and portabellas. If using fresh mushrooms, use 1 1/2 cups.

• Substitute sun-dried tomatoes for some of the dried shiitake stems.

TIP . . .

Although you can use entire mushrooms for flavoring vinegars and oils, I prefer to steep the tough stems and save the caps for other recipes!

Ginger Rice Vinegar

*For Asian-style recipes that call for rice vinegar and ginger,
you will have all that you need in this bottle. Use it in
the dressing for the Baked Ginger-Arame Rolls on page 75.*

1. Place the ginger in a clean pint jar, and add enough vinegar to cover. Put the cap on the jar, and add a label that includes the jar's contents, date prepared, and approximate date the vinegar will be ready (5 or 6 weeks from the preparation date). Store in a kitchen cabinet or another cool, dark place.

2. Give the jar a daily shake for the first few days. If needed, add more vinegar to keep the ginger covered.

3. After 5 or 6 weeks, taste the vinegar. If a stronger flavor is desired, let it steep another week.

4. When the vinegar is ready, pour it through a fine mesh strainer or cheesecloth into a bowl, wide-mouth jar, or measuring cup. Before discarding the strained ginger, either squeeze it through the cheesecloth or press it against the strainer with the back of a spoon to get every last drop of vinegar.

5. Transfer the vinegar to a clear bottle or jar, and label it with the type of vinegar and date. Store in a cool, dark place, where it will keep for at least a year.

Yield: About 1 cup

• • • • • • •

1 $\frac{1}{3}$ cups coarsely chopped ginger

1 $\frac{1}{3}$ cups rice vinegar

FOR A CHANGE . . .

• Use apple cider vinegar instead of rice vinegar.

• Add 1 teaspoon orange or lemon zest to the jar.

• For an even stronger Asian accent, add a peeled, chopped stalk of lemon grass.

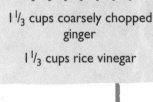

Nettles Vinegar

According to herbalist Susun Weed, nettles—which taste similar to fresh peas or parsley—are loaded with minerals, vitamins, and amino acids. They enhance energy, aid digestion, and are deeply nourishing for women during pregnancy, lactation, menses, and menopause.

Yield: About 2 cups

• • • • • • •

2 cups nettle leaves

2 cups cider vinegar

1. Wearing garden gloves, hold the nettles over a pint jar. Snip them into the jar with a pair of scissors, and add enough cider vinegar to cover. Put the cap on the jar, and add a label that includes the jar's contents, date prepared, and approximate date the vinegar will be ready (5 or 6 weeks from the preparation date). Store in a kitchen cabinet or another cool, dark place.

2. Give the jar a daily shake for the first few days. If needed, add more vinegar to keep the nettles covered.

3. After 5 or 6 weeks, taste the vinegar. If a stronger flavor is desired, let it steep another week.

4. When the vinegar is ready, pour it through a fine mesh strainer or cheesecloth into a bowl, wide-mouth jar, or measuring cup. Before discarding the strained nettles, either squeeze them through the cheesecloth or press them against the strainer with the back of a spoon to get every last drop of vinegar.

5. Transfer the vinegar to a clear bottle or jar, and label it with the type of vinegar and date. Store in a cool, dark place, where it will keep for at least a year.

FOR A CHANGE . . .

- Add 1 soft vanilla bean, snipped into ⅛-inch pieces (about 1 teaspoon).

- Add a sliced fig.

Pine Needle Vinegar

This rather exotic-tasting vinegar is particularly wonderful when made with apple cider or white wine vinegar.

1. Place the pine needles in a clean pint jar, and add enough vinegar to cover. Put the cap on the jar, and add a label that includes the jar's contents, date prepared, and approximate date the vinegar will be ready (5 or 6 weeks from the preparation date). Store in a kitchen cabinet or another cool, dark place.

2. Give the jar a daily shake for the first few days. If needed, add more vinegar to keep the needles covered.

3. After 5 or 6 weeks, taste the vinegar. If a stronger flavor is desired, let it steep another week.

4. When the vinegar is ready, pour it through a fine mesh strainer or cheesecloth into a bowl, wide-mouth jar, or measuring cup. Before discarding the strained needles, either squeeze them through the cheesecloth or press them against the strainer with the back of a spoon to get every last drop of vinegar.

5. Transfer the vinegar to a clear bottle or jar, and label it with the type of vinegar and date. Store in a cool, dark place, where it will keep for at least a year.

Yield: 1²/₃ cups

• • • • • • •

2 cups pine needles

1³/₄ cups white wine vinegar

TIP . . .

Unsure how a particular combination of herbs and spices will taste? Experiment by making a small batch in a baby food jar.

Cherry Vinegar

This vinegar takes only two weeks to achieve a sweet cherry flavor.
If you let the cherries steep for the full six weeks, the vinegar will
have a strong sherry-like taste. Either way it's delicious!

1. Place the cherries in a clean pint jar. Add 1 cup of the vinegar, leaving a few inches of space at the top of the jar for the cherries to expand. Put the cap on the jar, and add a label that includes the jar's contents, date prepared, and approximate date the vinegar will be ready (2 to 6 weeks from the preparation date). Store in a kitchen cabinet or another cool, dark place.

Yield: About 1¼ cups
• • • • • • •
1 cup dried cherries
1⅔ cup apple cider vinegar

2. The next day, add the remaining vinegar. Give the jar a daily shake for the first few days. If needed, add more vinegar to keep the cherries covered.

3. After 2 weeks, check the flavor. If a stronger flavor is desired, let it continue to steep. Continue to check the flavor once a week until the desired strength is reached.

4. When the vinegar is ready, pour it through a fine mesh strainer or cheesecloth into a bowl, wide mouth jar, or measuring cup. Before discarding the strained cherries, either squeeze them through the cheesecloth or press them against the strainer with the back of a spoon to get every last drop of vinegar.

5. Transfer the vinegar to a clear bottle or jar, and label it with the type of vinegar and date. Store in a cool, dark place, where it will keep for at least a year.

FOR A CHANGE . . .

• Use white wine or balsamic vinegar instead of apple cider vinegar.

• Cut up a vanilla bean and add it to the jar.

• Instead of dried cherries, use 2 cups fresh pitted cherries, wild black cherries, raspberries, or other berry variety.

A Splash of Color

A number of ingredients will turn certain vinegars—white wine, rice, and apple cider—lovely hues. Brighten up the color (and flavor) of your homemade vinegars with the following additions.

	INGREDIENT	RESULTING COLOR
FRUITS	Raspberries, strawberries, cranberries, wild cherries, black cherries (fresh or dried)	Red
	Blackberries	Dark purple
	Blueberries	Deep blue
	Black figs	Black
	Elderberries	Purple
	Pears	Amber
HERBS	Purple basil	Magenta
	Shiso leaves	Red
SPICES	Ginger	Golden
FLOWERS	Chive blossoms	Pink
	Dandelion flowers	Golden
	Lavender flowers	Slight lavender tint
MUSHROOMS	Most varieties	Brown
WILD FOODS	Nettles	Brilliant green
	Pine needles	Golden
	Burdock	Tan

Orange-Pear Vinegar

Pears are a delightful addition to salads—I love them in goat cheese salads with figs. I also enjoy the flavor of orange-flavored olive oils and dressings. I thought vinegar that combined the flavors of pears and oranges would be delicious—and it is.

1. Fill a quart jar with alternating layers of pears and orange zest, and add enough vinegar to completely cover. Put the cap on the jar, and add a label that includes the jar's contents, date prepared, and approximate date the vinegar will be ready (5 or 6 weeks from the preparation date). Store in a kitchen cabinet or another cool, dark place.

2. Give the jar a daily shake for the first few days. If needed, add more vinegar to keep the pears covered.

3. After 5 or 6 weeks, taste the vinegar. If a stronger flavor is desired, let it steep another week.

4. When the vinegar is ready, pour it through a fine mesh strainer or cheesecloth into a bowl, wide-mouth jar, or measuring cup. Before discarding the strained ingredients, either squeeze them through the cheesecloth or press them against the strainer with the back of a spoon to get every last drop of vinegar.

Yield: About 2 1/2 cups

• • • • • • •

3 cups coarsely diced Anjou pears

1/4 cup orange zest

2 1/4 cups apple cider vinegar

5. Transfer the vinegar to a clear bottle or jar, and label it with the type of vinegar and date. Store in a cool, dark place, where it will keep for at least a year.

FOR A CHANGE . . .

- Omit the orange zest and add another 1/4 cup pears.
- Instead of orange zest, use 1/4 cup fresh cherries or figs.
- Substitute 3 cups cranberries for the pears.
- Use rice vinegar instead of apple cider vinegar.

Orange-Pear Vinegar with Nettles and Ginger

This outstanding flavored vinegar adds a fresh spark to salads and cooked vegetables.

1. Wearing garden gloves, hold some of the nettles over a 3-cup jar. Snip them into the jar, followed by layers of pears, zest, and ginger. Continue layering the remaining ingredients, then add enough vinegar to cover.

2. Put the cap on the jar, and add a label that includes the jar's contents, date prepared, and approximate date the vinegar will be ready (5 or 6 weeks from the preparation date). Store in a kitchen cabinet or another cool, dark place.

3. Give the jar a daily shake for the first few days. If needed, add more vinegar to keep the ingredients covered.

4. After 5 or 6 weeks, taste the vinegar. If a stronger flavor is desired, let it steep another week.

Yield: About 2 cups

• • • • • • •

2 cups nettle leaves

1 cup coarsely diced Anjou pears

1 tablespoon orange zest

1 $\frac{1}{2}$ teaspoons chopped ginger

2 cups apple cider vinegar

5. When the vinegar is ready, pour it through a fine mesh strainer or cheesecloth into a bowl, wide-mouth jar, or measuring cup. Before discarding the strained ingredients, either squeeze them through the cheesecloth or press them against the strainer with the back of a spoon to get every last drop of vinegar.

6. Transfer the vinegar to a clear bottle or jar, and label it with the type of vinegar and date. Store in a cool, dark place, where it will keep for at least a year.

TIP . . .

Fresh nettles have tiny stingers, which dissolve when cooked or steeped in vinegar. Be sure to wear garden gloves when handling them.

Strawberry-Vanilla Vinegar

Wow! Drizzle a little extra virgin olive oil along with this sweet vinegar over fresh salad greens, toss in a handful of pine nuts, and sprinkle on some crumbled feta for a quick-and-easy main-course meal. When this vinegar is ready, instead of discarding the strawberries, you can add them to salads, or purée them with a little olive oil and pinch of sea salt for a delicious dressing.

Yield: About 2$\frac{1}{3}$ cups

• • • • • • •

4 cups thinly sliced strawberries

I soft vanilla bean, snipped into $\frac{1}{8}$-inch pieces (about I teaspoon)

1$\frac{2}{3}$ cups balsamic vinegar

1. Place a $\frac{1}{2}$-inch layer of strawberries in a quart jar. Sprinkle a few pieces of vanilla bean on top. Continue alternating the remaining strawberries and vanilla, then add enough vinegar to cover.

2. Put the cap on the jar, and add a label that includes the jar's contents, date prepared, and approximate date the vinegar will be ready (5 or 6 weeks from the preparation date). Store in a kitchen cabinet or another cool, dark place.

3. Give the jar a daily shake for the first few days. If needed, add more vinegar to keep the strawberries covered.

4. After 5 or 6 weeks, taste the vinegar. If a stronger flavor is desired, let it steep another week.

5. When the vinegar is ready, pour it through a fine mesh strainer or cheesecloth into a bowl, wide-mouth jar, or measuring cup. Before discarding the strawberries (or saving for later use), squeeze them through the cheesecloth or press them against the strainer with the back of a spoon to get every last drop of vinegar.

6. Transfer the vinegar to a clear bottle or jar, and label it with the type of vinegar and date. Store in a cool, dark place, where it will keep for at least a year.

Taste of Spring

*This aromatic blend of spring's first herbs and flowers
is delicious any time of the year.*

1. Fill a pint jar with alternating layers of sorrel, dandelion petals, chives, and garlic chives, then add enough vinegar to completely cover.

2. Put the cap on the jar, and add a label that includes the jar's contents, date prepared, and approximate date the vinegar will be ready (5 or 6 weeks from the preparation date). Store in a kitchen cabinet or another cool, dark place.

3. Give the jar a daily shake for the first few days. If needed, add more vinegar to keep the ingredients covered.

4. After 5 or 6 weeks, taste the vinegar. If a stronger flavor is desired, let it steep another week.

5. When the vinegar is ready, pour it through a fine mesh strainer or cheesecloth into a bowl, wide-mouth jar, or measuring cup. Before discarding the strained ingredients, either squeeze them through the cheesecloth or press them against the strainer with the back of a spoon to get every last drop of vinegar.

6. Transfer the vinegar to a clear bottle or jar, and label it with the type of vinegar and date. Store in a cool, dark place, where it will keep for at least a year.

Yield: About 1 1/2 cups
· · · · · · ·
1/3 cup ripped sorrel leaves

2 tablespoons ripped dandelion flower petals

1/2 cup coarsely chopped chives

1/3 cup coarsely chopped garlic chives

1 1/2 cups cider vinegar

FOR A CHANGE . . .

- Substitute violets or pansies for the dandelions.

- In the summer, use basil instead of sorrel, and calendula flowers instead of dandelions.

- Use this ingredient combination to make flavored oil.

MIX AND MATCH

The following herbs, spices, mushrooms, fruits, wild foods, and edible flowers are excellent choices (and among my favorites) for making flavored oils and vinegars. Choose one or combine any number of these ingredients to satisfy your creativity and sense of adventure!

Go Wild with Vinegars and oils

HERBS	Arugula, basil, chives, cilantro, dill, fennel, lemon thyme, marjoram, mints, oregano, parsley, rosemary, sage, sorrel, tarragon, and thyme.
SPICES	Chili peppers, garlic varieties, and ginger.
EDIBLE FLOWERS	Bee balm, calendula, chive flowers, chrysanthemums, dandelion flowers, Johnny-jump-ups, lavender, marigolds, nasturtiums, pansies, red clover, rose petals, violets, and wild mustard (for vinegar only).
FRUITS	FOR OILS: Lemons, limes, and sun-dried tomatoes.
	FOR VINEGARS: Apricots, black cherries (wild and domestic), blackberries, blueberries, cranberries, elderberries, figs, lemons, limes, peaches, pears, pomegranates, plums (wild and domestic), raspberries, and strawberries.
WILD FOODS	FOR OILS: Dandelion greens, nettles, and wild horseradish (garlic mustard).
	FOR VINEGARS: Burdock, dandelion greens, nettles, motherwort, pine needles, wild horseradish, and yellow dock root.
ZEST	Lemon, lime, orange, tangelo, and tangerine.

FLAVORED OILS

When I first discovered flavored oils, I was so in love with them I just about stopped using my usual sesame and extra virgin olive oils. The first flavored oil I made was basil oil, which I drizzled on salads, soups, and vegetables. Then I began cooking with it, using it to sauté and roast vegetables and even to fry eggs. I added it to sauces and used it as a dip for bread, as well as a marinade for sun-dried tomatoes and grilled eggplant.

I began by ripping up enough basil leaves to fill a pint jar, but quickly graduated to quarts and then half gallons. The technique for making flavored oils was so simple that I found myself becoming more and more creative with each type I made. Soon I had an assortment of pints and quarts with various herbs, spices, and edible flowers. In addition to basil oil, I made garlic oil, garlic-basil oil, calendula oil, garlic-basil-calendula oil, chili pepper oil, and garlic-fennel oil, among many others. Currently, I have over a dozen assorted flavors. I have also given up drying basil in favor of preserving its freshness in oil.

Every summer, I try new flavored-oil combinations with basil, cilantro, oregano, chili peppers, garlic scapes, calendula flowers, thyme, rosemary, bay leaves, garlic chive flowers, and whatever else I come across. As far as I can tell, no matter what the combination, you can't go wrong. Like flavored vinegars, I recommend choosing fresh ingredients over dried. With the exception of some dried vegetables and mushrooms, fresh ingredients offer stronger flavor and aroma. The "Mix and Match" chart on page 96 offers plenty of suggestions.

Olive oils will not turn rancid, so I recommend using them as the base for flavored oils. (Remember, these oils are being infused for weeks without refrigeration.) There is also an added health bonus. A heart-healthy monounsaturated fat, olive oil is rich in antioxidants and has been shown to actually help lower LDL (bad) cholesterol. While my preference is to use extra virgin olive oil, sometimes its strong flavor can overpower delicate-flavored herbs like marjoram and nettles. For these herbs, I use light olive oil.

FOR THE BEST RESULTS

As you will see, it is easy to "go wild" when concocting flavored oils. For the best results, keep the following tips in mind:

❏ Use a clean glass jar with a lid.

❏ When using fresh ingredients—herbs, spices, flowers, fruits, mushrooms—fill the jar, leaving about an inch of space at the top, and cover completely with oil. This head space will help prevent the oil from oozing out of the jar.

❏ When using strong ingredients like mint, tarragon, or chilies, fill one-third of the jar with these ingredients and two-thirds with oil.

❏ When using dried mushrooms or sun-dried tomatoes, fill the jar only halfway with these ingredients, as they will absorb the oil and expand, eventually filling the jar. As the ingredients steep and expand, you will have to continue adding oil to keep them covered.

❏ Before screwing on the lid, try to eliminate any air holes by pressing the ingredients down gently with a butter knife.

❏ Once you have prepared the jar, label it with

the contents, including the type of oil, and the date it was prepared. Also include the date it will be ready to use—two to six weeks later.

❏ Place the jar on a small plate and set it on a windowsill. After two weeks, check the flavor of the oil, and continue checking it once a week after that. The oil is ready when you are. I have found that a sunny window tends to shorten the steeping time.

❏ As the ingredients steep, the oil may expand and leak from the jar—especially when set on a sunny windowsill. No Problem! Keep the jar on a small plate to catch the flavorful overflow, and then use the oil to cook with, add to salads, or enjoy as a dip for bread. Delicious!

❏ When the oil is ready and has been strained into a clean bottle or jar, add a label with the type of oil and the date—for example: *Basil Oil, August 2004*. As a decorative touch, consider adding a fresh herb or another ingredient that was used to flavor the oil. Store in a cool dry place, where it will keep for at least a year.

Following these guidelines will help to insure successful results with your flavored oils. Be sure to check out the inset below for some pointers on bottling this precious liquid for gift giving.

GIVING THE GIFT OF FLAVORED OILS AND VINEGARS

Walk into any upscale gourmet shop, health food store, farmers market, or department store, and you're sure to notice bottles of flavored oils and vinegars on the shelves. Although wonderful to have on hand in the kitchen, these specialty items can be rather pricey. Knowing how to make your own can certainly be a money-saving effort (as well as an opportunity to choose the best ingredients), especially if you have your own garden or belong to a CSA—community supported agriculture—group (see page 130). As an added bonus, these flavorful liquids make great gifts!

Unlike homemade pickles, preserves, and tomato sauces, which also make wonderful gifts, infused oils and vinegars need no cooking and cause very little mess. A few creative touches are all you need. Although your family and friends will be just as pleased if the precious liquid comes in a plain jar, a decorative bottle offers a more "gift-like" presentation. Whether tall and slim, round or short, clear or colored, the bottle you choose needs only a lid or cork. Chances are, you already have one from a previously purchased bottle of spring water, oil, or vinegar.

If you have used an herb to flavor the oil or vinegar, consider inserting a fresh sprig into the bottle along with the liquid. After filling the bottle, tie a decorative ribbon around its neck, and add a tag or label that includes the type of oil or vinegar within.

Be creative and have fun decorating.

Garlic Flower Oil

Capture summer in a bottle with the mild garlicky flavor of garlic scapes. Use this oil to add the essence of garlic to marinated sun-dried tomatoes, roasted vegetables, pizza, pasta, eggs, sauces, soups, and dressings—on anything you would use fresh garlic and olive oil.

1. Loosely pack the scapes in a clean pint jar, leaving about an inch of space at the top. Add enough oil to cover (still leaving an inch of space). Using a butter knife, gently press down the scapes to eliminate any air pockets.

2. Put the cap on the jar, and add a label that includes the contents, date prepared, and approximate date the oil will be ready (2 to 6 weeks from the preparation date).

3. Place the jar on a small plate and set on a windowsill. After 2 weeks, taste the oil. If stronger flavor is desired, let it continue to steep. Continue to check once a week.

4. When the oil is ready, pour it through a fine mesh strainer or cheesecloth into a bowl, wide-mouth jar, or measuring cup. Before discarding the strained scapes, either squeeze them with your hands (with or without the cheesecloth) or press them against the strainer with the back of a spoon to get every last drop of oil.

5. Transfer the oil to a clean bottle or jar with a lid or cork, and label it with the type of oil and date. Store in a cool dry place, where it will keep for at least a year.

Yield: About 1 cup
• • • • • • •
2 cups coarsely chopped garlic scapes (stems and blossoms)

1 1/4 cups extra virgin olive oil

FOR A CHANGE . . .

• Instead of garlic scapes, use garlic chive flowers or calendula flowers (the petals and daisy-like centers).

Basil oil

*Basil oil has become a staple in my kitchen. I use it to marinate
sun-dried tomatoes, roast vegetables, and flavor salad
dressings—be sure to try it with Cherry Vinegar (page 90).
I also drizzle it over pasta with a little salt and fresh garlic
for a quick meal that's loved by kids of all ages.*

Yield: About 3½ cups

· · · · · · ·

4 cups ripped
basil leaves

3½ cups extra virgin
olive oil

1. Loosely pack the basil in a clean quart jar, leaving about an
inch of space at the top. Add enough oil to cover (still allowing an
inch of space). Using a butter knife, gently press down the basil to
eliminate any air pockets.

2. Put the cap on the jar, and add a label that includes the contents, date prepared, and approximate date the oil will be ready
(2 to 6 weeks from the preparation date).

3. Place the jar on a small plate and set on a windowsill. After
2 weeks, taste the oil. If stronger flavor is desired, let it continue
to steep. Continue to check once a week.

4. When the oil is ready, pour it through a fine mesh strainer or
cheesecloth into a bowl, wide-mouth jar, or measuring cup. Before
discarding the strained basil leaves (or saving for later use), either
squeeze them with your hands (with or without the cheesecloth)
or press them against the strainer with the back of a spoon to get
every last drop of oil.

5. Transfer the oil to a clean bottle or jar with a lid or cork, and
label it with the type of oil and date. Store in a cool dry place,
where it will keep for at least a year.

FOR A CHANGE . . .

• Add a bay leaf or chili pepper for added flavor interest.

Basil-Cilantro- Lemon Oil

Drizzle this tasty oil on a crisp green salad or over a platter of fresh mozzarella, sliced tomatoes, and fresh basil.

1. Place $\frac{1}{2}$ cup of basil in the bottom of a clean pint jar. Sprinkle on $\frac{1}{2}$ tablespoon of lemon zest, and $\frac{1}{4}$ cup cilantro. Continue layering the remaining basil, zest, and cilantro, leaving about an inch of space at the top of the jar. Add enough oil to cover (still allowing an inch of space).

2. Using a butter knife, gently press down the mushrooms to eliminate any air pockets. Put the cap on the jar, and add a label that includes the contents, date prepared, and approximate date the oil will be ready (2 to 6 weeks from the preparation date).

3. Place the jar on a small plate and set on a windowsill. After 2 weeks, taste the oil. If stronger flavor is desired, let it continue to steep. Continue to check once a week.

4. When the oil is ready, pour it through a fine mesh strainer or cheesecloth into a bowl, wide-mouth jar, or measuring cup. Before discarding the strained ingredients (or saving for later use), either squeeze them with your hands (with or without the cheesecloth) or press them against the strainer with the back of a spoon to get every last drop of oil.

5. Transfer the oil to a clean bottle or jar with a lid or cork, and label it with the type of oil and date. Store in a cool dry place, where it will keep for at least a year.

FOR A CHANGE . . .

- Use a chili pepper instead of lemon zest for a spicy flavored oil.
- Substitute lime zest for the lemon.

Yield: About $1\frac{1}{2}$ cups

. . . .

$1\frac{1}{3}$ cups ripped basil leaves

2 tablespoons lemon zest

$\frac{2}{3}$ cup coarsely chopped cilantro leaves

$1\frac{1}{2}$ cups extra virgin olive oil

Fennel-Calendula Oil

When it's August in New England, bright yellow-orange calendula flowers and feathery fresh fennel abound. Versatile and fragrant, this oil is especially wonderful drizzled over salads with raspberry vinegar. Use it all year round to jazz up sautés and stews, grilled vegetables, and sun-dried tomatoes.

Yield: About 2 cups

• • • • • • •

2 1/2 cups coarsely chopped fennel stalks and hearts

2 cups fresh calendula flower heads (18 to 20)

1 1/2–2 cups extra virgin olive oil

1. Place 1/2 cup of fennel in the bottom of a clean quart jar. Top with 1/2 cup of calendula flowers, ripping up their petals and daisy-like centers as you add them. Continue layering the remaining fennel and calendula, leaving about an inch of space at the top of the jar. Add enough oil to cover (still allowing an inch of space).

2. Using a butter knife, gently press down the fennel and calendula to eliminate any air pockets. Put the cap on the jar, and add a label that includes the contents, date prepared, and approximate date the oil will be ready (2 to 6 weeks from the preparation date).

3. Place the jar on a small plate and set on a windowsill. After 2 weeks, taste the oil. If stronger flavor is desired, let it continue to steep. Continue to check once a week.

4. When the oil is ready, pour it through a fine mesh strainer or cheesecloth into a bowl, wide-mouth jar, or measuring cup. Before discarding the strained ingredients (or saving for later use), either squeeze them with your hands (with or without the cheesecloth) or press them against the strainer with the back of a spoon to get every last drop of oil.

5. Transfer the oil to a clean bottle or jar with a lid or cork, and label it with the type of oil and date. Store in a cool dry place, where it will keep for at least a year.

FOR A CHANGE . . .

• Add 1 or 2 bay leaves.

• Instead of fennel, use thyme or cilantro for a more subtle flavor.

Garlic Basil Oil

This fragrant oil always reminds me of fresh hot pizza. It's one of my kitchen staples, and once you see how easy it is to make, I'm betting it will become one of yours, too. With this oil on hand, there's no need to peel garlic or chop basil. A healthy splash gives flavorful interest to croutons, soups, dressings, marinades, sautés, and eggs. Or simply sprinkle some on warm pasta for a quick meal.

1. Place ½ cup of garlic scapes in the bottom of a clean quart jar. Top with ½ cup of basil and ½ cup of calendula flowers, ripping up their petals and daisy-like centers as you add them. Continue layering the remaining scapes, basil, and calendula, leaving about an inch of space at the top of the jar. Add enough oil to cover (still allowing an inch of space).

2. Using a butter knife, gently press down the ingredients to eliminate any air pockets. Put the cap on the jar, and add a label that includes the contents, date prepared, and approximate date the oil will be ready (2 to 6 weeks from the preparation date).

3. Place the jar on a small plate and set on a windowsill. After 2 weeks, taste the oil. If stronger flavor is desired, let it continue to steep. Continue to check once a week.

4. When the oil is ready, pour it through a fine mesh strainer or cheesecloth into a bowl, wide-mouth jar, or measuring cup. Before discarding the strained ingredients (or saving for later use), squeeze them with your hands (with or without the cheesecloth) or press them against the strainer with the back of a spoon to get every last drop of oil.

5. Transfer the oil to a clean bottle or jar with a lid or cork, and label it with the type of oil and date. Store in a cool dry place, where it will keep for at least a year.

Yield: About 2 cups

• • • • • • •

1½ cups coarsely chopped garlic scapes (stems and blossoms)

1½ cups ripped basil leaves

1 cup calendula flower heads (9 or 10)

2 cups extra virgin olive oil

FOR A CHANGE . . .

- Instead of garlic scapes, use garlic cloves, garlic chives, or garlic chive flowers.

- Use sun-dried tomatoes or mushrooms instead of calendula flowers.

- Add a chili pepper for a "spark" of flavor.

Mushroom Orange Oil

If you love mushrooms, you'll love the flavor of this oil. You can use the stems of any wild and/or domestic mushroom, and save the caps for another use. Shiitakes, white button, crimini, morel, black trumpets, chanterelles, and portabellas are good choices.

1. Place ½ cup of mushroom stems in the bottom of a clean pint jar. Sprinkle with 1 tablespoon orange zest. Continue layering the remaining mushrooms and zest, leaving about an inch of space at the top of the jar. Add enough oil to cover (still allowing an inch of space).

Yield: About 1⅓ cups

• • • • • • •

1½ cups fresh mushroom stems (any variety)

¼ cup orange zest

1⅓ cups extra virgin olive oil

2. Using a butter knife, gently press down the mushrooms to eliminate any air pockets. Put the cap on the jar, and add a label that includes the contents, date prepared, and approximate date the oil will be ready (2 to 6 weeks from the preparation date).

3. Place the jar on a small plate and set on a windowsill. After 2 weeks, taste the oil. If stronger flavor is desired, let it continue to steep. Continue to check once a week.

4. When the oil is ready, pour it through a fine mesh strainer or cheesecloth into a bowl, wide-mouth jar, or measuring cup. Before discarding the mushrooms, either squeeze them with your hands (with or without the cheesecloth) or press them against the strainer with the back of a spoon to get every last drop of oil.

5. Transfer the oil to a clean bottle or jar with a lid or cork, and label it with the type of oil and date. Store in a cool dry place, where it will keep for at least a year.

FOR A CHANGE . . .

- Omit the zest.
- Use caps and stems from a combination of mushroom varieties.

Hot Pepper Oil

I like to make this oil very hot, so a little bit goes a long way.
Feel free to use a larger proportion of oil to chilies for a milder taste.

1. Place the peppers in a clean 1-cup jar. Cover with oil, leaving an inch of space at the top. Using a butter knife, gently press down the peppers to eliminate any air pockets.

2. Put the cap on the jar, and add a label that includes the contents, date prepared, and approximate date the oil will be ready (2 to 6 weeks from the preparation date).

3. Place the jar on a small plate and set on a windowsill. After 2 weeks, taste the oil. If stronger flavor is desired, let it continue to steep. Continue to check once a week.

Yield: About $\frac{2}{3}$ cup

• • • • • • •

$\frac{1}{3}$ cup seeded, coarsely chopped cayenne peppers

$\frac{3}{4}$ cup extra virgin olive oil

4. When the oil is ready, pour it through a fine mesh strainer or cheesecloth into a bowl, wide-mouth jar, or measuring cup. Before discarding the strained peppers (or saving for later use), either squeeze them with your hands (with or without the cheesecloth) or press them against the strainer with the back of a spoon to get every last drop of oil.

5. Transfer the oil to a clean bottle or jar with a lid or cork, and label it with the type of oil and date. Store in a cool dry place, where it will keep for at least a year.

FOR A CHANGE . . .

• Use combinations of hot and mild chili peppers.

TIP . . .

Certain ingredients used to flavor your oil can be saved for later use. Add steeped basil to pesto, salad dressings, and tomato-based sauces; use hot peppers in spicy dishes like chili; and toss calendula flowers into stir-fries or purée them before adding to sauces or dressings.

Tarragon and Thyme Oil

Tarragon and thyme lend a wonderful French accent to this flavorful oil. This herbal combination is also good for flavoring red or white wine vinegar.

Yield: About 1 1/3 cups

- - - - - - -

2/3 cup coarsely chopped
thyme leaves

1/3 cup coarsely chopped
tarragon leaves

1 1/3 cup extra virgin
olive oil

1. Place some of the thyme in the bottom of a clean pint jar, and top with some tarragon. Continue layering, leaving about an inch of space at the top of the jar. Add enough oil to cover (still allowing an inch of space).

2. Using a butter knife, gently press down the herbs to eliminate any air pockets. Put the cap on the jar, and add a label that includes the contents, date prepared, and approximate date the oil will be ready (2 to 6 weeks from the preparation date).

3. Place the jar on a small plate and set on a windowsill. After 2 weeks, taste the oil. If stronger flavor is desired, let it continue to steep. Continue to check once a week.

4. When the oil is ready, pour it through a fine mesh strainer or cheesecloth into a bowl, wide-mouth jar, or measuring cup. Before discarding the strained herbs, either squeeze them with your hands (with or without the cheesecloth) or press them against the strainer with the back of a spoon to get every last drop of oil.

5. Transfer the oil to a clean bottle or jar with a lid or cork, and label it with the type of oil and date. Store in a cool dry place, where it will keep for at least a year.

FOR A CHANGE . . .

- Instead of tarragon, use cilantro; and add a bay leaf to the mixture as it steeps.

Lemon-Mint Oil

Here is a perfect oil for seasoning tabouli salad.

1. Place half the lemon balm in the bottom of a clean pint jar, sprinkle with half the mint, and then half the violets. Repeat the layers, leaving about an inch of space at the top of the jar. Add enough oil to cover (still allowing an inch of space).

2. Using a butter knife, gently press down the lemon balm, mint, and violets to eliminate any air pockets. Put the cap on the jar, and add a label that includes the contents, date prepared, and approximate date the oil will be ready (2 to 6 weeks from the preparation date).

3. Place the jar on a small plate and set on a windowsill. After 2 weeks, taste the oil. If stronger flavor is desired, let it continue to steep. Continue to check once a week.

4. When the oil is ready, pour it through a fine mesh strainer or cheesecloth into a bowl, wide-mouth jar, or measuring cup. Before discarding the strained ingredients, either squeeze them with your hands (with or without the cheesecloth) or press them against the strainer with the back of a spoon to get every last drop of oil.

5. Transfer the oil to a clean bottle or jar with a lid or cork, and label it with the type of oil and date. Store in a cool dry place, where it will keep for at least a year.

Yield: About $1^2/_3$ cups

• • • • • • •

1 cup coarsely ripped lemon balm

$^1/_4$ cup coarsely ripped mint leaves

$^3/_4$ cup purple and white violet flowers

$1^2/_3$ cups extra virgin olive oil

FOR A CHANGE . . .

• Omit the violet flowers and increase the mint to 1 cup.

• Instead of violets, use chives or garlic chives.

• Substitute thyme for the mint.

• Replace the mint and lemon balm with nettles.

6

Salads and "Wraps"

The salad is one of the most versatile of foods. It can be a simple combination of fresh baby greens crowned with a splash of flavorful dressing, an impressive prelude to a meal, or a simple side dish. As a main course, salads can be a spectacular feast of beans, grains, goat and sheep cheeses, fruits, and vegetables. And you can really go wild by adding edible flowers, wild greens, and a wide array of herbs.

This chapter presents a number of delectable salads; many offer new takes on old favorites. There is Quinoa Tabouli—a delicious sesame-flavored change from the traditional salad made with couscous or bulgur wheat. Pressed cabbage gets a tasty jolt in the Crisp Cabbage Salad with Watercress and Caraway Seeds, while the Feta Cheese Salad with Kamut Pasta is a summertime salad favorite. The colorful contrast of carrots and parsley against black arame and white noodles gives the Japanese Sea Vegetable and Noodle Salad its remarkable beauty.

This chapter also presents a number of my favorite "wraps," which can be partnered with salads or enjoyed on their own. They do, however, go far beyond the traditional sandwich wrap in which a tortilla is piled high with a filling and then rolled into a neatly sealed package. The "wraps" in this chapter include quesadillas, sushi, egg rolls, and even knishes that are unconventionally covered with egg-roll wrappers before they are baked or fried. Be sure to try the Seitan Quesadillas or Baked Ginger Arame Rolls when a satisfying entrée is what you're craving. And when company is coming, serve some Potato-Olive Knishes or Ginger Tempeh Sushi. The Cabbage, Scallion, and Cilantro Egg Rolls are other showstoppers.

I'm getting hungry just thinking about these delicious foods. Come on, let's get started!

The creative art of cooking lies in being adaptable. You can substitute ingredients by colors, seasons, flavors, and textures. Use the choices below as a swap chart to concoct your own variations of this chapter's recipes.

EDIBLE FLOWERS	Anise hyssop, bee balm, borage, blueberry, calendula, chive flowers, comfrey, dandelions, day lily flowers and pods, garlic chive flowers, Johnny-jump-ups, mallow, marigolds, nasturtiums, pansies, purple vetch (pea), red clover, rose petals, violets, wild daisies, and wild mustard.
DOMESTIC/ WILD GREENS	Romaine, green leaf, red leaf, red oak, Boston, and bibb lettuce. Baby chard, bok choy, chickweed, dandelion greens, frisee, garlic mustard, lambs quarters, mache, mizuna, purslane, red mustard greens, sheep sorrel, spinach, tat soi, and watercress.
ONION VARIETIES	Chives, chive blossoms, ramps (wild leeks), red onions, and scallions.
TOMATO VARIETIES	Plum, beefsteak, vine-ripe, and other heirloom tomato varieties; cherry tomatoes; grape tomatoes; and sun-dried tomatoes.
BEANS	Anasazi beans, chickpeas, Great Northern beans, kidney beans, navy beans (cannellini), and pinto beans.
SEA VEGETABLES	LEAFY VARIETIES: Alaria, digitata kelp, dulse, kelp, ocean ribbons kombu, and wakame.
	NOODLE-LIKE VARIETIES: Arame, hiziki, and sea palm.
CHILI PEPPERS	VERY HOT: Cayenne peppers, habañero chilies, and Scotch bonnets.
	MODERATELY HOT: Serrano chilies.
	MILDLY HOT: Anaheim chilies, ancho chilies, jalapeño peppers, and poblano chilies.
HERBS AND SPICES	See "Spice It Up!" (page 8) for substitutions.
OILS	IN DRESSINGS: Extra virgin olive oil, flavored oil varieties (see Chapter 5).
	FOR FRYING: Canola oil, peanut oil.
	FOR BAKING: Canola oil, light olive oil.
SALTY SEASONINGS	Dulse flakes, kelp granules, miso, nori flakes, sea salt, shoyu, tamari, umeboshi vinegar, and Bragg Liquid Aminos.

Corn Salad With Strawberries, Chèvre, and Raspberry Vinaigrette

*Layer the ingredients or mix them together.
Either way, this salad, with its honey-sweetened dressing,
is both beautiful and delicious.*

1. In a large salad bowl, combine the lettuce, cabbage, corn, and cheese. Garnish with strawberries.

2. Place all of the dressing ingredients in a blender and purée until smooth. Adjust the seasonings, if desired.

3. Pour the dressing over the salad and serve.

FOR A CHANGE . . .

• Instead of strawberries, use blackberries, blueberries, boysen-berries, or huckleberries.

• Try crumbled blue cheese instead of chèvre.

• For a vegan version, omit the cheese.

• Replace the lettuce and/or red cabbage with mesclun salad mix.

Yield: 6 to 8 servings

4 cups tightly packed lettuce leaves, torn into bite-sized pieces

2 cups thinly sliced red cabbage

1 cup fresh or frozen corn kernels

4.5 ounces chèvre, crumbled

10 strawberries

Raspberry Vinaigrette

1 cup fresh or frozen raspberries

$1/2$ cup water

2 tablespoons balsamic vinegar

4 teaspoons honey, or to taste

$1/4$ teaspoon sea salt

Feta Cheese Salad

No matter which type of feta—goat, sheep, or cow's milk—you use, you are sure to score with this quick and easy-to-prepare main-course salad. It's an ideal dish for a picnic lunch or potluck dinner.

Yield: 4 servings

4 cups green leaf lettuce, torn into bite-sized pieces

1 pint (about 2 cups) cherry tomatoes, stems removed

2$\frac{1}{2}$ cups seedless cucumber slices, quarters or half moons

1 cup coarsely chopped red bell peppers

1 cup coarsely chopped red radishes

$\frac{1}{2}$ cup pitted kalamata olives

5–8 ounces feta cheese, crumbled

$\frac{1}{4}$ cup extra virgin olive oil

4 teaspoons coarsely chopped fresh oregano, or 2 teaspoons dried

$\frac{1}{2}$ teaspoon sea salt, or to taste

$\frac{1}{2}$ cup coarsely chopped scallions or chives

1. Place the lettuce, tomatoes, cucumbers, peppers, radishes, and olives in a large bowl. Toss gently.

2. Add the feta, oil, oregano, and salt. Mix well. Adjust the seasonings, if desired.

3. Garnish with scallions and serve.

FOR A CHANGE . . .

• Replace the scallions with one or more edible flowers, such as borage, nasturtiums, calendula, day lilies, and bee balm.

• Use marjoram instead of oregano, or a combination of oregano and mint.

• Instead of red radishes, try radicchio, daikon radish, or cauliflower florets.

FYI . . .

In Greece, delicious feta cheese is made from a combination of goat and sheep milk. Feta from France is made with goat's milk, and in the USA, you may be familiar with cow's milk feta. All have slightly different sweet and salty flavors.

White Bean Salad with Fresh Fennel and Capers

The first time I made this salad was also the first time I used fresh fennel. I chopped up and used the tough celery-like stalks and outer leaves of the fennel, and threw away the bulb's inner heart. The exquisite dressing still provided delicious results. Years later, I learned that the heart of the bulb is the preferred part—as it is sweeter and more tender. For a quicker, easier version of this salad, use 4 cups canned Great Northern beans.

Yield: 6 to 8 servings

4½ cups water

1½ cups dried Great Northern beans, presoaked (page 14), rinsed, and drained

5-inch strip ocean ribbons kombu or kelp

1 small fennel bulb (about 8 ounces)

1½ cups thinly sliced red or green bell pepper

1 cup coarsely chopped zucchini

½ cup coarsely chopped red radishes

¼ cup capers (rinse if packed in salt)

½ cup orange juice

2 tablespoons extra virgin olive oil

1 tablespoon balsamic vinegar

1 teaspoon grated orange zest

1 teaspoon ground cumin

1 teaspoon white wine or champagne vinegar, optional

1. Bring the water, beans, and kombu to boil in a 2-quart stockpot. Reduce the heat to medium-low and simmer covered for 1½ hours, or until the beans are tender. Drain and set aside to cool.

2. Discard the celery-like stalks and fronds from the fennel. Peel away and discard any tough outer leaves. Cut the bulb in half, then slice the halves into thin strips.

3. Combine the beans, fennel, pepper, zucchini, radishes, and capers in a large mixing bowl.

4. In a small bowl, whisk together the orange juice, oil, balsamic vinegar, zest, cumin, and vinegar (if using) until well combined. Drizzle over the salad ingredients and toss. Adjust the seasonings, if desired.

5. Serve immediately.

Japanese Sea Vegetable and Noodle Salad

The colorful contrast of the carrots and parsley against the black arame and white noodles gives this Asian-style salad its remarkable beauty. It is also rich in calcium and quick to make.

Yield: 8 servings

1 cup dried arame

4 cups thinly sliced green cabbage

4 cups coarsely chopped parsley

1 1/2 cups julienned carrots

1/4 cup coarsely chopped lovage leaves or celery

1/4 cup coarsely chopped chives, including blossoms

5.3-ounce package bifun noodles, or 3 cups cooked udon noodles

3 tablespoons toasted sesame oil

3 tablespoons umeboshi vinegar

3 tablespoons rice vinegar

6 ounces baked or smoked tofu, cut into 1-inch cubes

1. In a large bowl, cover the arame with water and soak for 5 to 7 minutes, or until tender. Drain and return to the bowl. Discard the soaking water or save it for soup stock or use to water plants.

2. Add the cabbage, parsley, carrots, lovage, and chives to the arame. Mix gently and set aside.

3. Cook the noodles according to package directions, rinse in cold water, and drain.

4. Add the noodles to the vegetables along with the oil, umeboshi vinegar, and rice vinegar. Toss well. Adjust the seasonings, if desired.

5. Garnish with tofu and serve.

FOR A CHANGE . . .

• Replace bifun or udon noodles with soba noodles or angel hair pasta.

• Instead of green cabbage, use snow peas, snap peas, or a combination of red and green cabbage. Steamed vegetables, such as beets, carrots, broccoli, cauliflower, and green beans are other good choices.

Quinoa Tabouli

Foolproof! Even when I have left out the lemon juice, mint, or tomatoes, this recipe works. The sesame-flavored quinoa stands in beautifully for the bulgur or couscous traditionally used in tabouli. Mixed with fragrant olive oil, olives, chives, and parsley, this main-course salad is one of my family's summertime favorites.

1. Bring the water to boil in a 2-quart pot.

2. Place the quinoa in an unoiled skillet over medium-low heat. Stirring constantly, dry-roast the quinoa about 3 minutes, or until it pops and smells like sesame seeds. Turn off the heat.

3. Add the boiling water and salt to the quinoa. Turn the heat back to medium-low, cover, and simmer 15 minutes, or until the water is absorbed.

4. Transfer the quinoa to a large mixing bowl and cool to room temperature. Stir often to hasten cooling.

5. Add the tomatoes, cucumbers, parsley, mint, olives, chives, lemon juice, and oil to the quinoa, and mix well. Adjust the seasonings, if desired.

6. Garnish with fresh flowers, if desired, and serve.

FOR A CHANGE . . .

• If you're out of mint, try cooking the quinoa in mint tea. When the water comes to a boil, add 2 mint tea bags, turn off the heat, and let steep at least 10 minutes. Bring the tea to a boil before adding to the dry-roasted quinoa.

• Instead of parsley, use lettuce, baby red kale, mizuna, tat soi, or other leafy salad green.

• Substitute spelt cous, spelt bulgur, couscous, or bulgur wheat for the quinoa. If using spelt cous or spelt bulgur, use only $2\frac{1}{4}$ cups water.

Yield: 4 to 6 servings

3 cups water

$1\frac{1}{2}$ cups quinoa, rinsed and drained

1 teaspoon sea salt

3 cups coarsely chopped red or yellow tomatoes

2 cups quartered cucumber

1 cup coarsely chopped parsley

$\frac{1}{2}$ cup coarsely chopped mint

$\frac{1}{2}$ cup pitted kalamata olives

$\frac{1}{2}$ cup chopped chives

$\frac{1}{3}$ cup lemon juice

5 tablespoons extra virgin olive oil

$\frac{1}{3}$ cup nasturtium, borage, calendula, or bee balm flower petals, optional

Crisp Cabbage Salad with Watercress and Caraway Seeds

Yield: 6 to 8 servings

• • • • • • • •

7 1/2 cups thinly sliced green cabbage

2 1/2 cups thinly sliced red cabbage

1 1/2 cups coarsely chopped watercress

1 cup thinly sliced red radishes

1 cup coarsely chopped scallions

2 tablespoons caraway seeds

2 tablespoons sea salt

Adding salt before pressing these vegetables helps release their juices. The result is a crisp, somewhat pickle-flavored salad.

1. Place all the ingredients in a vegetable press or large mixing bowl and stir well. If using a press, tighten it; if using a bowl, place a large plate on top of the ingredients and weigh it down with a large rock, a gallon jar filled with beans or some other weight.

2. Press the ingredients for at least 30 minutes and as long as 1 1/4 hours. Toss before serving.

MORE CREATIVE SALAD IDEAS

Consider the following salad recommendations:

✔ Substitute *similar-tasting* vegetables for each other. Use *cauliflower* for cabbage, *daikon radishes* for red radishes, and *green peas* for snow peas or snap peas.

✔ Change the flavor and color of a salad by substituting *radicchio* for some of the lettuce or other salad greens.

✔ Substitute *similar-textured* vegetables for each other. Try radish varieties instead of *jicama* or *turnips*, cucumbers instead of *zucchini*, and green beans instead of *carrots*.

✔ Change the appearance of a dish by *choosing among different colored varieties* of the same vegetable. Use red or green cabbage; or various bell pepper varieties—red, yellow, green, and orange.

Marinated Sun-Dried Tomatoes with Calendula Flowers

These tomatoes are one of my kitchen staples. I add them to pizza, roast them with vegetables and beans, blend them into pesto, and toss them in stir-fries and salads.

1. Place the tomatoes and vinegar in a bowl. Stirring occasionally, marinate for two hours, or until the tomatoes absorb most of the vinegar and soften.

2. Add the garlic, basil, and oregano. Toss in the calendula flowers whole, or gently remove the petals before adding them to the bowl along with the flower centers. Mix the ingredients well.

3. Transfer the mixture to a clean pint jar, and add enough oil to cover.

4. Store in the kitchen pantry, where it will keep for at least a year.

FOR A CHANGE . . .

• Substitute garlic chive flowers or coarsely chopped garlic scapes for the garlic cloves.

• Layer the ingredients directly in the jar, instead of mixing them in a bowl first.

• Add 1 tablespoon fresh thyme to the mixture.

• Omit the calendula flowers.

Yield: About 2 cups

• • • • • • •

1 1/2 cups sun-dried tomatoes

1/2 cup balsamic vinegar or wine

5 cloves garlic, thickly sliced

2–3 tablespoons coarsely chopped fresh basil

2–3 tablespoons fresh oregano leaves

3 calendula flower heads

1 cup extra virgin olive oil, Basil Oil (page 100), or Garlic Basil Oil (page 103)

TIP . . .

When adding edible flowers to salads or sandwiches, choose only varieties that come from an organic garden, have been grown in the wild, or come in a package labeled "pesticide-free." They are the safest to eat and the most flavorful.

Feta Cheese Salad with Kamut Pasta

This summer fresh salad highlights hearty kamut spirals, flavorful marinated sun-dried tomatoes, feta cheese, olives, and fresh juicy tomatoes. It's so tasty, there is no need to add salt.

1. Bring a 4-quart pot of water to a rolling boil. Add the kamut spirals and cook according to package directions. Rinse under cold water, drain well, and place in a large mixing bowl.

2. Add the fresh tomatoes, bell peppers, feta, capers, sun-dried tomatoes, oil, and half the olives. Mix well. Adjust the seasonings, if desired.

3. Garnish with the remaining olives and serve.

FOR A CHANGE . . .

• Instead of kamut, try this salad with other types of pasta, such as rice, wheat, spinach, tomato, and basil-garlic. And use different shaped pasta like penne and bow ties.

Yield: 4 to 6 servings

• • • • • • •

12-ounce package kamut spirals

2 cups coarsely chopped tomatoes

1 $\frac{1}{2}$ cups coarsely chopped green bell peppers

8 ounces feta cheese, crumbled

$\frac{1}{2}$ cup capers (rinse if packed in salt)

$\frac{1}{2}$ cup tightly packed sun-dried tomatoes in oil, or Marinated Sun-Dried Tomatoes with Calendula Flowers (page 117)

$\frac{1}{4}$ cup extra virgin olive oil

$\frac{1}{4}$ cup pitted kalamata olives

TIP . . .

Edible flowers are delicate and wilt easily. Always dress and toss the salad before adding them.

Marinated Red Peppers with Lemon and Garlic

Grilling and marinating many pounds of red, orange, and yellow bell peppers is one of the best antidotes I know for the changing seasons—when lush green summer turns into colorful New England fall. Like my flavored oils, these marinated peppers have become a welcomed staple in my kitchen. They're wonderful in chili, hummus, sushi, polenta, omelets, and tofu scrambles.

1. Place the peppers on a heated grill, and rotate several times until lightly charred on all sides. Transfer to a large bowl.

2. When the peppers are cool enough to handle, scrape off and discard the charred skin with your fingers, and lightly rinse under running water.

3. Make a slit down the side of each pepper, and remove and discard the seeds and veins. Tear or cut the peppers into wide strips ($\frac{1}{8}$ to $\frac{1}{2}$ inch), and place in a mixing bowl.

4. Heat the lemon juice, oil, garlic, and salt in a small pot over medium-high heat until almost boiling. Pour over the peppers, cover, and let marinate overnight on the kitchen counter.

5. Transfer to a clean pint jar, and store in the refrigerator, where it will keep up to four months.

Yield: About 2 cups

• • • • • • •

$2\frac{1}{2}$ pounds red, orange, and/or yellow bell peppers

I cup fresh squeezed lemon juice

$\frac{1}{4}$ cup extra virgin olive oil

10 cloves garlic, crushed

$1\frac{1}{2}$ tablespoons sea salt

FOR A CHANGE . . .

• Instead of grilling, cook the peppers in an oven broiler, or over the open flame of a gas burner.

• Slightly vary the amounts of lemon juice, olive oil, garlic, and/or salt.

• Use umeboshi vinegar for some of the lemon juice and salt.

Seitan Quesadillas

Seitan that has been fried with onions and peppers in chili pepper oil tastes great. Add some roasted red peppers and marinated sun-dried tomatoes (like the Marinated Sun-Dried Tomatoes with Calendula Flowers on page 117), wrap it all up in a tortilla with melted cheese, and you have an easy, satisfying meal.

Yield: 6 quesadillas
. . . .

2 tablespoons Hot Pepper Oil (page 105)

1 1/2 cups coarsely chopped onions

2 cups seitan, sliced into 1-x-1-inch pieces

1 cup coarsely chopped green peppers

6 spinach or plain tortillas (12-inch rounds)

2 cups shredded Muenster cheese or crumbled feta

1/2 cup roasted red pepper strips, or Marinated Red Peppers with Lemon and Garlic (page 119)

1/3 cup marinated sun-dried tomatoes

1. Heat the oil in a medium-sized skillet over medium heat. Add the onions and sauté, stirring occasionally for 5 minutes, or until the onions begin to soften and become translucent.

2. Add the seitan and continue to sauté, stirring occasionally for 5 minutes, or until it is slightly crisp.

3. Add the green peppers and cook another 3 minutes, or until they become bright green. Turn off the heat and set aside.

4. Heat each tortilla in a large skillet over medium-low heat for about 1 minute, or until warm and soft. Flip the tortilla over and cover with 1/3 cup of cheese. Add 2 tablespoons of the seitan-vegetable mixture, 1 1/3 tablespoons roasted peppers, and 1 tablespoon sun-dried tomatoes.

5. Fold the tortilla in half and continue to heat 30 seconds. Flip over and heat another 30 seconds, or until the cheese is melted. Remove from the pan.

6. Slice the hot quesadillas in half and serve immediately.

FOR A CHANGE . . .

• Vary the amounts of cheese, marinated peppers, and sun-dried tomatoes.

• Instead of Meunster, try chèvre, goat cheddar, goat gouda, or Manchego cheese.

Cabbage, Scallion, and Cilantro Egg Rolls

Here is an Asian stir-fry that is fabulous served as a side dish and even better stuffed into egg roll wrappers and then baked.

1. To make the filling, heat a wok over medium-high heat. Add the oil, mirin, tamari, garlic, ginger, onions, and carrots. Stir-fry 5 minutes, or until the onions are soft and carrots are bright orange.

2. Add the cabbage and celery, and continue to cook, stirring occasionally for 5 minutes, or until bright green. Stir the scallions and cilantro into the mixture and let cook another 3 minutes. Adjust the seasoning, if desired. Transfer the mixture to a large bowl, and let cool to room temperature (about 20 minutes).

3. In a small bowl, dissolve the arrowroot in the water.

4. Place an egg roll wrapper diagonally on a large cutting board, so it appears diamond-shaped. Place 2 tablespoons of the filling in the center. Fold first the right and left sides of the wrapper over the filling, then fold up the bottom corner, and roll up tightly. Dab some of the arrowroot mixture on the open flap, and then seal the egg roll. Repeat with the remaining wrappers and filling.

5. Place the rolls on an unoiled baking sheet in a single layer, and brush the tops with canola oil. Bake in a preheated 350°F oven for 15 to 20 minutes, or until golden brown.

6. Arrange the egg rolls on a platter and serve with your favorite dipping sauce. Sweet-and-Sour Dipping Sauce (page 73) and Mustard Sauce with Maple Syrup and Miso (page 76) are recommended.

Yield: 12 egg rolls

• • • • • • • •

1 tablespoon canola or peanut oil

2 tablespoons mirin

2 tablespoons tamari

3 cloves garlic, minced

1 tablespoon grated ginger

1 cup diced onions

1 cup diced carrots

4 cups thinly sliced cabbage

1 cup diced celery

$3/4$ cup chopped scallions

$1/4$ cup chopped cilantro

$1/2$ teaspoon arrowroot powder

$1/2$ teaspoon water

12 egg roll wrappers (6-inch squares)

FOR A CHANGE . . .

• Instead of baking the rolls, deep-fry them. Heat $1/2$ cup canola oil (about $1/2$ inch) in a medium-sized skillet over medium heat. Add the rolls and fry, rotating them as they cook, until golden brown on all sides.

Baked Ginger-Arame Rolls

Tofu, garlic, and ginger bring a taste of Asia to these rolls. The addition of Blackberry-Pear Sauce (page 75) offers another flavorful dimension. A sprinkling of cilantro makes this a picture-perfect dish.

Yield: 12 egg rolls

• • • • • • • •

$^1/_2$ cup dried arame

8 ounces firm tofu, diced

3 cups thinly sliced green cabbage

1 cup diced celery

4 cloves garlic

1 tablespoon grated ginger

$^1/_4$ cup tamari

2 tablespoons toasted sesame oil

1 tablespoon unsulfured molasses or honey

1 teaspoon arrowroot powder

1 teaspoon water

12 egg roll wrappers (6-inch squares)

1 tablespoon canola oil

$^1/_2$ cup coarsely chopped cilantro, optional

1. Preheat the oven to 350°F.

2. Place the arame in the bottom of a large mixing bowl, and layer the tofu on top (the water from the tofu will hydrate the arame). Add the cabbage and celery, and set aside.

3. Place the garlic and ginger in a blender. Add the tamari, sesame oil, and molasses, and purée until smooth. Adjust the seasonings, if desired. Combine the dressing and arame-vegetable mixture.

4. In a small bowl, dissolve the arrowroot in the water.

5. Place an egg roll wrapper diagonally on a large cutting board or plate, so it appears diamond-shaped. Place 2 tablespoons of the arame mixture in the center. Fold the right and left sides of the wrapper over the filling, then fold up the bottom corner, and roll up tightly. Dab some of the arrowroot mixture on the open flap, and then seal the egg roll. Repeat with the remaining wrappers and filling.

6. Place the rolls on an unoiled baking sheet, and brush the tops with canola oil. Bake 15 to 20 minutes, or until golden brown.

7. Arrange the egg rolls on a platter and serve plain or topped with your favorite sauce and a sprinkling of cilantro.

FOR A CHANGE . . .

• Instead of baking the rolls, deep-fry them. Heat $^1/_2$ cup canola oil (about $^1/_2$ inch) in a medium-sized skillet over medium heat. Add the rolls and fry, rotating them as they cook, until golden brown on all sides.

Potato-olive Knishes

*I have discovered the easiest way to make knishes. Use egg roll wrappers.
This recipe's mashed potato filling is flavored with black olives,
scallions, and olive oil. Delicious!*

1. Preheat the oven to 375°F.

2. In a large mixing bowl, combine the mashed potatoes with $\frac{1}{2}$ cup of the oil, the olives, scallions, and sea salt. Adjust the seasonings, if desired.

3. Place an egg roll wrapper diagonally on a large cutting board or plate, so it appears diamond-shaped. Place 2 tablespoons of the potato mixture in the center. Fold the top and bottom corners over the filling to meet in the middle, then fold the right and left corners to meet in the middle. Pick up the knish and place it in the palm of both hands as if it were a ball and gently squeeze to make it round in shape. Repeat with the remaining ingredients.

4. Arrange the knishes on an unoiled baking sheet, and brush the tops with the remaining oil. Bake 15 to 20 minutes, or until golden brown.

5. Arrange the knishes on a platter and serve plain or with your favorite dipping sauce. Mustard Sauce with Maple Syrup and Miso (page 76) is recommended.

Yield: 14 knishes

• • • • • • •

6 cups mashed potatoes

$\frac{1}{2}$ cup plus 2 tablespoons
extra virgin olive oil

$\frac{1}{2}$ cup pitted kalamata
olives

1 cup coarsely chopped
scallions

$\frac{3}{4}$ teaspoon sea salt,
or to taste

14 egg roll wrappers
(6-inch squares)

Curried Vegetable Knishes with Chickpeas

Enjoy these savory knishes as appetizers or light entrées.

Yield: 13 knishes

• • • • • • • •

4½ cups water

1 cup dried chickpeas, presoaked (page 14), rinsed, and drained

1 dried cayenne pepper

1 cinnamon stick

5-inch strip kelp, optional

1 tablespoon dried nettles, optional

5 tablespoons extra virgin olive oil

1 cup coarsely chopped onions

3 cloves garlic, minced

1 tablespoon grated ginger

1 teaspoon fennel seeds

1 teaspoon cumin seeds

4 cups potatoes, cut into 1-inch cubes

3 cups butternut squash, cut into 1-inch cubes

½ cup raisins

1 teaspoon sea salt, or to taste

13 egg roll wrappers (6-inch squares)

1 teaspoon canola oil

1. Bring 3 cups of the water, the chickpeas, cayenne, cinnamon, kelp, and nettles (if using) to boil in a 4-quart pot. Reduce the heat to low, cover, and simmer 1 hour, or until the chickpeas are soft.

2. Heat the oil in a 6-quart stockpot over medium heat. Add the onions, garlic, ginger, fennel seeds, and cumin seeds. Sauté about 5 minutes, or until the onions begin to soften.

3. Add the chickpeas, potatoes, squash, raisins, and remaining water to the pot. Bring to a boil, then reduce the heat to medium-low. Simmer 20 minutes, or until the potatoes are soft. Add the salt and turn off the heat. Adjust the seasonings, if desired.

4. Preheat the oven to 375°F.

5. Place an egg roll wrapper diagonally on a large cutting board or plate, so it appears diamond-shaped. Place 2 tablespoons of the chickpea mixture in the center. Fold the top and bottom corners over the filling to meet in the middle, then fold the right and left corners to meet in the middle. Pick up the knish and place it in the palm of both hands as if it were a ball and gently squeeze to make it round in shape. Repeat with the remaining ingredients.

6. Place the knishes on an unoiled baking sheet, and brush the tops with the remaining oil. Bake 15 to 20 minutes, or until golden brown. Serve immediately.

FOR A CHANGE . . .

• Instead of chickpeas, use quicker-cooking beans, such as lentils or mung beans.

• Try Butternut Squash with Indian Spices (page 138) as filling.

Melted Goat Cheese Sandwich with Arugula and Sun-Dried Tomatoes

If you don't have the marinated tomatoes called for in this recipe, use any variety. And although I am partial to goat cheeses, feel free to use other cheeses that melt well, such as mozzarella, cheddar, or gouda.

1. Mix the cheeses together and crumble half over each slice of bread. Place under the broiler or in a toaster oven for 1 minute, or until the cheese melts. Transfer the open-faced slices to a large plate.

2. On one slice, add the tomatoes, olives, and arugula, then cover with the other slice.

3. Cut the sandwich in half diagonally, and serve immediately.

Yield: 1 sandwich
• • • • • • •
$^1/_4$ cup grated goat cheddar

$^1/_4$ cup grated goat gouda

2 large slices sourdough bread

1 tablespoon Marinated Sun-Dried Tomatoes with Calendula Flowers (page 117), or other marinated variety

1 tablespoon pitted kalamata olives

$^1/_2$ cup coarsely chopped arugula

FYI . . .

Stuff fresh calendula flowers or nasturtiums inside sandwiches and wraps like slices of pickle.
Feel like a kid again with each bite.

Ginger Tempeh Sushi

Tempeh, grated beets, and carrots combine with rice to create a beautiful mosaic pattern in each slice of this vegan sushi, which travels well, whole or sliced. Perfect for a summer picnic.

Yield: 48 pieces

2 cups white sushi rice, rinsed and drained

3 cups plus 1 tablespoon cold water

1 tablespoon sesame oil

1 tablespoon mirin

1 tablespoon tamari

8 ounces soy tempeh, cut into 6 long strips

1 cup grated carrots

$\frac{1}{2}$ cup grated beets

6 sheets toasted nori

1–2 tablespoons umeboshi paste

1 tablespoon wasabi powder

1. Place the rice and 3 cups of water in a 4-quart pot, and let soak 20 minutes. Bring to a boil over medium-high heat, then reduce the heat to low and simmer covered for 15 minutes, or until the water is absorbed. Remove from the heat, and let stand 1 hour, or until the rice is cool enough to handle.

2. While the rice cools, heat up the oil, mirin, and tamari in a medium-sized skillet over medium heat. Add the tempeh and fry about 5 minutes, or until golden brown on both sides. If the pan gets too dry, add a teaspoon or two of water.

3. Mix the carrots and beets together in a bowl, and set aside.

4. Lay a sushi mat on a clean work surface with the bamboo strips running horizontally. Place a piece of nori on the mat, shiny side down. Spread $\frac{1}{2}$ cup of rice on the nori leaving a $1\frac{1}{2}$-inch space at the top. Lay a strip of tempeh on the rice, followed by some of the carrot-beet mixture, and gently press onto the rice. Spread some umeboshi paste over the top inch of the nori.

5. Starting at the end closest to you (and using even pressure), use the sushi mat to roll the nori tightly and evenly around the rice and filling. (Be sure to pull the leading edge of the mat back so it does not get incorporated into the roll.) Once the rolling is completed, give the mat a gentle squeeze and let sit for a minute to ensure a tight roll. Gently unroll the mat and slice each roll into 8 rounds. Repeat with the remaining ingredients.

6. In a small bowl, stir the wasabi powder and 1 tablespoon water to form a paste. For a thinner, less spicy dip, add a little more water. (Make additional wasabi, if desired.)

7. To serve, place the bowl of wasabi on of a platter surrounded by the sushi rounds.

FOR A CHANGE . . .

- Replace the carrots and beets with red pepper, mesclun salad, or avocado and cucumber.

7

Super Sides

Although main dishes are cast in starring roles, side dishes can be just as impressive and inspiring. Several seasonal dishes served side-by-side can make a meal festive and fun, especially if they are colorful and visually appealing.

The side dishes in this chapter—made with a variety of domestic and wild vegetables, mushrooms, beans, grains, and sea vegetables—are among those my family enjoys the most. You'll find quick and easy stir-fries like String Beans in Garlic Sauce with Cashews, Bok Choy and Mushroom Stir-Fry, and Sea Palm with Red Peppers and Lime. A delicious lemon and caper dressing gives my Lemon-Roasted Beets, Brussels Sprouts, and Yams delectable Mediterranean-style flavor; the Moroccan-Style Carrots and Yams benefit from a delicate honey-sweetened sauce; while chili pepper flakes add a flavorful spark to Spicy Jamaican Beans. A variety of healthy, delicious grain dishes, such as Millet with Cilantro and Red Peppers, Racy Rice Pilaf, and Pasta with Fresh Garlic and Basil are versatile and easy to make.

Mushrooms are among my favorite foods, and in this chapter I have shared some special side dishes that spotlight these earthy-flavored gems. If you enjoy mushrooms, too, be sure to experience the Carrots with Wild Mushrooms and Basil—a virtual mushroom feast—or try the Wild Mushroom Stew with Tomatoes and Capers in which a medley of wild porcini, button, and crimini mushrooms take center stage in a tomato-based sauce. In the Mushroom Festival, juicy portabellas, shiitake, and enokis are tossed with spinach and soba noodles.

Ready? It's time to experience the incomparable tastes and textures of the special side dishes that follow.

MIX AND MATCH

Create sensational side dishes! Try different ingredients and ingredient combinations from the ones typically called for in your favorite sides, or vary those used in this chapter's recipes. The chart below offers some ideas.

Go Wild With Side Dishes

FALL/WINTER VEGETABLES	Carrots, butternut squash, delicata squash, Jerusalem artichokes, sweet potatoes, and yams.
SPRING/SUMMER VEGETABLES	Asparagus, broccoli, green beans, patty pan squash, yellow summer squash, and zucchini.
DOMESTIC/ WILD GREENS	Bok choy, chard, collards, dandelion greens, fiddleheads, kale, lamb's quarters, mizuna, mustard greens, napa cabbage, nettles, purslane, spinach, tat soi, and watercress.
BEANS	Anasazi beans, chickpeas, fava beans, kidney beans, lentils, lima beans, mung beans, navy beans (cannellini), and split peas.
MUSHROOMS	DOMESTIC VARIETIES: Crimini, portabella, shiitake, and white button.
	WILD VARIETIES: Black trumpet, chanterelles, lobster, maitake, matsutake, morels, mousseron, porcini,* and wood ears.
SEA VEGETABLES	LEAFY VARIETIES: Alaria, digitata kelp, dulse, kelp, ocean ribbons kombu, and wakame.
	NOODLE-LIKE VARIETIES: Arame, hiziki, and sea palm.
ONION VARIETIES	Chives, leeks, onions, ramps (wild leeks), scallions, and shallots.**
GARLIC VARIETIES	Garlic, elephant garlic, and garlic scapes.
CHILI PEPPERS	VERY HOT: Cayenne peppers, habañero chilies, and Scotch bonnets.
	MODERATELY HOT: Serrano chilies.
	MILDLY HOT: Anaheim chilies, ancho chilies, jalapeño peppers, and poblano chilies.
HERBS AND SPICES	See "Spice It Up!" (page 8) for substitutions.
OILS	FOR FRYING: Coconut butter, ghee, extra virgin olive, peanut, sesame, hi-oleic sunflower, and flavored oils (see Chapter 5).
	FOR ROASTING: Extra virgin olive oil, light olive oil, and flavored oils.
SALTY SEASONINGS	Dulse flakes, kelp granules, miso, nori flakes, sea salt, shoyu, tamari, umeboshi vinegar, and Bragg Liquid Aminos.

* Only 2 tablespoons dried porcini are equivalent to 2 cups fresh, milder-flavored mushrooms like white button.
** Approximately 1/3 cup coarsely chopped shallots is equivalent to 1 cup onions or leeks.

Carrots With Wild Mushrooms and Basil

In this virtual mushroom feast, porcini, shiitake, and portabella mushrooms are roasted with carrots and fragrant basil. Serve as a warm side dish or as a savory topper for pasta or toasted bread.

1. Preheat the oven to 425°F.

2. Place the porcini and shiitake mushrooms in a small mixing bowl and cover with water. Let sit for 20 minutes or until they soften. Remove and slice. Discard the soaking water, or save for soup stock or to water plants.

3. Transfer the sliced porcini and shiitake to a covered crock or baking dish, along with the portabella mushrooms, carrots, onions, garlic, basil, oil, and salt. Toss well.

4. Cover and bake for 35 minutes, or until the carrots are tender. Adjust the seasonings, if desired.

5. Add the parsley to the vegetables, stir, and serve.

FOR A CHANGE . . .

• Soak the dried porcini and shiitake mushrooms in wine or stock instead of water.

Yield: 4 to 6 servings

• • • • • • •

$1/4$ cup dried porcini mushrooms

1 cup dried shiitake mushroom caps

3 cups coarsely chopped portabella mushrooms

2 cups coarsely chopped carrots

$2/3$ cup coarsely chopped onions

7 cloves garlic, thickly sliced

$4^1/2$ tablespoons fresh basil, or $1^1/2$ tablespoons dried

$1/4$ cup extra virgin olive oil

1 teaspoon sea salt

$1/4$ cup chopped parsley

COMMUNITY SUPPORTED AGRICULTURE

Going wild in the kitchen means having access to a good selection of fresh organic foods. Maintaining your own garden or living near a natural foods supermarket certainly helps. You can also become involved in Community Supported Agriculture (CSA). CSA creates a partnership between consumers and local organic or biodynamic farmers. In exchange for paying for a share in the farm, consumers receive the freshest produce throughout the growing season. This covers the farmer's costs while he or she is able to make a fair wage.

On my CSA, there are plenty of pick-your-own crops in addition to the bounty that is harvested for me and distributed at the barn. On farm-shop days, many other products are for sale, including fresh breads, honey, eggs, pickles, maple syrup, cow and goat cheese, milk, ice cream, fresh fruits, and so much more. It's like a mini farmer's market!

At a cost of $400, my CSA provides me with fresh produce from June through December. Winter produce, such as butternut squash, cabbage, potatoes, carrots, beets, celeriac, leeks, and rutabagas, is stored at the farm from December until March (until April on a good year). That comes to about $40 a month—an incredible bargain for organic fruit and vegetables for a family of four.

To find out more about Community Supported Agriculture or to locate a CSA farm in your area, call the hotline at 1-800-516-7797. You can also visit the following website: http://www.nal.usda.gov/afsic/csa.

Yield: 6 to 8 servings

- - - - - - - -

5 cups carrot chunks

5 cups yams, cut in chunks

2 cups onion chunks

1 ½ cups pitted prunes

¾ cup honey

7 tablespoons extra virgin olive oil

2 teaspoons cinnamon

1 teaspoon black pepper

1 teaspoon ground ginger

1 teaspoon sea salt

Moroccan-style carrots and Yams

This honey-sweetened carrot-and-yam medley is a perfect accompaniment to richer dishes.

1. Preheat the oven to 400°F. Place all the ingredients in a large bowl and mix well. Transfer to a large covered baking dish.

2. Bake for 1 hour, or until the carrots and yams are tender. Adjust the seasonings, if desired.

3. Serve immediately.

Orange-Scented Yams with chestnuts

Presoaking the dried chestnuts results in a delicious smoky flavored stock in which to bake these orange-scented yams. Dried chestnuts are available in most Asian markets, specialty shops, and natural foods stores.

1. Place the chestnuts and water in a small bowl, and let sit several hours or overnight until the chestnuts have softened.

2. Preheat the oven to 400°F.

3. Transfer the chestnuts and soaking water to a large mixing bowl along with the remaining ingredients. Mix well.

4. Place the ingredients in a baking dish; cover and bake 45 minutes, or until the yams are tender. Adjust the seasonings, if desired.

5. Serve immediately.

FOR A CHANGE . . .

• Substitute nutmeg or mace for the cardamom.

Yield: 4 to 6 servings

• • • • • • •

$1/3$ cup dried chestnuts

$2/3$ cup water

6 cups yams, cut into 1-inch cubes

$1\ 1/2$ cups coarsely chopped oyster or white button mushrooms

$1\ 1/2$ cups coarsely chopped onions

3 tablespoons dried orange peel

1 teaspoon cinnamon

$1/2$ teaspoon sea salt

$1/4$ teaspoon dried cardamom

Wild Mushroom Stew with Tomatoes and Capers

Yield: 4 to 6 servings

· · · · · · · · · ·

$^1/_2$ cup water

$^1/_2$ cup dried porcini mushrooms

2 tablespoons extra virgin
olive oil

7 cloves garlic, thickly sliced

I cup coarsely chopped onions

4 cups cauliflower florets

$^1/_4$ cup capers
(rinse if packed in salt)

3 bay leaves

3 cups coarsely chopped
white button mushrooms

$2^1/_2$ cups coarsely chopped
crimini mushrooms

28-ounce can diced tomatoes,
or $3^1/_2$ cups coarsely chopped
plum tomatoes

2 tablespoons balsamic vinegar

Pinch saffron

I teaspoon fresh rosemary,
or $^1/_2$ teaspoon dried

$^1/_2$ teaspoon sea salt,
or to taste

$^1/_4$ teaspoon black pepper,
or to taste

*The first time I cooked with porcini mushrooms, I was
surprised and delighted by their sherry-like aroma.
They are spotlighted along with white button and crimini
mushrooms in this delectable Mediterranean
tomato-based stew. Enjoy as is, mixed with beans,
or spooned on top of pasta or grains.*

1. Bring the water to boil in a small pan, and add the
porcini mushrooms. Turn off the heat, and let sit 20 minutes, or until the mushrooms have softened.

2. While the mushrooms soak, heat the oil in a medium-
sized skillet over medium heat. Add the garlic, onions, cauliflower, capers, and bay leaves. Stirring occasionally, sauté
5 minutes, or until the ingredients are fragrant.

3. Over a bowl, strain the soaking porcini mushrooms
through cheesecloth, then add the strained soaking water
to the sautéing vegetables. Slice the porcini and add to the
skillet along with the button and crimini mushrooms.

4. Stirring occasionally, simmer the ingredients for 15 minutes, or until the fresh mushrooms are soft. Add the tomatoes, vinegar, saffron, and rosemary, and continue to
simmer 25 minutes, or until the cauliflower is tender.

5. Season with salt and pepper, and serve.

HUNTING FOR MUSHROOMS IN THE WILD

Learning to hunt for edible wild mushrooms was an education that rewarded my adventurous spirit. It began one autumn day a few years ago when I and a few other interested locals explored the woods with three mushroom experts. One by one, we brought our finds to the guides, who carefully examined them before giving us mostly the thumbs-down sign. We were, however, advised to hold onto the rejects and study them for the purposes of identifying them again and again.

Amidst the gray of the day, one woman found a beautiful apricot-colored chanterelle. I found a few white puff mushrooms, which I later sautéed with garlic and olive oil (they were scrumptious!). We also came across honey mushrooms, which thrived in the creek bed we explored. They grew on the roots of fallen dead trees. We each picked a handful to cook at home.

Although we managed to find a few edible mushrooms that day, mostly we came away from the experience learning what not to pick. (Many poisonous mushrooms look similar to edible varieties.) Lucky for us, our teacher guides had filled the trunk of their car with plenty of wild edible mushrooms, which they had found on a trek through the woods the day before. There were maitake, oyster, chicken of the woods, chanterelles, and morels. After show and tell, they generously divvied them up, and we all rushed home to cook our free samples.

So inspired, I began a true love affair with mushrooms, and eventually developed what turned out to be an unending parade of recipes that both spotlight mushrooms and incorporate them with other ingredients into delicious, easy-to-prepare dishes. And I am constantly changing and reinventing these recipes.

If you are as wild about these delectable gems as I am, and you find yourself exploring the woods for edible varieties, just be sure that you know what you are picking. Learn about foraging for mushrooms from an expert.

Green Beans in Garlic Sauce with cashews

Try this saucy side dish alongside or over quinoa, rice, or noodles. Serve with Spicy Tempeh Strips (page 143) for a quick Asian-style dinner.

Yield: 4 to 6 servings

- 1 tablespoon sesame oil
- 5 tablespoons tamari
- 3 tablespoons mirin
- 9 cloves garlic, sliced
- 2 cups coarsely chopped onions
- 1 1/2 cups whole cashews (unsalted)
- 4 cups green beans, sliced into 1-inch diagonals
- 1 cup coarsely chopped red bell pepper
- 3/4 cup coarsely chopped shiitake mushrooms caps

1. Heat up a wok over high heat, then add the oil, tamari, and mirin. Toss in the garlic and stir-fry 1 minute, or until fragrant. (Be careful not to burn the garlic.)

2. Add the onions and cashews, continuing to stir-fry, then add the beans, pepper, and mushrooms. Stir-fry another 5 minutes for crisp, brightly colored beans and bell peppers, or longer for more tender vegetables. Adjust the seasonings, if desired.

3. Serve immediately.

FOR A CHANGE . . .

- Replace the onions with wild leeks. Because leeks are quick cooking, add them to the wok along with the beans.

Bok Choy and Mushroom Stir-Fry

*This quick and easy Asian-inspired stir-fry makes
a great topping for rice or udon noodles.*

1. Heat up a wok over high heat, then add the oil and mirin. Toss in the leeks and garlic, and stir-fry 2 minutes or until the garlic is fragrant and the leeks are bright green. (Be careful not to burn the garlic.)

2. Add the mushrooms and celery, continuing to stir-fry for 2 minutes, then add the bok choy. Stir-fry another 2 or 3 minutes.

3. Gather the grated ginger in your hands, and squeeze the juice into the wok. Stir in the tamari. Adjust the seasonings, if desired.

4. Serve immediately.

FOR A CHANGE . . .

• Substitute Chinese cabbage for some or all of the bok choy.

• Instead of celery, use red bell pepper for added taste and color.

Yield: 6 to 8 servings
• • • • • • •
1 tablespoon sesame oil

3 tablespoons mirin

1 1/2 cups coarsely chopped leeks

8 cloves garlic, thickly sliced

3 cups coarsely chopped white button mushrooms

2 cups coarsely chopped celery

8 cups coarsely chopped bok choy

2 tablespoons grated ginger

1 tablespoon tamari

FYI . . .

Bok choy is a crisp, sweet Asian vegetable that looks similar to celery. Its smooth white stalks are topped with dark green crinkly leaves. Perfect for stir-fries, bok choy is also delicious sautéed as a side dish, added to soups, or tossed raw into salads.

Butternut Squash Purée With Sun-Dried Tomatoes and Sage

This dish is one of my Thanksgiving staples. It is also delightful served as a pâté on crackers or thin slices of toasted baguettes.

Yield: 8 to 12 servings

• • • • • • •

1 cup water

1 1/2 cups sun-dried tomatoes

1 1/2 cups sunflower seeds

4 1/2-pound butternut squash, cut into 1/2-inch cubes (about 9 1/2 cups)

2 tablespoons extra virgin olive oil

7 cloves garlic, thickly sliced

4 cups coarsely chopped red onions

3 cups coarsely chopped white button mushrooms

1/4 cup coarsely chopped fresh sage, or 4 teaspoons dried

1 tablespoon chopped fresh oregano, or 1 teaspoon dried

2 teaspoons sea salt, or to taste

1. Bring the water to boil in a small pan, and add the sun-dried tomatoes. Turn off the heat, and let sit 20 minutes, or until the tomatoes have softened. Drain and set aside.

2. While the tomatoes soak, place the sunflower seeds in an un-oiled skillet over medium-low heat. Stirring occasionally, dry-roast the seeds for 5 minutes, or until they begin to pop and have a nutty aroma. Remove from the heat and set aside to cool.

3. Place the squash on a steamer basket set over boiling water. Cover and steam 15 minutes, or until fork tender.

4. While the squash cooks, heat the oil in a medium-sized skillet over medium heat. Add the garlic and onions, and sauté 5 minutes, or until the onions begin to soften. Add the mushrooms, and continue to cook another 5 minutes, or until they begin to soften.

5. Place the sunflower seeds in a food processor and grind. Add half the sun-dried tomatoes, half the squash, half the sautéed vegetables, and half the sage, oregano, and salt. Purée until smooth, then transfer to a large mixing bowl. Repeat with the remaining ingredients. Adjust the seasonings, if desired.

6. Transfer the purée to a serving bowl, and enjoy.

FOR A CHANGE . . .

• Use pecans, walnuts, or pumpkin seeds instead of sunflower seeds.

• Instead of steaming the squash, bake it whole for 1 hour in a 400°F oven.

Mushroom Festival

*Portabella, shiitake and enoki mushrooms
give this dish its subtle earthy flavor.*

1. Bring a 4-quart pot of water to a rolling boil. Add the soba noodles, and cook according to package directions. Drain, rinse under cold water, and set aside. Cut off and discard the bottom inch of the enoki mushroom stems, then set the mushrooms aside.

2. Heat a wok or medium-sized skillet over high heat. Add the oil, wine, tamari, and mirin. Toss in the portabella mushrooms and stir-fry 2 minutes, or until they begin to soften. Add the shiitake mushrooms and continue to stir-fry for 5 minutes. Turn off the heat.

3. Add the spinach to the mushrooms, stirring until it wilts. Add the soba noodles and toss to combine. Adjust the seasonings, if desired. Garnish with enoki mushrooms, and serve.

Yield: 8 servings

1 pound soba noodles

6 ounces fresh enoki mushrooms

4 teaspoons sesame oil

7 tablespoons white wine

6 tablespoons tamari

4 tablespoons mirin

3 cups coarsely chopped portabella mushrooms

5 cups coarsely chopped fresh shiitake caps

4 cups spinach leaves

Lemon-Roasted Beets, Brussels Sprouts, and Yams

In this colorful dish, a vegetable medley is roasted in a delicious Mediterranean-style lemon and caper sauce.

1. Preheat the oven to 400°F. Place all the ingredients in a large bowl and mix well. Transfer to a large covered baking dish.

2. Bake for 1 hour, or until the beets are tender. Adjust the seasonings, if desired.

3. Serve immediately.

Yield: 4 to 6 servings

2 cups cubed beets

2 cups Brussels sprouts, cut in half

2 cups yams, cut in chunks

2 cups leeks, cut into 2-inch diagonals

$1/2$ cup chopped parsley

$1/3$ cup lemon juice

$1/4$ cup extra virgin olive oil

2 tablespoons capers (rinse if packed in salt)

Butternut Squash with Indian Spices

When I asked my friend Fredrique, who has been to India many times, how she came to cook such a wonderful spicy Indian stew, she replied that she deep-fries her mustard seeds until they pop. Thanks goes to Fredrique for inspiring this sweet and spicy side dish, which also makes a fabulous knish filling.

Yield: 6 to 8 servings

• • • • • • •

6 tablespoons extra virgin olive oil

6 cloves garlic, thinly sliced

2 tablespoons grated ginger

1 1/2 teaspoons chili pepper flakes

1 teaspoon brown mustard seeds

1 teaspoon cumin seeds

1 teaspoon fennel seeds

5 1/2-pound butternut squash, cut into 1-inch cubes (about 12 cups)

1 teaspoon sea salt

1. Place the oil, garlic, ginger, chili pepper, mustard seeds, cumin seeds, and fennel seeds in a 6-quart stockpot over medium heat. Cover and fry for 3 to 5 minutes, or until you hear the mustard seeds pop. Turn off the heat.

2. Add the squash and salt to the pot. Simmer covered over medium-low heat, stirring occasionally for 20 minutes, or until squash is very soft. Adjust the seasonings, if desired.

3. Serve immediately.

FOR A CHANGE . . .

• Try ghee or coconut oil instead of extra virgin olive oil.

• Replace the butternut squash with a combination of potatoes, carrots, sweet potatoes, yams, green beans, and onions.

Millet with Cilantro and Red Peppers

Cooked millet is soft, moist, and versatile. In this colorful side dish, it can be served as is or pressed into burgers. You can also combine millet with teff or quinoa in this recipe.

1. Bring all of the ingredients to boil in a 4-quart stockpot. Reduce the heat to low and simmer covered for 15 minutes, or until the water is absorbed.

2. Stir the millet, and serve immediately. To make burgers, cover the cooked millet and cool for 30 minutes. Form into burgers and serve.

Yield: 4 to 6 servings

6 cups water

2 cups millet, rinsed

2 cups coarsely chopped red bell peppers

1 $\frac{1}{2}$ cups chopped cilantro

$\frac{2}{3}$ cup sunflower seeds

$\frac{1}{2}$ teaspoon sea salt, or to taste

Racy Rice Pilaf

Simmering dry-roasted rice in wine with vegetables and spices results in this special dish.

1. Heat the oil in a medium-sized skillet over medium heat. Add the garlic, shallots, rice, carrots and celery, and sauté, stirring occasionally for 5 minutes, or until the ingredients are fragrant and well mixed.

2. Stir the oregano, salt, and cayenne pepper into the skillet and combine with the rice mixture. Turn off the heat, and add the boiling water and wine.

3. Bring the ingredients to a boil, then reduce the heat to medium-low. Simmer covered for 45 minutes, or until the rice is tender. Adjust the seasonings, if desired, and serve.

* Four Chimneys Organic Farm Winery brand is recommended.

Yield: 4 to 6 servings

1 tablespoon extra virgin olive oil

6 cloves garlic, thickly sliced

$\frac{2}{3}$ cup chopped shallots

1 $\frac{1}{2}$ cups long grain brown rice

1 cup julienned carrots

$\frac{1}{2}$ cup diced celery

$\frac{1}{4}$ cup chopped oregano

$\frac{3}{4}$ teaspoon sea salt, or to taste

$\frac{1}{4}$ teaspoon cayenne pepper, or to taste

2 $\frac{1}{4}$ cups boiling water

$\frac{3}{4}$ cup peach or white wine*

Roasted Vegetables Bombay

This highly flavorful dish of roasted pumpkin and potatoes is seasoned with Indian spices.

Yield: 4 to 6 servings

• • • • • • •

1 tablespoon brown mustard seeds

1 teaspoon fennel seeds

$1/2$ cup extra virgin olive oil

2-pound pumpkin, cut into 1-inch cubes (about $4^{1}/_{2}$ cups)

4 cups potatoes, cut into 1-inch cubes

1 teaspoon sea salt

$1/2$ teaspoon ground coriander

$1/4$–$1/2$ teaspoon chili pepper flakes, or to taste

$1/2$ cup coarsely chopped parsley or cilantro

1. Place the mustard seeds in an unoiled skillet over medium-low heat. Cover and dry-roast for 1 to 2 minutes, or until the seeds start to pop. Turn off the heat and add the fennel and oil. Fry over medium heat for 2 minutes, or until fragrant.

2. Place the pumpkin and potatoes in a large mixing bowl. Add the hot oil mixture, salt, coriander, and chili pepper, and mix well. Transfer to a large covered baking dish.

3. Bake for 1 hour, or until the pumpkin and potatoes are tender. Adjust the seasonings, if desired.

4. Garnish with parsley and serve.

FOR A CHANGE . . .

• Instead of dry-roasting the mustard seeds, add them to the skillet along with the oil and fennel seeds. Cover and fry for 3 to 5 minutes, or until you hear the mustard seeds pop.

FYI . . .

In Indian cooking, roasted whole mustard seeds lend a nutty texture and creamy flavor to many vegetable dishes. The ground seeds are popular additions to pastes, curries, and marinades.

Sea Palm With Red Peppers and Lime

This innovative noodle-like stir-fry with chunks of red bell pepper and green California sea palm is a dazzling addition to any menu. I often serve this side dish with broiled or baked tofu.

1. Soak the sea palm in the water for 5 to 10 minutes, or until it expands and softens.

2. Heat a wok over medium-high heat. Add the oil, sea palm, and soaking water. Simmer while stirring occasionally for 15 minutes, or until sea palm is tender.

3. Add the bell pepper and snow peas, and stir-fry for 2 minutes, or until the peppers are bright red and the snow peas turn bright green. Turn off the heat.

4. Add the cilantro, lime juice, and tamari to the wok and toss well. Adjust the seasonings, if desired.

5. Garnish with scallions and serve.

FOR A CHANGE . . .

• Instead of sea palm, use hiziki.

• Replace the snow peas with green beans or fiddleheads.

• For added spark, stir 1 teaspoon dried chili pepper flakes or 1 tablespoon grated ginger into the dish.

Yield: 4 to 6 servings

1 cup dried sea palm

1 cup water

1 tablespoon sesame oil

2 cups coarsely chopped red bell pepper

1 cup snow peas, cut into 1-inch diagonals

1 cup tightly packed coarsely chopped cilantro

$1/_3$ cup lime juice

1 tablespoon tamari, or to taste

1 cup chopped scallions or chives

Sea Palm Stir-Fry

Yield: 6 to 8 servings

• • • • • • •

1 cup dried sea palm

2 cups water

1 tablespoon toasted sesame oil

2 cups broccoli florets and coarsely chopped stems

1 ½ cups cauliflower florets

1 ½ cups julienned daikon

2 cups coarsely chopped orange bell peppers

1 ½ cups coarsely chopped yellow peppers

2 tablespoons umeboshi vinegar

1 tablespoon rice vinegar

This colorful Asian-inspired side dish of silky sea palm—the fettuccine of sea vegetables—with daikon radish, cauliflower, and orange and yellow bell peppers is delicious both hot from the wok and cold as a salad.

1. Soak the sea palm in the water for 5 to 10 minutes, or until it expands and softens. Drain and set aside.

2. Heat a wok over medium heat. Add the oil, sea palm, broccoli, cauliflower, and daikon. Stirring occasionally, sauté the vegetables for 5 minutes or until tender.

3. Add the bell peppers, umeboshi vinegar, and rice vinegar. Turn off the heat, and stir the ingredients together. Adjust the seasonings, if desired.

4. Serve immediately, or refrigerate and serve chilled as a salad.

FOR A CHANGE . . .

• Try purple cauliflower instead of broccoli.

Spicy Tempeh Strips

This quick and easy dish is a snap to prepare, yet special enough for guests. I often serve it as an appetizer, or as a side dish along with Green Beans in Garlic Sauce with Cashews (page 134) and a serving of brown rice.

1. Heat a medium-sized skillet or wok over medium-high heat. Add the oil, Anaheim chili, and garlic, and fry for 1 minute, or until the garlic is fragrant. (Be careful not to burn the garlic or it will become bitter.)

2. Add the tempeh, and fry about 5 minutes on each side until golden brown. Toss in the tamari and half the scallions, and mix until well combined.

3. Transfer the strips to a serving bowl. Garnish with the remaining scallions, add a sprinkling of cayenne pepper (if desired), and serve.

FOR A CHANGE . . .

• Try other flavored tempeh varieties.

Yield: 4 servings
. . . .
$1/4$ cup sesame oil

1 tablespoon seeded, coarsely chopped Anaheim chili

3 cloves garlic, thickly sliced

1 pound soy tempeh, sliced into $1/2$-x-3-inch long strips

1–2 tablespoons tamari, or to taste

1 cup chopped scallions or chives

$1/4$ teaspoon ground cayenne pepper, optional

TIP . . .

Fresh chili peppers, which range from mildly warm to fiery hot, make food even hotter when the seeds are also used.

Spicy Jamaican Beans

When I visited Jamaica, I was treated to beans and rice that were cooked in coconut milk. I serve this spicy variation of that dish over millet or rice. A slice of baked butternut squash on the side helps balance the spiciness and complete the meal.

Yield: 4 to 6 servings

• • • • • • • • • • •

1 cup dried kidney beans, presoaked (page 14), rinsed, and drained

3 cups water

3-inch-piece kelp

1 tablespoon dried nettles, optional

14-ounce can coconut milk

1 cup coarsely chopped onions

1 cup coarsely chopped scallions

2 cloves garlic, finely minced or pressed

1 teaspoon chili pepper flakes

1 teaspoon dried thyme

1/2 teaspoon dried coriander

1/2 teaspoon ground cloves

1/2 teaspoon sea salt, or to taste

1. Place the beans in a 4-quart stockpot with the water, kelp, and nettles (if using). Bring to a boil, then reduce the heat to medium-low. Simmer covered for 1 hour, or until beans are soft.

2. Add the coconut milk, onions, scallions, garlic, chili pepper, thyme, coriander, and cloves to the pot. Stirring occasionally, simmer for 20 to 30 minutes, or until the onions are soft.

3. Add the sea salt to the pot, and adjust the seasonings, if desired.

4. Transfer the beans to a serving bowl and enjoy.

FOR A CHANGE . . .

• Do one or more of the following: Increase the nettles to 2 tablespoons; replace the scallions with 2 cups coarsely chopped collards; use 3/4 teaspoon allspice instead of the cloves and coriander.

• Swap dulse for the kelp.

Refried Beans with Tomatillos

Serve these spicy beans over rice, topped with a dollop of sour cream or guacamole. Or wrap them up in a heated corn or whole wheat tortilla. Ole!

1. 1. Heat the oil in a medium-sized skillet over medium heat. Add the cumin seeds and fry for 4 minutes, or until fragrant and slightly brown.

2. Add the garlic and onions, and sauté, stirring occasionally for 5 minutes, or until the onions begin to soften.

3. Toss the ancho and cayenne peppers into the skillet, sauté 5 minutes, then add the tomatillos, beans, and bell peppers. Mix the ingredients together and cook another 5 minutes, or until the tomatillos are soft and juicy.

4. Stir the basil and salt into the mixture. Adjust the seasonings, if desired.

5. Transfer the beans to a serving bowl and enjoy.

Yield: 4 to 6 servings

3 tablespoons extra virgin olive oil

1 tablespoon cumin seeds

3 cloves garlic, coarsely chopped

1 1/2 cups coarsely chopped onions

1/4 cup seeded, coarsely chopped ancho chili pepper

1 teaspoon seeded, coarsely chopped cayenne pepper

2 cups husked, coarsely chopped tomatillos

2 cups cooked pinto beans

1 cup coarsely chopped red bell peppers

1/2 cup coarsely chopped basil

1/2 teaspoon sea salt, or to taste

Kasha With Leeks and Collards

Yield: 4 to 6 servings

1 teaspoon sesame oil

2 cups coarsely chopped leeks

2 cups coarsely chopped collards

1 1/2 cups kasha

Pinch sea salt

3 cups boiling water

1/2 cup coarsely chopped parsley

When I was growing up, kasha with onions was a standard dish in my house. In this healthy variation, leeks replace the onions, and greens are added for color and nutrition.

1. Heat the oil in medium-sized skillet over medium heat. Add the leeks, collards, kasha, and salt, and sauté, stirring occasionally for 5 minutes, or until the ingredients are fragrant and well mixed. Turn off the heat.

2. Add the boiling water, and bring the ingredients to a boil over high heat. Reduce the heat to medium-low, and simmer covered for 10 minutes, or until the water is absorbed. Adjust the seasonings, if desired. Garnish with parsley and serve immediately.

Pasta With Fresh Garlic and Basil

Yield: 4 to 6 servings

1 pound spaghetti

3 ounces extra virgin olive oil

1/4 cup minced garlic

3/4 cup tightly packed fresh basil

1/2 teaspoon sea salt

6 calendula flower heads, optional

When fresh basil is unavailable, I sprinkle some Garlic Basil Oil (page 103) and a little salt on the hot pasta.

1. Bring a 4-quart pot of water to a rolling boil. Add the pasta, and cook according to package directions. Drain, rinse under cold water, and transfer to a bowl.

2. In the same pot, heat the oil over medium-low heat. Add the garlic, and sauté 1 to 2 minutes or until fragrant. Add the basil and salt, and sauté 2 minutes. Transfer the pasta to the pot and toss with the oil. Adjust the seasonings, if desired.

3. Serve hot. If using calendula flowers, break them up before adding to individual servings.

8

Ancient Wisdom, Ancient Grains

Grains are one of nature's gifts that have nurtured people all over the world for centuries. Through an increased awareness of the benefits of a healthy diet, ancient grains, such as quinoa, spelt, kamut, teff, sorghum, Bhutanese red rice, and Chinese "forbidden" black rice, are growing in popularity.

These ancient grains offer new options for those whose diets demand rotation—not just to escape boredom, but because of wheat and corn allergies. They permit even the most restricted dieter to feast. And, if you are looking for grains with more flavor and protein, these grains have it.

More and more, in my own kitchen, I find myself replacing common grains like brown rice, barley, and millet with quinoa, teff, and spelt. Rich in protein, amino acids, B vitamins, calcium, and fiber, each ancient grain has its own unique flavor and nutritional profile. Let's take a closer look at them now.

❑ **QUINOA.** Revered by the ancient Incas of South America, quinoa (pronounced keen-wah) is among the most popular of the ancient grains. The small, flattened quinoa grains have a look and taste that is similar to sesame seeds, and they are easily substituted for bulgur or couscous. This nutty-flavored choice has become a regular part of my weekly dinner repertoire—and not just because of its superlative nutritional qualities. (Quinoa is the only grain that is a complete protein; it is also a good source of B vitamins, vitamin E, calcium, iron, zinc, and potassium.) Quinoa is also quick cooking, and blends well with a wide variety of vegetables and spices.

Although quinoa is simple to cook, it must be rinsed well first. The grains are covered with a bitter-tasting protective coating called *saponin,* which deters birds and insects from eating them. Quinoa that is imported from South America is cream colored and about the size of millet. American quinoa is tinier in size and darker in color (beige to dark tan); it also requires less liquid to cook. Bolivian quinoa is black and believed to be especially strengthening to the kidneys.

❏ **TEFF.** Originally from Ethiopia, sweet-tasting teff has a subtle hazelnut, almost chocolate-like flavor and a moist texture that is similar to millet, only more exotic. Brown and ivory varieties of this grain are tinier than poppy seeds.

Safe for wheat-free diets, teff is a nutritional powerhouse. With all grains, nutrients are concentrated in the germ and the bran. With teff, the germ and bran make up almost the entire grain. Since the grains are too small to hull, teff can't be refined or lose its nutritional value. An eight-ounce serving provides 32 percent of the RDA for calcium and 80 percent for iron. Although teff is not a complete protein like quinoa, a two-ounce serving of teff contains 7 grams of protein, which is equal to an extra-large egg. Teff is also low in fat, high in fiber, and a good source of niacin, thiamin, riboflavin, zinc, magnesium, copper, manganese, boron, phosphorous, and potassium. If I sound excited, I am; teff is my favorite grain.

With the versatility of cornmeal and millet, teff can be enjoyed alone or in combination with other grains and vegetables. It is delicious in porridges, stews, stuffings, loaves, and polenta. It is also quick cooking (ready in twenty minutes), and there is no need for pre-rinsing. Season with cinnamon, ginger, garlic, cardamom, chilies, basil, and/or cilantro for a tasty dish.

Teff now grows and thrives in Idaho, thanks to Wayne Carlson. In 1973, Carlson had been working as a biologist in the Ethiopian highlands where he developed a taste for *injera*—the two-foot round sourdough flatbread made of teff flour. Three years later, when Carlson was working for the Idaho health department, he noted the similarity of the state's landscape to Ethiopia's highlands. He began experimenting with growing this ancient grain and succeeded. Today, Carlson's teff is sold in natural food markets under a variety of popular brand names. It is enjoyed by a growing number of consumers, particularly the wheat-free crowd, as well as the country's Ethiopian population.

❏ **SPELT.** Also known as *farro* or *dinkel,* spelt was originally harvested in the Middle Eastern area known as the Fertile Crescent over 9,000 years ago. Considered an ancient wheat, spelt contains a more-digestible form of gluten than common (hybrid) wheat, making it easily digestible and tolerated by many people with wheat allergies.

Spelt is also a high-fiber, high-energy grain—an excellent source of amino acids, complex carbohydrates, protein, iron, and potassium. Nutty-flavored spelt berries have a chewy texture (chewier than wheat berries) that works well in pilafs, salads, and soups.

This ancient grain also comes in the form of flour and flakes, a pearled grain (similar to pearled barley), and a cracked grain (similar to bulgur). Spelt pasta is also available.

❏ **KAMUT.** Harvested in ancient Egypt over 2,000 years ago, kamut, like spelt, is considered an ancient form of wheat. And like spelt, it is easily digested by most people who have wheat sensitivities.

Kamut has sweet, nutty taste and chewy texture. It is a high-energy grain—richer in protein, fiber, complex carbohydrates, B vitamins, iron, and potassium than common wheat. Available as whole berries, which are ideal in hot cereals and pilafs, kamut is also sold as pasta, flakes, and flour.

❏ **BHUTANESE RED RICE.** Earthy red in color, this short-grained rice is a staple in Bhutan, a small kingdom in the Himalayas. It has a delicious earthy flavor, soft texture, and cooks in just twenty minutes. Try it plain or in pilafs, puddings, and stir-fries. One cup of Bhutanese red rice has 12 grams of protein and contains 8 percent of the RDA for iron.

❏ **CHINESE "FORBIDDEN" BLACK RICE.** Once grown exclusively for Chinese emperors to insure their good health, medium-grained Chinese black rice is high in protein and iron. One cup contains 20 grams of protein and offers 16 percent of the RDA for iron. Delicious plain, or in pilafs, soups, puddings, and stir-fries, this chewy rice has a nutty flavor and turns a purplish black color when cooked. "Forbidden" rice requires only thirty minutes cooking time.

❏ **SORGHUM.** Also known as *milo,* sorghum—a small round grain with the texture of pearled barley—has been grown and served extensively in Africa, India, and China for thousands of years. Sorghum's flavor is quite bland, so when serving it plain, drizzle it with olive oil or season it well with herbs and spices. Sorghum is good in pilafs, porridges, soups, casseroles, and marinated salads. A half-cup serving contains 11.3 grams of protein, which is higher than the protein content of corn and almost as high as wheat.

On the following pages, you will find a tempting selection of my favorite recipes made with these delicious grains, including pilafs, loaves, roasted vegetables dishes, stir-fries, and polenta. I use a wide variety of nuts, seeds, mushrooms, vegetables, herbs, and spices to complement the subtle earthy flavors, colors, and textures of these ancient grains. In addition to the "Mix and Match" chart of ingredient substitutions (page 150), the "Cooking Ancient Grains" table (page 159) will help guide you in preparing these age-old gifts of nature for your own recipes.

MIX AND MATCH

The following ingredients are excellent choices (and among my favorites) to use in flavorful grain dishes. Choose one or combine any number of these ingredients to create your own recipe variations and satisfy your sense of adventure!

COOKING LIQUIDS	Coconut milk, fruit juice, vegetable stock, and water; combinations of beer, mirin, nut milk, water, and wine.
FALL/WINTER VEGETABLES	Carrots, butternut squash, delicata squash, Jerusalem artichokes, sweet potatoes, and yams.
SPRING/SUMMER VEGETABLES	Asparagus, broccoli, green beans, patty pan squash, yellow summer squash, and zucchini.
DOMESTIC/ WILD GREENS	Bok choy, chard, collards, dandelion greens, fiddleheads, kale, lamb's quarters, mizuna, mustard greens, napa cabbage, nettles, purslane, spinach, tat soi, and watercress.
MUSHROOMS	DOMESTIC VARIETIES: Crimini, portabella, shiitake, and white button.
	WILD VARIETIES: Black trumpet, chanterelles, lobster, maitake, matsutake, morels, mousseron, porcini,* and wood ears.
ONION VARIETIES	Chives, leeks, onions, ramps (wild leeks), scallions, and shallots.**
GARLIC VARIETIES	Garlic, elephant garlic, and garlic scapes.
NUTS AND SEEDS	Raw and toasted almonds, hazelnuts, pecans, pine nuts, pistachios, pumpkin seeds, sunflower seeds, and walnuts.
CHILI PEPPERS	VERY HOT: Cayenne peppers, habañero chilies, and Scotch bonnets.
	MODERATELY HOT: Serrano chilies.
	MILDLY HOT: Anaheim chilies, ancho chilies, jalapeño peppers, and poblano chilies.
MISO VARIETIES	SWEET, MELLOW: Aduki, barley, brown rice, chickpea, corn, and millet.
	SALTY, DARK: Hearty brown rice, aged barley, chickpea-barley, black soybean-barley, and red soybean.
HERBS AND SPICES	See "Spice It Up!" (page 8) for substitutions.
OILS	Almond, canola, coconut butter, corn, extra virgin olive, ghee, hi-oleic safflower and sunflower, peanut, sesame, toasted sesame, walnut, and flavored oils (see Chapter 5).
SALTY SEASONINGS	Dulse flakes, kelp granules, miso, nori flakes, sea salt, shoyu, tamari, umeboshi vinegar, and Bragg Liquid Aminos.

* Only 2 tablespoons dried porcini are equivalent to 2 cups fresh, milder-flavored mushrooms like white button.
** Approximately $1/3$ cup coarsely chopped shallots is equivalent to 1 cup onions or leeks.

Quinoa with corn, cinnamon, and Almonds

Exquisite. That's how I describe this sweet-tasting side dish, which always draws raves.

1. Preheat the oven to 375°F.

2. Place all of the ingredients except the water in a large bowl and mix well. Transfer to a covered baking dish, and add the water.

3. Bake for 45 minutes, or until the liquid is absorbed and the squash is tender. Adjust the seasonings, if desired.

4. Serve hot.

Yield: 4 to 6 servings

• • • • • • • •

1 cup quinoa, rinsed

4 cups butternut squash, cut into 1-inch cubes

2 cups corn kernels

1 cup onions, cut in chunks

$\frac{1}{2}$ cup almonds

3 tablespoons extra virgin olive oil

1 teaspoon cumin seeds

1 teaspoon cinnamon

$\frac{1}{2}$ teaspoon sea salt

2 cups water

Chinese Black Rice with Coconut Milk and Garlic

Serve this delicious dish with Szechwan Tofu with Mustard Greens and Chinese Cabbage (page 181) for a fine meal.

1. Bring the coconut milk, water, and salt to boil in a 4-quart pot.

2. Add the rice and garlic, reduce the heat to low, and simmer covered for 30 minutes, or until the liquid is absorbed. Adjust the seasonings, if desired.

3. Serve hot.

Yield: 4 servings

• • • • • • • •

14-ounce can coconut milk

1 cup water

Pinch sea salt

1 cup Chinese "forbidden" black rice, rinsed and drained

2 cloves garlic, minced

Quinoa with Wine, Tomatoes, and Mousseron Mushrooms

Yield: 4 to 6 servings

. . . .

.35-ounce package dried mousseron mushrooms ($\frac{1}{2}$ cup)

1 cup peach or white wine*

2 tablespoons extra virgin olive oil

1 head garlic or 10 cloves, thickly sliced

1 cup coarsely chopped onions

$\frac{1}{2}$ teaspoon sea salt

$\frac{1}{4}$–1 teaspoon ground cayenne pepper or chili pepper flakes, optional

1 $\frac{1}{2}$ cups quinoa, rinsed and drained

28-ounce can diced tomatoes, or 3 $\frac{1}{2}$ cups coarsely chopped plum tomatoes

$\frac{1}{4}$ cup water

1 teaspoon dried basil

$\frac{1}{2}$ teaspoon dried oregano

$\frac{1}{2}$ teaspoon dried sage

* Four Chimneys Organic Farm Winery brand is recommended.

Mousserons, also known as "fairy rings," are wild mushrooms with a delicate, sweet flavor. Here, they are cooked with tomatoes, peppers, quinoa, and white wine. Enjoy this fragrant dish as is or garnished with fresh cracked pepper, chopped parsley, grated Parmesan, crumbled feta, or slices of chèvre.

1. Place the mushrooms in a small mixing bowl and cover with wine. Let sit for 20 to 30 minutes to soften.

2. Heat the oil in a 4-quart stockpot over medium heat. Add the garlic, onions, salt, and cayenne (if using), and sauté, stirring occasionally for 5 minutes, or until the onions begin to soften. Add the quinoa, tomatoes, water, softened mushrooms, and wine.

3. Bring the ingredients to a boil, and then reduce the heat to medium-low. Simmer covered for 10 minutes, or until the liquid is almost absorbed.

4. Add the basil, oregano, and sage, and simmer another 5 minutes, or until the liquid is completely absorbed.

5. Turn off the heat, keep the pot covered, and let sit 15 to 20 minutes to allow the flavors to mingle.

6. Serve immediately.

Shiitake Mushrooms, Summer Squash, and Quinoa Pilaf

Fragrant herbs and a touch of curry enliven this juicy main-course pilaf.

1. Bring the water to boil in a teakettle or small pot.

2. Heat the oil in a medium-sized skillet over medium heat. Add the mushrooms, and sauté for 3 to 4 minutes, or until browned.

3. Add the garlic, onions, squash, and carrots to the skillet. Sauté, stirring occasionally for 4 minutes, or until the onions begin to soften and the ingredients become fragrant. Stir in the quinoa, thyme, curry powder, salt, rosemary, and cayenne.

4. Add the boiling water, and bring the ingredients to a boil over high heat. Reduce the heat to medium-low, and simmer covered for 10 to 15 minutes, or until the water is absorbed. Adjust the seasonings, if desired.

5. Serve immediately.

Yield: 4 to 6 servings

2$\frac{1}{2}$ cups water

I teaspoon extra virgin olive oil

1$\frac{1}{2}$ cups coarsely chopped fresh shiitake mushroom caps

6 cloves garlic, thickly sliced

1$\frac{1}{2}$ cups coarsely chopped onions

2 cups yellow summer squash, cut into bite-sized pieces

$\frac{1}{2}$ cup julienned carrots

1$\frac{1}{4}$ cups quinoa, rinsed and drained

I tablespoon fresh thyme, or I teaspoon dried

1$\frac{1}{2}$ teaspoons curry powder

$\frac{1}{2}$ teaspoon sea salt

$\frac{3}{4}$ teaspoon fresh rosemary, or $\frac{1}{4}$ teaspoon dried

Pinch cayenne pepper, or to taste

FYI . . .

The delicious woodsy-flavored shiitake mushroom has been considered potent medicine by Asian herbologists for thousands of years. In addition to its anti-viral properties, the shiitake is known for strengthening the immune system, reducing the risk of some cancers, and lowering cholesterol and high blood pressure.

Roasted Wild Mushrooms and Quinoa

Yield: 4 to 6 servings

. . . .

1 tablespoon dried chanterelle mushrooms

1 tablespoon dried porcini mushrooms

2 1/2 cups boiling water

1 1/4 cups quinoa, rinsed and drained

3 1/2 cups celery root, peeled and cut into 1-inch cubes

1 1/2 cups parsnips, cut into 2-inch chunks

2 1/2 cups coarsely chopped white button mushrooms

3 cups red or green bell peppers, cut into 2-inch strips

1 cup onions, cut into 2-inch chunks

4 cloves garlic, thickly sliced

1 teaspoon dried thyme

1/2 teaspoon sea salt

The incomparable flavors of chanterelles, white button, and porcini mushrooms result in a dish that is rich and inviting.

1. Preheat the oven to 400°F.

2. Place the dried chanterelles and porcini in a large mixing bowl, add the boiling water, and let sit 20 minutes. Add the quinoa and all of the remaining ingredients. Mix and transfer to a large covered baking dish.

3. Bake for 40 minutes, or until the vegetables are tender.

4. Stir the ingredients and serve immediately.

FYI . . .

To alter the texture of grains, before adding the cooking liquid, you can:

✔ Dry-roast them (either alone or with spices, nuts, or seeds). This will make them fluffy, light, and nutty.

✔ Sauté them in a little oil (either alone or with spices, nuts, or seeds). This will make them moist, tender, rich, and flavorful.

Spicy Pumpkin-Seed Quinoa

In this dish, toasted pumpkin seeds add a tasty crunch to quinoa that is flavored with chilies and dill.

1. Bring the water to boil in a teakettle or small pot.

2. Place the pumpkin seeds in a medium-sized unoiled skillet over medium-low heat. Stirring occasionally, dry-roast the seeds for 5 minutes, or until they begin to pop and smell fragrant. Add the quinoa and salt to the skillet and dry roast for 2 to 3 minutes, stirring occasionally, until quinoa begins to crackle.

3. Add the oil, garlic, onions, cumin, and chili flakes. Sauté, stirring occasionally for 5 minutes, or until onions begin to soften.

4. Turn off the heat and add the beans, dill, and boiling water. Simmer over medium-low heat for 10 minutes, or until the water is absorbed. Adjust the seasonings, if desired.

5. Serve immediately.

Yield: 4 to 6 servings

• • • • • • •

$2^2/_3$ cups water

$3/_4$ cup shelled pumpkin seeds

$1^1/_3$ cups quinoa, rinsed and drained

$1/_2$ teaspoon sea salt, or to taste

1 tablespoon extra virgin olive oil

5 cloves garlic, thickly sliced

1 cup coarsely chopped onions

1 teaspoon cumin seeds or ground cumin

$1/_4$–1 teaspoon chili pepper flakes, or to taste

$3/_4$ cup green beans, cut into 1-inch pieces

$1/_4$ cup chopped fresh dill

Quinoa with Cauliflower and Feta

A wonderful garnish of tangy feta cheese is the perfect crown for this melt-in-your-mouth quinoa dish. Enjoy it as a light main-course or scrumptious side, or use it as a filling for tomatoes, squash, or bell peppers.

Yield: 4 to 6 servings

3 cups water

1 tablespoon extra virgin olive oil

1 cup coarsely chopped onions

4 cloves garlic, thickly sliced

4 cups cauliflower florets

1 1/2 cups quinoa, rinsed and drained

6 cups coarsely chopped kale

1 1/2 cups coarsely chopped red bell pepper

1 teaspoon fresh thyme, or 1/2 teaspoon dried

1/2 teaspoon sea salt

5 ounces crumbled feta cheese

1. Bring the water to boil in a teakettle or small pot.

2. Heat the oil in a medium-sized skillet over medium heat. Add the onions and garlic, and sauté 5 minutes, or until the garlic is fragrant and onions begin to soften.

3. Add the cauliflower and continue to sauté 5 minutes, or until it becomes bright white. Add the quinoa, kale, red pepper, thyme, salt, and boiling water.

4. Bring the ingredients to a boil, then reduce the heat to low and simmer 15 minutes, or until the water is absorbed.

5. Stir the mixture, top with feta cheese, and serve.

FOR A CHANGE . . .

• Substitute 2 cups coarsely chopped parsley for the kale, and add 1 teaspoon dried chili pepper flakes.

Teff Polenta

*Flavored with sweet juicy tomatoes, green bell peppers, fresh basil,
and garlic, this teff dish is an irresistible summer repast.
Serve plain or garnished with sliced rounds of chèvre,
or grated fontina, Parmesan, or Manchego cheese.*

1. Bring the water to boil in a teakettle or small pot.

2. Heat the oil in a medium-sized skillet over medium heat. Add the garlic and onions, and sauté, stirring occasionally for 5 minutes, or until the garlic is fragrant and the onions begin to soften.

3. Add the peppers to the skillet, and sauté for 2 minutes, then stir in the teff. Add the boiling water and salt, and bring the ingredients to a boil. Stir in the tomatoes and basil.

4. Reduce the heat to low, and simmer covered for 10 to 15 minutes, stirring occasionally, until the teff is soft and most or all of the water is absorbed. Adjust the seasonings, if desired.

5. Transfer the mixture to an unoiled 9-inch pie plate, and let cool for about 30 minutes.

6. Slice into wedges and serve.

Yield: 4 to 6 servings

• • • • • •

2 cups water

2 tablespoons extra virgin olive oil

8 cloves garlic, thickly sliced

1 cup coarsely chopped onions

1 cup coarsely chopped green bell peppers

$^2/_3$ cup teff

$^1/_2$ teaspoon sea salt

2 cups coarsely chopped plum tomatoes

1 cup coarsely chopped fresh basil

FYI . . .

Nutrient-rich teff is low in fat and high in fiber. An eight-ounce serving contains 32 percent of the Recommended Daily Allowance of calcium and 80 percent of iron, which is why I've nicknamed teff "the women's grain."

Ethiopian Grain Loaf

*Yams and collards combine with teff, herbs, and spices,
creating a beautiful mosaic pattern
in this robust grain loaf.*

Yield: 8 servings

. . . .

3 cups water

3 1/2 cups thinly sliced yams

1 cup teff

1/2 teaspoon sea salt,
or to taste

1 tablespoon extra virgin
olive oil

1 1/2 cups coarsely chopped
leeks

1 teaspoon fennel seeds

1 teaspoon cumin seeds

2 cups coarsely chopped
collard greens

1/2 cup coarsely chopped
basil

1/2 cup coarsely chopped
cilantro

1. Bring the water, yams, teff, and salt to boil in a 4-quart stock-pot. Reduce the heat to low and simmer covered for 20 minutes.

2. While the teff mixture simmers, heat a medium-sized skillet over medium heat. Add the oil, leeks, fennel, and cumin, and sauté 2 to 3 minutes or until fragrant. Stir in the collard greens and sauté about 3 minutes, or until bright green.

3. Transfer the collard mixture to the teff mixture, cover, and continue to simmer another few minutes, or until all of the liquid is absorbed.

4. Turn off the heat and stir the basil and cilantro into mixture. Adjust the seasonings, if desired.

5. Spoon the mixture into an 8-inch unoiled loaf pan, and let stand about 30 minutes, or until firm.

6. Remove the loaf onto a platter (or leave in the pan). Cut into slices and serve.

Cooking Ancient Grains

The chart below provides the amount of water needed and the cooking times for preparing 1 cup of the ancient grains used in this chapter. To cook, bring the liquid to a boil, stir in the grain, and reduce the heat to low. Cover and simmer until the liquid is absorbed and the grain is tender.

When combining grains and cooking them in one pot, use the *total* amount of liquid needed for each grain. For example, if you wanted to cook 1 cup of quinoa together with 1 cup of sorghum in the same pot, you would need 2 cups of liquid for the quinoa and 3 cups for the sorghum for a total of 5 cups liquid. This same principle works when cooking other grains, such as brown rice and millet. Also, when cooking two grains in one pot, always follow the longer cooking time.

GRAIN (1 CUP)	AMOUNT OF WATER/LIQUID	COOKING TIME	APPROXIMATE YIELD
Quinoa,* rinsed well	2 cups	15 minutes	$2\frac{1}{2}$ cups
Teff, unrinsed	3 cups	20 minutes	2 cups
Spelt, presoaked**	$1\frac{1}{2}$ cups	1 hour	2 cups
Kamut, presoaked**	3 cups	1 hour	$2\frac{1}{2}$ cups
Sorghum	3 cups	1 hour	4 cups
Bhutanese red rice	$1\frac{3}{4}$ cups	20 minutes	$2\frac{1}{2}$ to 3 cups
Chinese "forbidden" black rice	$1\frac{3}{4}$ cups	30 minutes	$2\frac{1}{2}$ to 3 cups

* If preparing American quinoa, which is tinier in size and darker in color than standard South American varieties, use less liquid—about $1\frac{1}{2}$ cups.

** Either presoak overnight, or add to boiling water and soak at least 1 hour.

Tempeh with Dried Cherry Tomatoes and Teff

This is one of my favorite main-course meals made with teff.

Yield: 6 to 8 servings

3 cups water

1 tablespoon cumin seeds

1 tablespoon mustard seeds

3 tablespoons extra virgin olive oil

3 packages (8 ounces each) soy tempeh, cut into 1-inch cubes

2 cups coarsely chopped red onions

1 cup dried cherry tomatoes*

²/₃ cup teff

1 teaspoon sea salt

1 cup coarsely chopped cilantro or parsley, optional

* If dried cherry tomatoes are unavailable, use sun-dried tomato halves.

1. Bring the water to boil in a teakettle or small pot.

2. While the water comes to a boil, place the cumin and mustard seeds in a medium-sized unoiled skillet over medium-low heat. Stirring occasionally, dry-roast the seeds for 1 or 2 minutes, or until they begin to pop.

3. Add the oil to the skillet along with tempeh, onions, tomatoes, and teff. Sauté briefly, add the boiling water and salt, and simmer covered 15 to 20 minutes, or until the water is absorbed. Adjust the seasonings, if desired.

4. Garnish with cilantro, and serve immediately.

FOR A CHANGE . . .

• Fry the mustard and cumin seeds in the oil before adding the remaining ingredients.

• Try different varieties of tempeh, such as vegetable or grain.

Spring Teff Loaf

Asparagus, bell peppers, and thyme create a tasty spring variation of the Ethiopian Grain Loaf (page 158).

1. Heat the oil in a 4-quart stockpot over medium heat. Add the teff, leeks, peppers, asparagus, and collard greens. Sauté 5 minutes, or until the vegetables are bright green.

2. Add the boiling water to the sautéing vegetables, and stir in the basil, cumin, and thyme. Bring the ingredients to a boil, then reduce heat to low and simmer 15 to 20 minutes, or until the water is absorbed. Adjust the seasonings, if desired.

3. Spoon the mixture into an 8-inch unoiled loaf pan, and let stand about 30 minutes, or until firm.

4. Remove the loaf onto a platter (or leave in the pan). Cut into slices and serve.

Yield: 8 servings

· · · · · · · ·

I tablespoon olive oil

1 $\frac{1}{3}$ cups teff

$\frac{1}{2}$ cup coarsely chopped leeks

1 $\frac{1}{2}$ cups coarsely chopped green bell peppers

I cup asparagus, cut into I-inch pieces

$\frac{2}{3}$ cup coarsely chopped collard greens

4 cups boiling water

I cup coarsely chopped basil

I teaspoon ground cumin

I tablespoon fresh thyme, or I teaspoon dried

I teaspoon sea salt, or to taste

Kamut Berries with Fennel and Red Peppers

The chewiness of kamut berries offers a nice change of pace from rice and other softer grains. Substitute kamut for wheat berries and spelt in pilafs, salads, and stuffings. Many folks who are allergic to wheat are able to enjoy kamut.

Yield: 4 servings

• • • • • • •

1 cup kamut berries

3 cups water

1 bay leaf

$\frac{1}{2}$ teaspoon sea salt

1 tablespoon extra virgin olive oil

1 teaspoon fennel seeds

3 cloves garlic, minced

1 cup coarsely sliced leeks

$1\frac{1}{2}$ cups diced celery root

$1\frac{1}{3}$ cups diced red bell peppers

1. Place the kamut in a 2-quart unoiled pot over medium-low heat. Stirring occasionally, dry-roast the kamut berries for 4 minutes, or until they begin to pop and smell fragrant. Transfer to a strainer, rinse, and drain well. Return the berries to the pot, cover with 3 cups water, and let soak at least 1 hour.

2. Add the bay leaf and salt to the kamut, and bring to a boil. Reduce the heat to medium-low, and simmer covered about 30 minutes.

3. While the kamut is simmering, heat the olive oil in a medium-sized skillet over medium heat. Add the fennel seeds and fry 1 or 2 minutes, or until they begin to pop and become fragrant. Add the garlic and leeks to the fennel, and sauté, stirring occasionally for 5 minutes, or until the garlic and leeks are soft but not browned.

4. Add the celery root to the skillet, cook 10 minutes, then transfer the sautéed vegetables to the pot with the kamut. Cover and simmer another 20 minutes.

5. Add the bell peppers to the pot but do not stir with the kamut. Continue to simmer 10 minutes or until the water is absorbed and the kamut is tender but still chewy. (Total kamut cooking time is about 1 hour.)

6. Stir the peppers into the kamut, and adjust the seasonings, if desired.

7. Serve immediately.

Basmati Rice Pilaf with Spelt and Red Wine

This delicious nutty pilaf is infused with garlic and red wine.

1. Place the spelt in a small bowl, cover with $\frac{3}{4}$ cup boiling water, and let sit at least 1 hour. Drain, reserving $\frac{2}{3}$ cup of the soaking water.

2. Bring the 2 cups of fresh water to boil in a teakettle or small pot.

3. Heat a 4-quart stockpot over medium heat. Add the oil, garlic, onions, celery, and sea salt. Sauté, stirring occasionally for 5 minutes, or until the onions begin to soften and the celery turns bright green.

4. Add the spelt and basmati rice, and sauté, stirring occasionally 2 to 3 minutes until well mixed. Turn off the heat. Add the boiling water, the reserved spelt soaking water, and the wine.

5. Simmer covered over low heat for 50 minutes, or until the liquid is absorbed and the spelt and rice are tender.

6. Serve immediately.

FOR A CHANGE . . .

- Replace the spelt with $\frac{1}{3}$ cup kamut berries.

Yield: 4 to 6 servings
• • • • • • • •
$\frac{1}{2}$ cup spelt berries, rinsed and drained

$\frac{3}{4}$ cup boiling water

2 cups water

1 tablespoon extra virgin olive oil

3 cloves garlic, thickly sliced

$\frac{2}{3}$ cup coarsely chopped onions

$\frac{3}{4}$ cup diced celery or celeriac

$\frac{1}{4}$ teaspoon sea salt

1 cup basmati rice, rinsed and drained

$\frac{3}{4}$ cup red wine

Spelt Spaghetti with Dairy-Free Pesto

Serve this vegan version of a summertime favorite either warm or chilled.
It can be ready in about the time it takes to boil a pot of pasta.

Yield: 4 to 6 servings

• • • • • • • •

1 pound spelt spaghetti

$^1/_2$ cup almonds

$^1/_2$ cup sunflower seeds

5 tablespoons umeboshi vinegar

$^1/_2$ cup water

$2^1/_2$ cups basil leaves

6 cloves garlic

$^1/_2$ cup edible flowers such as bee balm, calendula, day lilies, or nasturtiums, optional

1. Bring a 4-quart pot of water to a rolling boil. Add the spelt spaghetti, and cook according to package directions.

2. While the spaghetti is cooking, place the almonds and sunflower seeds in a food processor and grind to a fine meal. Add the umeboshi vinegar, water, basil, and garlic, and purée to form a smooth pesto. Adjust the seasonings, adding more umeboshi vinegar for a saltier, tangier flavor.

3. Drain the cooked spaghetti and place in a serving bowl. Add the pesto and toss well.

4. Garnish with edible flowers, if desired, and serve warm.

FOR A CHANGE . . .

• Instead of spelt pasta, use kamut spaghetti or spirals.

• Substitute cilantro for some or all of the basil.

TIP . . .

When cooking any type or shaped pasta:

✔ Always bring the water to a rolling boil before adding the uncooked pasta.

✔ Drain and serve cooked pasta immediately, or rinse under cold water to stop the cooking process.

✔ Don't overcook the pasta or it will become mushy. Properly cooked pasta should be *al dente*—firm to the bite, but not hard.

Asian Vegetable Stir-Fry With Bhutanese Red Rice

Ginger-flavored rice and vegetables make a very satisfying side dish. Serve with baked yams and tofu for a wonderful and simple meal.

1. Place the rice in a bowl, cover with the water, and soak at least 45 minutes.

2. Heat a wok over high heat. Add the oil, ginger, garlic, and onions, and stir-fry 5 minutes, or until the onions begin to soften.

3. Add the mirin, then toss in the carrots and stir-fry 3 minutes, or until they turn bright orange.

4. Stir the celery, tamari, rice, and soaking water into the wok, and bring to a boil. Reduce the heat to low, and simmer covered for 15 to 20 minutes, or until the water is absorbed.

5. Let stand 5 minutes, stir, and serve.

Yield: 4 servings

• • • • • • •

$^3/_4$ cup Bhutanese red rice, rinsed and drained

1 $^1/_4$ cups water

2 tablespoons sesame oil

2 tablespoons grated ginger

2 cloves garlic, minced

1 $^1/_2$ cups coarsely chopped onions

2 tablespoons mirin

1 cup julienned carrots

1 cup diagonally sliced celery

1 tablespoon tamari

Spelt Loaf With Almonds and Sunflower Seeds

There is nothing more basic than meat loaf flavored with thyme and sage. Here is a meatless version made with nutty-flavored spelt bulgur. Ground almonds and sunflower seeds add richness. Serve slices of this savory loaf with ketchup, Mustard Sauce with Maple Syrup and Miso (page 76), or a side of Cranberry-Orange Sauce (page 75).

Yield: 8 servings

• • • • • • • •

3 cups water

Pinch sea salt

2 cups spelt bulgur

1 tablespoon sesame oil

4 cloves garlic, minced

1 cup coarsely chopped leeks

1 cup diced carrots

1 1/2 cups diced celery root

1 cup finely ground almonds

1 cup finely ground sunflower seeds

3 tablespoons barley miso, or to taste

2 tablespoons fresh sage, or 1 tablespoon dried

2 teaspoons fresh thyme, or 1 teaspoon dried

1. Preheat the oven to 375°F. Lightly oil a 2-quart loaf pan and set aside.

2. Place the water and salt in a 4-quart pot and bring to a rolling boil. Add the spelt, reduce the heat to low, and simmer 3 minutes, or until the water is absorbed. Transfer the spelt to a large bowl to cool.

3. Heat a wok or medium-sized skillet over medium heat. Add the sesame oil, garlic, leeks, carrots, and celery root. Sauté, stirring occasionally for 5 minutes, or until the leeks begin to soften and the carrots turn bright orange.

4. Add the leek-carrot mixture and all of the remaining ingredients to the spelt, and mix well. Adjust the seasonings, if desired.

5. Spoon the mixture into the loaf pan and press it down firmly. Cover and bake 45 minutes, remove the cover, and continue to bake another 10 minutes. Remove from the oven and let cool for 30 minutes.

6. Remove the loaf onto a platter (or leave in the pan). Cut into slices and serve.

FOR A CHANGE . . .

- Use bulgur wheat instead of spelt. When doing so, increase the water to 4 cups.

- Substitute 1½ teaspoons of sea salt for the miso.

- Replace the almonds and sunflower seeds with ground hazelnuts or hazelnut flour; ground walnuts, pistachios, or pecans; or a combination of ground nuts and seeds.

- Instead of celery root, use wild or domestic mushrooms, such as portabella, crimini, shiitake, white button, oyster, or maitake.

Spicy Sorghum with Peas and Orange Zest

The hot, enticing flavors of African spices are balanced with sweet orange zest in this beautiful side dish. Serve with the Curried Lentil Soup with Coconut Milk (page 53), or another coconut-flavored dish.

1. Bring the water to boil in a 2-quart pot. Stir in the sorghum and salt, reduce the heat to low, and simmer 1 hour, or until the water is absorbed.

2. Melt the ghee in a medium-sized skillet over medium-high heat. Add the zest, garlic, cumin, cayenne, and fennel. Fry for 2 minutes, or until the garlic begins to brown and the spices become fragrant.

3. Add the sorghum and peas to the skillet and mix with the spices. Adjust the seasonings, if desired.

4. Serve immediately.

Yield: 4 to 6 servings

3 cups water

1 cup sorghum, rinsed and drained

Pinch sea salt

2 tablespoons ghee

2 tablespoons dried orange peel or zest

4 cloves garlic, thickly sliced

1 teaspoon cumin seeds

1 teaspoon coarsely chopped dried cayenne pepper

½ teaspoon fennel seeds

2 cups fresh or frozen peas

9

Main Attractions

Here's my mantra: let the food guide the recipe. Let me further explain through an example. One evening I went down to the kitchen to make dinner. Since it was already late, my idea was to make a quick meal of curried tofu with tomatoes. When I opened the refrigerator, I discovered some fresh picked broccoli, chard, and lots of garlic scapes. Suddenly, everything changed. With fresh thyme and oregano growing outside my kitchen door, I decided to conjure up an Italian feast.

With a splash of extra virgin olive oil in the pot, I quickly sautéed the garlic scapes, added chopped tomatoes, broccoli, and tofu. After letting the dish simmer for a while, I added the chard and some coarsely chopped thyme and oregano leaves. Tasting the vegetables, I found them disappointedly bland, so I sprinkled on a bit of sea salt, which brought out the juice and flavor of the tomatoes. Instinctively, I took a few sprigs off my rosemary plant, and added some leaves. I tasted the dish again and—Ah, Bellissima!

I had taken my cues from nature, blending vegetables and herbs that were in season for a delicious ingredient combination. I improvised, making the dish up as I went along. Easy and delicious, the sauté evolved into a stew.

Often an idea for a main course will come to me at the market, in a restaurant, or on a walk through the garden. Combinations of ingredients sometimes come to me in my dreams. Creative impulses often steer me into the kitchen. I have had my fair share of delicious one-night stands. I just can't help myself—I like to play around.

When I first started cooking, I looked to recipes to tell me how much of this herb or that spice to use. Now, I try different combinations of foods and seasonings. I alter recipe ingredients, using more or less of what is typically called for; I omit and/or substitute; I give dishes ethnic flavor by using certain seasonings. For me, it is always fun to create new dishes!

Although the recipes in this chapter call for simple cooking techniques and basic ingredients, the results are both satisfying and delicious. The Goat Cheese Mushroom Strudel, for instance, is an elegant entrée that will make you feel as if you're dining in a five-star restaurant, while the warming Moroccan Black Bean Stew will transport you to another continent. When you're feeling tired and weary, the Hiziki with Shiitake Mushrooms and Butternut Squash is the perfect energizer. And keep in mind that Linguine a la Sweet Putanesca is a crowd pleaser, especially with the kids.

Whether you prepare the dishes as outlined on the following pages, or use the recipes as springboards for creating your own versions, have fun! Remember, cooking is easy. What's hard is having faith in your own preferences, jumping from indecision to trial and success. Once you bridge that gap (the "Mix and Match" chart on the next page will help), you'll find it becoming second nature to creatively bring together delicious ingredient blends.

MIX AND MATCH

A little of this . . . a little of that. I feel pure joy whenever I come up with a delicious new version of a favorite dish. The chart below will help you create spinoffs of the entrées in this chapter, as well as your own main-dish favorites.

Go Wild with Main Courses

FALL/WINTER VEGETABLES	Butternut squash, carrots, delicata squash, Jerusalem artichokes, sweet potatoes, and yams.
SPRING/SUMMER VEGETABLES	Asparagus, broccoli, green beans, patty pan squash, yellow summer squash, and zucchini.
DOMESTIC/ WILD GREENS	FOR ASIAN DISHES: Bok choy, chard, collards, lamb's quarters, mizuna, mustard greens, napa cabbage, nettles, spinach, tat soi, and watercress.
	FOR MEDITERRANEAN DISHES: Chard, dandelion greens, kale, lamb's quarters, and nettles, spinach.
BEANS	Anasazi beans, black beans, cannellini (navy) beans, chickpeas, fava beans, kidney beans, lentils, lima beans, navy beans, and pinto beans.
ONION VARIETIES	Chives, leeks, onions, scallions, shallots,* and wild leeks (ramps).
GARLIC VARIETIES	Garlic, elephant garlic, garlic scapes.
SEA VEGETABLES	LEAFY VARIETIES: Dulse, kelp, ocean ribbons kombu, wakame, and alaria.
	NOODLE-LIKE VARIETIES: Arame, hiziki, and sea palm.
MUSHROOMS	DOMESTIC VARIETIES: Crimini, portabella, shiitake, and white button.
	WILD VARIETIES: Black trumpet, chanterelles, lobster, maitake, matsutake, morels, mousseron, porcini,** and wood ears.
OILS	Canola, extra virgin olive, sesame, hi-oleic sunflower, and flavored oils (see Chapter 5); coconut butter; and ghee.
CHILI PEPPERS	VERY HOT: Cayenne peppers, habañero chilies, Scotch bonnets.
	MODERATELY HOT: Serrano chilies.
	MILDLY HOT: Anaheim chilies, ancho chilies, jalapeño peppers, poblano chilies.
SALTY SEASONINGS	Dulse flakes, kelp granules, nori flakes, miso, sea salt, shoyu, tamari, umeboshi vinegar, and Bragg Liquid Aminos.
HERBS AND SPICES	See "Spice It Up!" (page 8) for substitutions.

* Approximately $\frac{1}{3}$ cup coarsely chopped shallots is equivalent to 1 cup onions or leeks.
** Only 2 tablespoons dried porcini are equivalent to 2 cups fresh, milder-flavored mushrooms like white button.

Lasagna With Chèvre, Arugula, and Crimini Mushrooms

*Lasagna is very versatile. In this version, chèvre stands in for the
more commonly used ricotta cheese, and goat cheddar subs for mozzarella.
Other cheeses that melt well, such as goat Gouda, French petite
Basque or Spanish Manchego, are good choices, too.*

Yield: 4 to 6 servings

· · · · · · · ·

2 cups tomato sauce

9 uncooked
lasagna noodles
(8 ounces)

6-ounce log chèvre
(plain or basil)

I cup coarsely chopped
crimini mushrooms

I $\frac{1}{2}$ cups coarsely chopped
arugula

2 cups grated
goat cheddar

1. Preheat the oven to 400°F.

2. Spread $\frac{1}{2}$ cup of the tomato sauce in the bottom of an 8-inch square baking dish. (You can use one of the lasagna noodles to do the spreading.) Lay 3 of the noodles over the sauce.

3. Spread the chèvre on top of the noodles, top with another 3 noodles, and cover with mushrooms and arugula.

4. Place the last 3 noodles over the mushrooms and arugula, and press gently. Top with the remaining sauce and grated cheese.

5. Cover with foil or a cookie sheet and bake for 45 minutes, or until the noodles are soft and the lasagna is hot and bubbly.

6. Remove from the oven and let sit about 10 minutes to set. Cut into squares and serve.

FOR A CHANGE . . .

• Instead of crimini mushrooms and arugula, try a combination of marinated sun-dried tomatoes, fresh or roasted bell peppers, chopped radicchio, sautéed shiitake mushrooms, and kale.

• Replace the layer of vegetables with another layer of grated cheese.

• Vary the type of lasagna noodles; use rice, whole wheat, spelt, spinach, or artichoke soy. Even penne or macaroni pasta works well.

• For a Mexican-style version, use jalapeño jack soy cheese instead of chèvre, and salsa in place of tomato sauce.

Pasta with Roasted Vegetables and Chèvre

Each bite of this savory pasta dish is jam-packed with vegetables and creamy chunks of chèvre.

1. Preheat the oven to 400°F.

2. Place the yellow squash, zucchini, onions, peppers, garlic, oil, rosemary, and sea salt in a large bowl and mix well. Transfer to a baking dish, cover, and bake 45 minutes, or until the vegetables are tender.

3. While the vegetables are baking, bring a pot of water to a rolling boil, and cook the penne according to package directions. Drain, rinse in cold water, and transfer to a large serving bowl.

4. Add the roasted vegetables to the pasta and toss well.

5. Garnish with chunks of chèvre, and serve. The steam from the veggies will slightly melt the cheese. Delicious!

Yield: 4 to 6 servings

• • • • • • •

6 cups yellow squash, sliced into half moons

3 cups zucchini, sliced into half moons

$1\frac{1}{2}$ cups coarsely chopped onions

1 cup red or green bell peppers, sliced into 1-inch wide strips

8 garlic scapes or garlic cloves, thickly sliced

5 tablespoons extra virgin olive oil

3 heaping tablespoons fresh rosemary leaves

1 teaspoon sea salt

1 pound penne pasta

6-ounce log chèvre, cut into chunks

FYI . . .

Looking for a farmer's market to buy fresh local produce? Visit the following website for a national map of market locations:

www.ams.usda.gov/farmersmarkets/map.htm

Moroccan
Black Bean Stew

Spicy ginger and habañero chili set off the natural sweetness of the yams in this savory dish, while cilantro and cumin balance the heat. A true celebration of flavors, this stew is best when served over rice or scooped up with warm flat bread.

Yield: 6 to 8 servings

2 tablespoons extra virgin olive oil

4 cloves garlic, thinly sliced

2 teaspoons grated ginger

1 teaspoon seeded, coarsely chopped habañero chili

1 teaspoon ground cumin

1 cup coarsely chopped onions

4 cups coarsely chopped yams

3 cups cauliflower florets

28-ounce can diced tomatoes

2 cups cooked black beans

1/2 cup water

Pinch saffron

1 cup coarsely chopped cilantro leaves

1 teaspoon sea salt, or to taste

1. Heat the oil in a 6-quart stockpot over medium heat. Add the garlic, ginger, habañero, and cumin, and sauté 2 minutes, or until fragrant.

2. Add the onions, yams, cauliflower, tomatoes, beans, water, and saffron to the pot. Bring the ingredients to a boil, then reduce the heat to medium-low. Cover and simmer, stirring occasionally, for 20 to 30 minutes, or until the vegetables are tender.

3. Add the cilantro and salt, and continue to simmer another 5 minutes. Adjust the seasonings, if desired.

4. Ladle the hot stew into bowls and serve.

FOR A CHANGE . . .

• Instead of black beans, use chickpeas or lentils. Fresh or frozen green beans or peas also work well.

Curried Coconut Seitan

The flavors of curry and coconut give this simple seitan dish a luxurious hint of India. I usually serve it over Chinese bifun noodles along with a green salad that is garnished with orange and grapefruit segments.

1. Reserving the liquid, cut the seitan into $1/2$-inch cubes. Heat the oil in a wok or medium-sized skillet over medium-high heat. Add the seitan and stir-fry for 5 minutes.

2. Add the seitan liquid and cabbage to the wok, and stir-fry 3 to 5 minutes, or until the cabbage becomes bright green. Toss in the carrots and stir-fry another 3 to 5 minutes, or until the carrots turn bright orange.

3. Stir the bell pepper (if using), curry powder, and coconut into the mixture. Adjust the seasonings, if desired. For a spicier taste, add more curry; for added sweetness, add more coconut.

4. Serve hot either as is or over noodles. Garnish with mung bean sprouts.

Yield: 4 servings

12-ounce package seitan

2 tablespoons sesame oil

2 cups coarsely chopped green cabbage

1 cup coarsely chopped carrots

1 cup coarsely chopped red bell pepper, optional

1 teaspoon curry powder

2 tablespoons shredded coconut

1 cup mung bean sprouts

FYI . . .

Seitan (pronounced SAY·tan) is a meat-like substitute made from the gluten in whole wheat flour. Depending on how it is cooked and seasoned, seitan (like tofu) can take on a variety of flavors. This allows cooks to use seitan to create vegetarian "meat" dishes.

Roasted Eggplant with Wine and Morel Mushrooms

Yield: 4 to 6 servings

• • • • • • • • • • • •

4 cups eggplant, cut into triangular pieces (about 1-inch wide and $1/4$-inch thick)

1 teaspoon sea salt, or 1 tablespoon umeboshi vinegar

1 pound soy tempeh, cut into 1-inch cubes

3 cups red bell pepper, sliced into 1-inch-wide strips

1 cup red onion, cut into 1-inch chunks

4 dried morel mushrooms

$1/2$ cup dry white wine

6 cloves garlic, thickly sliced

4 tablespoons extra virgin olive oil

1 teaspoon sea salt

Earthy flavored wild morel mushrooms are succulent and meaty. In this recipe, I combine them with roasted eggplant and tempeh—one of my favorite soy foods— for an exciting main course.

1. Place the eggplant in a large bowl and sprinkle with salt. Let sit for 45 minutes to release some of the eggplant's bitter juices. Drain and set aside.

2. Preheat the oven to 400°F.

3. Add the remaining ingredients to the eggplant, mix well, and transfer to a large covered baking dish.

4. Bake for 1 hour, or until vegetables are tender.

5. Serve hot over pasta.

Goat Cheese Mushroom Strudel

*It's easy to see why this strudel, with its crisp layers of flaky phyllo, surrounding
a luscious mushroom-chèvre filling, is the centerpiece of my Thanksgiving feast.
I serve it with Cranberry-Orange Sauce (page 75), roasted vegetables,
and some good wine. No one misses the turkey.*

1. Heat a large heavy skillet over medium heat. Add 2 table-spoons of the oil, the garlic, and shallots, and sauté, stirring occasionally for 5 minutes, or until the shallots begin to soften.

2. Add all of the mushrooms and continue to sauté 5 minutes, or until tender. Mix in the parsley and salt, then transfer the mixture to a bowl. Let cool 30 minutes.

3. Preheat the oven to 375°F. Place the remaining oil in a small bowl. Line a large baking sheet with parchment paper and set aside.

4. Place a sheet of phyllo on a clean work surface, brush with oil, and top with another sheet of phyllo. Repeat until you have used half the phyllo.

5. On the bottom 2 inches of the shorter end of the phyllo stack, place half the sautéed mushroom mixture, and sprinkle half the chèvre on top.

6. Roll up the strudel into a tight roll and brush with oil. Transfer to the baking sheet, and prepare a second strudel with the remaining ingredients.

7. Bake the strudels for 30 minutes, or until golden and crisp. Remove from the oven and let cool 5 minutes.

8. Cut with a serrated knife and serve.

FOR A CHANGE . . .

- Replace the parsley with dill or tarragon.
- Use toasted pecans, black walnuts, or hazelnuts instead of (or in addition to) the chèvre.
- Try basil-, garlic-, or dill-flavored chèvre.

Yield: 2 strudels
(6 to 8 servings)

• • • • • • • •

6 tablespoons extra virgin olive oil

4 cloves garlic, minced

1 cup diced shallots

3 cups coarsely chopped shiitake mushroom caps

3 cups coarsely chopped white button mushrooms

3 cups coarsely chopped crimini mushrooms

$1/3$ cup coarsely chopped parsley

$1/2$ teaspoon sea salt

20 to 24 sheets phyllo dough

6 ounces chèvre, crumbled

Hiziki with Shiitake Mushrooms and Butternut Squash

This savory stew can restore the weary and energize those who are feeling fine. Garlic, hiziki, and shiitake mushrooms are renowned for their immune-enhancing properties. Sweet butternut squash fills the pot with the delicious taste of autumn. Serve over rice, quinoa, or noodles.

Yield: 4 to 6 servings

12-ounce package seitan

2 cups dried hiziki

3 cups water

2 tablespoons sesame oil

2 cloves garlic, thickly sliced

1 cup coarsely chopped onions

1 1/2 cups coarsely chopped fresh shiitake mushroom caps

3 1/2 cups butternut squash, cut into cubes

1 tablespoon dried nettles, optional

2 tablespoons mirin

1. Reserving the liquid, cut the seitan into 1-inch cubes and set aside. Cover the hiziki with 2 cups of the water and soak 10 minutes, or until tender and triple in size.

2. While the hiziki is soaking, heat the oil in a 6-quart stockpot over medium heat. Add the garlic and onions, and sauté 5 minutes, or until onions begin to soften.

3. Add the hiziki and soaking water to the pot along with the remaining ingredients, including the reserved seitan liquid. Bring to a boil, then reduce the heat to low. Simmer covered for 20 minutes, or until the squash is tender. Add more water as needed.

4. Adjust the seasonings, if desired, and serve hot.

FOR A CHANGE . . .

• Substitute tofu or tempeh for the seitan.

• Add a tablespoon of grated ginger, and sauté along with the onion and garlic.

Black Bean Chili with Sun-Dried Tomatoes

*Sun-dried tomatoes melt into this super
black bean chili as it simmers.*

1. Bring the water, beans, and kelp to boil in a 6-quart stockpot. Reduce the heat to medium-low, and simmer covered for 1 hour, or until the beans are soft. Add the cauliflower, and continue to simmer 5 to 10 minutes, or until tender.

2. Heat the oil in a medium-sized skillet over medium heat. Add the garlic, onions, and cumin, and sauté 5 minutes, or until the onions begin to soften.

3. Add the sautéed onion mixture to the beans, along with the diced and sun-dried tomatoes, and continue simmering for 5 minutes. Add the zucchini and simmer another 10 minutes, or until tender.

4. Stir the chili powder, oregano, and salt into the chili, and simmer another 5 minutes to blend the flavors. Adjust the seasonings, if desired.

5. Ladle the hot chili into bowls and enjoy.

TIP . . .

When substituting fresh tomatoes for dried,
use twice the amount.

Yield: 6 to 8 servings

• • • • • • • • • • •

4 cups water

$1\frac{1}{4}$ cups dried black beans, presoaked (page 14), rinsed, and drained

3-inch strip kelp

3 cups cauliflower florets

1 tablespoon extra virgin olive oil

6 cloves garlic, thickly sliced

$1\frac{1}{2}$ cups sliced onions

1 tablespoon cumin seeds

14-ounce can diced tomatoes

10 sun-dried tomatoes (not oil-packed)

3 cups zucchini, quartered and cut into $\frac{1}{2}$-inch pieces

1 tablespoon chili powder

2 tablespoons dried oregano

1 teaspoon sea salt, or to taste

Tempeh Stew with Wine and Shiitake Mushrooms

Yield: 4 to 6 servings

2 tablespoons extra virgin olive oil

1 pound tempeh, cut into $1/2$-inch cubes

$2 1/2$ cups water

$1/2$ cup dry white wine

2 tablespoons mustard

8 dried shiitake mushrooms

2 cups coarsely chopped yams

$1 1/2$ cups coarsely chopped carrots

$1 1/2$ cups halved Brussels sprouts

1 cup coarsely chopped red onion

$1 1/2$ tablespoons dark miso

2 teaspoons dried thyme

$1 1/2$ teaspoons dried sage

1 teaspoon dried rosemary

Just about any type of tempeh—soy, quinoa, sesame, 3-grain, wild rice—works well in this stew, which tastes even better the next day. For a complete-protein meal, use a grain variety of tempeh; otherwise, spoon the stew over rice or millet. Cranberry-Orange Sauce (page 75) is a perfect accompaniment.

1. Heat the oil in a 6-quart stockpot over medium heat. Add the tempeh and cook 5 to 10 minutes, or until golden brown.

2. Add the water, wine, and mustard to the pot, along with the shiitake. "Bury" the shiitake under the yams, carrots, Brussels sprouts, and onion. Bring the ingredients to a boil, then reduce the heat to medium-low. Simmer covered about 20 minutes, or until the vegetables are soft.

3. Dissolve the miso in some of the hot broth, then add to the pot, along with the thyme, sage, and rosemary. Simmer another 5 minutes to blend the flavors. Adjust the seasonings, if desired.

4. Ladle the hot stew into bowls and enjoy.

Szechwan Tofu with Mustard Greens and Chinese Cabbage

If you can handle the heat, cook this dish with plenty of ginger and chilies, which add zip to the calcium-rich tofu and leafy green vegetables. Serve with steamed brown rice or quinoa.

1. Heat the oil in a wok or medium-sized skillet over medium-high heat. Add the chili peppers and sauté for 30 seconds. Add the tofu and stir-fry about 5 minutes, or until golden brown.

2. Add the onions to the wok. Gather the grated ginger in your hands, and squeeze the juice over the tofu and onions. Continue to stir-fry 3 minutes, or until the onions begin to soften.

3. Add the remaining ingredients, and continue to cook another 3 minutes or until the greens wilt and become bright in color.

4. Adjust the seasonings, if desired, and serve immediately.

Yield: 4 servings

• • • • • • • •

5 tablespoons canola oil

4 tablespoons minced, seeded jalapeño, poblano, or cayenne peppers, or 2 tablespoons dried chili pepper flakes

I pound firm or extra-firm tofu, cut into I-inch cubes

I cup coarsely chopped onions

I tablespoon grated ginger

6 cups coarsely chopped mustard greens

3 cups coarsely chopped Chinese cabbage

3 tablespoons tamari

2 tablespoons mirin

Roasted Eggplant and Tomatoes with Chickpeas

This Italian stew is a great late-summer main course, especially when served with a leafy salad and fresh bread. Leftovers make a great pasta sauce.

Yield: 6 to 8 servings

. . . .

10 cups eggplant, cut into triangular pieces (about 1-inch wide and $1/4$-inch thick)

$1 1/2$ teaspoons sea salt

3 cups coarsely chopped white button mushrooms

$1 1/2$ cups cooked chickpeas

14-ounce can diced tomatoes

1 cup coarsely chopped onions

10 sun-dried tomatoes

10 cloves garlic, coarsely chopped

2 bay leaves

4 tablespoons minced fresh basil

2 tablespoons extra virgin olive oil

2 tablespoons fresh thyme

2 tablespoons fresh oregano

Pinch cayenne pepper

1. Place the eggplant in a large bowl and sprinkle with salt. Let sit for 45 minutes to release some of the eggplant's bitter juices.

2. Preheat the oven to 500°F.

3. Drain the eggplant, add the remaining ingredients, and mix well. Transfer to a large baking dish.

4. Cover and bake for 50 minutes, or until the vegetables are tender.

5. Adjust the seasonings, and serve immediately.

FYI . . .

Popular in the cuisines of India, France, Italy, Africa, and the Middle East, nutty-tasting chickpeas (also called garbanzo beans) are the most widely consumed legumes in the world. They are commonly tossed whole into soups, stews, and salads, or ground into paste and used in sauces, dips, and spreads.

Soba With Stir-Fried Asparagus and Snow Peas

*Keep this exceptional noodle dish in mind
when asparagus is young and tender.*

1. Heat a wok over medium-high heat. Add the oil, mirin, tamari, garlic, and carrots. Stir-fry for 5 minutes, or until the carrots are bright orange and the garlic is fragrant.

2. Add the asparagus and snow peas, and stir-fry 2 minutes, or until they become bright green. Toss in the seitan and cook 2 minutes, or until slightly browned.

3. Add the noodles and mix well to combine with the vegetables. Adjust the seasonings, if desired.

4. Mound onto plates and serve h

Yield: 4 to 6 servings

• • • • • • •

1 tablespoon sesame oil

2 tablespoons mirin

2 tablespoons tamari

3 cloves garlic, thickly sliced

$1\frac{1}{2}$ cups julienned carrots

2 cups asparagus, cut into 1-inch diagonals

$1\frac{1}{4}$ cups snow peas, cut into 1-inch-diagonals

$1\frac{1}{2}$ cups thinly sliced seitan

3 cups cooked soba noodles

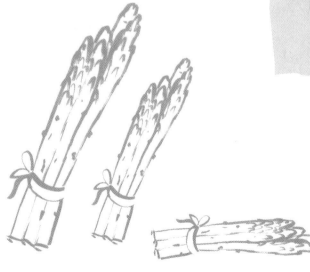

Linguine a la Sweet Putanesca

This linguine favorite—especially with kids—really comes alive with a sweet and hearty combination of capers, tomatoes, garlic, and olives.

Yield: 6 to 8 servings

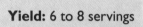

1 pound linguine

2 tablespoons extra virgin olive oil

14 cloves garlic, thickly sliced

1 cup capers
(rinse if packed in salt)

3 cups diced plum tomatoes

$^{1}/_{2}$ cup sliced black olives

2 cups tightly packed, coarsely chopped Italian parsley

1. Bring a 4-quart pot of water to a rolling boil. Add the linguine and cook according to package directions. Drain, rinse under cold water, and set aside.

2. While the water is coming to a boil, heat the oil in a 6-quart stockpot over medium heat. Add the garlic and sauté 3 minutes, or until golden brown.

3. Add the capers, continue to sauté 2 minutes, then stir in the tomatoes. Reduce the heat to medium-low, and simmer covered for 5 minutes.

4. Stir the olives into the pot and simmer uncovered for 5 minutes. Add the parsley and simmer 5 minutes more. Adjust the seasonings, if desired.

5. Transfer the cooked linguine to a serving bowl, top with the sauce, and toss well. Serve immediately.

Lentil Stew with Saffron and Porcini Mushrooms

I relish tomatoes, greens, and mushrooms that are seasoned with Italian herbs and spices. This delicious stew offers these ingredients and so much more. I usually serve it with a crisp green salad, ripe olives, and a loaf of whole grain bread to scoop up every flavorful bit.

1. Bring the lentils, kelp, bay leaves, nettles (if using), and 4 cups of the water to boil in a 6-quart stockpot. Reduce the heat to medium-low and simmer covered for 20 minutes, or until the lentils are tender.

2. While the lentils cook, place the mushrooms in a small mixing bowl. Bring the remaining water to boil and pour over the mushrooms. Let sit 20 minutes to soften, then drain through a filter and add the soaking water to the pot. Coarsely chop the mushrooms and set aside.

3. Heat a medium-sized skillet over medium heat. Add the oil, onions, garlic, and mushrooms, and sauté 5 minutes, or until the onions begins to soften.

4. Transfer the sautéed onion-mushroom mixture to the lentils, along with the cauliflower, tomatoes, kale, and saffron. Simmer covered for 10 minutes or until the cauliflower is tender.

5. Stir in the sage, thyme, rosemary, salt, and pepper, and simmer 5 minutes more to blend the flavors. Adjust the seasonings, if desired.

6. Ladle the hot stew into bowls and serve.

Yield: 4 to 6 servings

1 cup brown lentils, rinsed

4-inch piece kelp

2 bay leaves

1 tablespoon dried nettles, optional

$4\frac{1}{2}$ cups water

$\frac{1}{2}$-ounce package dried porcini mushrooms

2 tablespoons extra virgin olive oil

1 cup coarsely chopped onions

5 cloves garlic, thickly sliced

4 cups cauliflower florets

$3\frac{1}{2}$ cups coarsely chopped plum tomatoes

2 cups coarsely chopped kale

Pinch saffron

1 teaspoon dried sage

1 teaspoon dried thyme

1 teaspoon coarsely chopped fresh rosemary, or $\frac{1}{2}$ teaspoon dried

1 teaspoon sea salt, or to taste

Pinch black pepper, or to taste

Tempeh With Marinated Sun-Dried Tomatoes and Kale

Yield: 4 to 6 servings

• • • • • • • • • • •

3 tablespoons extra virgin olive oil, or Garlic-Basil Oil (page 103)

1 pound soy tempeh, cut into $\frac{1}{2}$-inch cubes

1 cup coarsely chopped leeks

5 cloves garlic, thickly sliced

8 cups coarsely chopped kale

$\frac{1}{3}$ cup red wine

$\frac{1}{3}$ cup capers (rinse if packed in salt)

15 marinated sun-dried tomatoes*

$\frac{1}{4}$ teaspoon fresh cracked black pepper, optional

1 cup grated Manchego or Parmesan cheese, optional

* Marinated Sun-Dried Tomatoes with Calendula Flowers (page 117) are recommended.

This quick Mediterranean-style dish is savory and delicious. Try it over pasta for a fun meal.

1. Warm a 6-quart stockpot over medium-high heat. Add the oil, tempeh, leeks, and garlic, and cook 5 minutes, or until the tempeh is golden brown.

2. Add the kale, wine, capers, and marinated sun-dried tomatoes to the pot. Cover and simmer for 5 minutes or until the kale wilts and is tender. Adjust the seasonings, if desired.

3. Serve immediately as is or garnished with cracked pepper and/or grated cheese.

FOR A CHANGE . . .

• Use seitan instead of tempeh.

• Add $\frac{1}{2}$ cup chopped fresh basil to the mixture as it simmers.

• Replace the capers with pitted kalamata olives or 2 teaspoons sea salt.

• Reduce the amount of kale to 6 cups, and add 2 cups white button mushrooms. Because the mushrooms will release some juice as they cook, use only 2 tablespoons wine or balsamic vinegar instead of $\frac{1}{3}$ cup wine.

Sweet and Spicy Udon Noodles with Tofu

Udon noodles and tofu are tossed with a honey-sweetened cilantro-peanut sauce that gets a spicy jolt from chili flakes. Delicious served at room temperature.

1. Preheat the oven to 375°F.

2. Place all of the sauce ingredients in a blender or food processor and blend until creamy. Adjust the seasonings, if desired.

3. Slit the tops of the tofu cubes, place in a baking dish, and cover with sauce. (The slits will allow the sauce to penetrate the tofu for more intense flavor.)

4. Bake uncovered for 15 to 20 minutes, or until the sauce is hot and bubbly and begins to dry around the edges of the baking dish. Remove and set aside to cool.

5. While the tofu bakes, bring a 4-quart pot of water to a rolling boil. Add the noodles and cook according to package directions. Drain, rinse, and place in a serving bowl. Spoon the baked tofu over the noodles and mix well.

6. Serve with a garnish of mint and nasturtium flowers, if desired.

FOR A CHANGE . . .

• Vary the type of udon noodles; use rice, whole wheat, or spelt.

Yield: 4 to 6 servings

• • • • • • • • • •

1 pound extra-firm tofu, cut into 1-inch cubes

8 ounces udon noodles

$1/4$ cup coarsely chopped mint

6 nasturtium flowers, optional

Sauce

2 cups cilantro leaves

$1/2$ cup water

$1/2$ cup tahini

3 tablespoons lime juice

2 tablespoons tamari

2 tablespoons peanut butter

2 tablespoons honey

2 cloves garlic

1 teaspoon chili pepper flakes

Yield: 4 servings

• • • • • • • • • • • •

2 tablespoons extra virgin olive oil

2 cloves garlic

1 cup finely chopped onions

Pinch saffron

5 cups diced butternut squash

1 1/2 cups coarsely chopped fresh
shiitake mushrooms caps

1 cup arborio or carnaroli rice

1 teaspoon sea salt

1 cup peach or white wine*

1/2 teaspoon dried thyme

1 cup freshly grated Manchego
or Parmesan cheese

Stock

6 cups water

1 1/2 cups celery root, cut into
1-inch chunks

1 1/2 cups carrots, cut into
1-inch chunks

1 cup onions, cut into
1-inch chunks

1 cup dried shiitake mushrooms

1/3 cup coarsely chopped burdock

2 bay leaves

* Four Chimneys Organic Farm
Winery brand is recommended.

Butternut Squash Risotto with Shiitake Mushrooms and Wine

*A stock, rich with shiitake mushrooms, is combined with peach
wine to give incredible deep flavor to this delectable risotto.*

1. Bring all of the stock ingredients to boil in a 4-quart pot.
Reduce the heat to medium-low and simmer covered for
1 hour. Strain the vegetables, reserving the stock—there
should be about 4 cups.

2. Transfer the stock to a 4-quart pot and gently simmer.

3. Heat the oil in a 6-quart stockpot over medium heat.
Add the garlic, onions, and saffron. Sauté for 5 minutes, or
until the onions soften. Add the squash, and continue to
sauté for 10 minutes, or until soft.

4. Stir the fresh shiitake, rice, and salt into the squash mixture, and continue to stir for 3 minutes.

5. Add 1/2 cup of the simmering stock to the rice mixture,
and adjust the heat to maintain a lively simmer. Stir continuously until the stock is absorbed. Add another 1/2 cup of
stock to the rice, and stir until it is absorbed. Repeat with
the remaining stock, 1/2 cup at a time.

6. Once the stock has been added to the rice, add the wine,
1/2 cup at a time, continuously stirring until completely
absorbed. The rice should be tender yet firm to the bite.

7. Stir the thyme into the risotto. Adjust the seasonings, if
desired.

8. Garnish with grated cheese and serve immediately.

Italian Lentil Stew with Creamy Grano

Grano is pearled Italian wheat that has the texture of pasta. It is quite delicious in Mediterranean stews like this one.

1. Bring the lentils, grano, bay leaves, and 8 cups of the water to boil in a 6-quart pot. Reduce heat to medium-low and simmer covered for 40 minutes, or until the lentils are soft and the grano is plump and tender.

2. While the ingredients are simmering, heat the oil in a medium-sized skillet over medium-low heat. Add the onions and celery, and sauté 5 minutes, or until they begin to soften.

3. When the lentils and grano are tender, add the sautéed onion-celery mixture along with cauliflower, tomatoes, and saffron to the skillet. Pour the remaining $1/2$ cup water into the empty tomato can, swish it around to get every last drop of the tomatoes, and add to the skillet. Continue to simmer covered for 20 minutes, or until the cauliflower is tender.

4. Stir the rosemary, basil, oregano, thyme, salt, and pepper into the pot, and simmer another 5 minutes to blend the flavors. Adjust the seasonings, if desired.

5. Ladle the hot stew into bowls and enjoy.

Yield: 4 to 6 servings

$3/4$ cup brown lentils, rinsed

1 cup grano, rinsed

2 bay leaves

$8^1/_2$ cups water

1 tablespoon extra virgin olive oil

1 cup coarsely chopped red onions

1 cup coarsely chopped celery

$4^1/_2$ cups cauliflower florets

28-ounce can diced tomatoes

Pinch saffron

1 tablespoon coarsely chopped rosemary

1 tablespoon dried basil

1 teaspoon dried oregano

1 teaspoon dried thyme

1 teaspoon sea salt, or to taste

$1/4$ teaspoon black pepper, or to taste

10

Just Desserts

Mmmmmm, dessert! From cookies and cakes to pastries, tarts, and pies, dessert is always welcomed. Now, imagine that these indulgences actually support a healthy lifestyle. In this chapter, I share lots of my favorite sweet treats made with the best dark chocolate, nuts, berries, a wide selection of sweeteners, plus a variety of whole grain flours.

You'll find healthy twists on a number of classic favorites, as well as some inspired originals. Be sure to try the Maple Cranberry Pecan Cake, some Mocha Chocolate Chunk Cookies, or the Apple-Blackberry Crumb Pie —they will encourage you to bake even when it isn't anyone's birthday. Easy-to-make crusts for recipes like rich Vegan Chocolate Mousse Pie and the luscious Lemon Tart can be made with exotic teff or Bhutanese red rice flour, as well as simple whole wheat pastry or spelt flour. Personally, I happen to love wheat-free desserts because of their amazing flavors and superior nutritional content. Further-more, the fillings are delicious enough to enjoy on their own.

When it comes to the recipes in this chapter that call for chocolate, I recommend using dark chocolate, which you can buy by the pound, chips, or bars. Dark chocolate has a higher cocoa content than milk chocolate, which has more sugar. I generally use chocolate that contains 60- to 70-percent cocoa, which I buy by the pound at whole food markets, gourmet shops, or fine chocolatiers. Brands I recommend are El Rey, Valrhona, Caulibaut, and Scharffenberger. Organic dark chocolate bars from Dagoba and Green & Black's are also recommended. Of course, feel free to use whatever brand and type of chocolate you prefer.

No matter what type of dessert you're craving—light and simple or rich and exotic, moist and fruity or crisp and crunchy, bursting with berries or oozing with chocolate—you are sure to find it on the following pages. Enjoy!

MIX AND MATCH

You can easily replace many of the ingredients called for in this chapter's dessert recipes, including nuts, berries, and flavorings, with your own product preferences. The substitution suggestions provided below will help.

MILK	Cow's milk, goat's milk, almond milk, plain or vanilla soymilk, plain or vanilla rice milk, and juice.*
JUICE	Apple, apricot, cherry, pear, and raspberry juices; cranberry nectar; and milk.*
NUTS	Almonds, hazelnuts, pecans, and walnuts.
BERRIES	Blackberries, blueberries, cranberries, raspberries, and strawberries.
CHOCOLATE/CAROB (CHIPS, BARS)	Dark, milk, and white chocolate;
	Dairy-free and sugar-free;
	Espresso, peanut butter, and vanilla flavored.
EXTRACTS**	Almond, hazelnut, orange, and vanilla.
OILS	Almond oil, canola oil, corn oil, hazelnut oil, light olive oil, safflower oil, sunflower oil, melted unsalted butter, and coconut oil (use $3/4$ the amount compared to other oils).

* For baked goods, substituting juice for milk offers sweeter results. You can also use a milk-juice combination.
** Substitute $1/2$ teaspoon of a flavored extract for 1 tablespoon vanilla.

Hot Fudge

You can use dark or milk chocolate for this scrumptious quick-and-easy hot fudge. Spoon it over ice cream or other frozen desserts, or drizzle it on cake, such as Dark Chocolate Cake (page 193).

Yield: About 1 cup
. . . .
$2/3$ cup dark chocolate chips or chunks

$1/2$ cup cocoa powder

$1/4$ cup water

$1/3$ cup maple syrup

1. Place all the ingredients in a 1-quart saucepan over low heat. Whisk for 2 minutes or until the chocolate has melted and the sauce is smooth. Taste and add more maple syrup, if desired.

2. Serve immediately.

Dark Chocolate Cake

Loved by vegans and non-vegans alike, this rich chocolate cake is the one I usually make for birthdays. Serve it plain, drizzled with Hot Fudge (page 192), or frosted with Vegan Chocolate Mousse (page 202).

1. Preheat the oven to 350°F. Lightly oil a 9-inch cake or loaf pan and set aside.

2. Combine the flour, baking powder, and salt in a large mixing bowl and set aside.

3. Place the flaxseeds in a blender and grind to a powder. Add the juice, oil, maple syrup, and vanilla, and blend well.

4. Heat the chocolate chips and soymilk in a double boiler or 1-quart saucepan over low heat. Stir constantly about 3 minutes, or until the chocolate melts.

5. Add the melted chocolate and flaxseed mixture to the flour mixture, and stir to form a smooth batter.

6. Pour the batter into the cake pan and bake 40 minutes, or until a toothpick inserted in the center comes out clean.

7. Let the cake cool 30 minutes before removing from the pan. Serve plain or frosted.

FOR A CHANGE . . .

• Replace the soymilk with $1\frac{1}{4}$ cups juice.

Yield: 8 servings

$1\frac{3}{4}$ cups whole wheat pastry flour

1 tablespoon baking powder

$\frac{1}{4}$ teaspoon sea salt

$2\frac{1}{2}$ tablespoons flaxseeds

$\frac{1}{2}$ cup apple juice

$\frac{1}{4}$ cup canola oil

$\frac{1}{2}$ cup maple syrup

$\frac{1}{2}$ tablespoon vanilla

$1\frac{1}{2}$ cups dark chocolate chips or chunks

$\frac{3}{4}$ cup vanilla soymilk

TIP . . .

Be sure your freshly baked cake is completely cool before adding frosting. If the cake is warm, the frosting will melt right in.

Banana-Chocolate Chip Cake

This simple cake is made with spelt and teff—one of my favorite flour combinations. Whether you use white, milk, or dark chocolate in this recipe, you are in for a treat.

Yield: 8 servings

2 cups spelt flour

1/2 cup teff flour

1 tablespoon baking powder

1/2 teaspoon sea salt

1 cup white, milk, or dark chocolate chips

3 ripe bananas, cut into 3-inch pieces (about 3 cups)

1 cup apple juice

1/3 cup applesauce

1/3 cup maple syrup

1/4 cup canola oil

1 tablespoon vanilla

1. Preheat the oven to 350°F. Lightly oil a 9-inch cake or loaf pan and set aside.

2. Combine the spelt flour, teff flour, baking powder, sea salt, and 3/4 cup of the chocolate chips in a large mixing bowl and set aside.

3. Place the bananas, apple juice, applesauce, maple syrup, oil, and vanilla in a blender, and purée. Add to the flour mixture and stir to form a smooth batter.

4. Pour the batter into the cake pan, sprinkle with the remaining chocolate chips, and bake 50 minutes, or until a toothpick inserted in the center comes out clean.

5. Let the cake cool 30 minutes before removing from the pan. Slice and serve.

Shortbread Cake

This sweet gluten- and wheat-free cake has great texture. Enjoy it plain or topped with Strawberry Cashew Cream (page 209). It's also delicious with a drizzle of Strawberry Sauce (page 73) and a dollop of whipped cream.

Yield: 8 servings

• • • • • • •

1 cup quinoa flour

1 cup brown rice flour, or Chinese "forbidden" black rice flour

1 tablespoon baking powder

$\frac{1}{4}$ teaspoon sea salt

$2\frac{1}{2}$ tablespoons flaxseeds

1 cup apple or cherry juice

$\frac{1}{4}$ cup canola oil

$\frac{1}{4}$ cup maple syrup

$\frac{1}{4}$ cup almond milk

1 tablespoon vanilla

1. Preheat the oven to 350°F. Lightly oil a 9-inch cake pan and set aside.

2. Combine the quinoa and brown rice flours, baking powder, and salt in a large mixing bowl, and set aside.

3. Place the flaxseeds in a blender and grind to a powder. Add the juice, oil, maple syrup, almond milk, and vanilla, and blend well. Add to the flour mixture and stir to form a smooth batter.

4. Pour the batter into the cake pan and bake 30 to 40 minutes, or until a toothpick inserted in the center comes out clean.

5. Let the cake cool 30 minutes before removing from the pan. Slice and serve.

FYI . . .

When ground into meal, nutty-flavored flaxseeds —rich in beneficial omega-3 fatty acids and vitamin E— can take the place of eggs in quick breads, pie crusts, and pancakes.

Maple Cranberry Pecan Cake

Yield: 6 to 8 servings

· · · · · · ·

2 cups spelt flour

$1/3$ cup maple sugar granules, or $1/2$ cup organic cane sugar

1 tablespoon baking powder

$1/4$ teaspoon sea salt

1 teaspoon orange zest

$2/3$ cup fresh or frozen cranberries

2 tablespoons flaxseeds

$3/4$ cup cranberry nectar or apple juice

$1/4$ cup freshly squeezed orange or tangelo juice

$1/4$ cup canola oil

Topping

$1/2$ cup pecans

1 tablespoon maple sugar granules, or to taste

Maple sugar is the perfect sweetener for adding distinctive flavor and fragrance to baked goods without any added moisture. Also, if you want to convert a maple syrup sweetened cake recipe from whole wheat flour to spelt flour, simply use maple sugar; all the other measurements remain the same.

1. Preheat the oven to 350°F. Lightly oil a 9-inch cake pan and set aside.

2. Place the topping ingredients in a food processor and pulse until coarsely ground. Transfer to a small bowl and set aside.

3. Combine the spelt flour, maple sugar, baking powder, salt, zest, and cranberries in a large mixing bowl, and set aside.

4. Place the flaxseeds in a blender and grind to a powder. Add the cranberry nectar, orange juice, and oil, and blend well. Add to the flour mixture and stir to form a smooth batter.

5. Pour the batter into the cake pan, sprinkle with the pecan topping, and bake 45 minutes, or until a toothpick inserted in the center comes out clean.

6. Let the cake cool 30 minutes before removing from the pan. Slice and serve.

FOR A CHANGE . . .

• Substitute chocolate chips, blackberries, or blueberries for some or all of the cranberries.

• Use walnuts instead of pecans.

• Use $2/3$ cup orange juice and $1/3$ cup apple juice for a stronger orange flavor.

Orange Ginger Cake

*Drizzle some Hot Fudge (page 192) over this sweet cake
or frost with Vegan Chocolate Mousse (page 202).
It's also delicious plain, especially when served warm.*

1. Preheat the oven to 350°F. Lightly oil a 9-inch cake pan and set aside.

2. Combine the spelt flour, teff flour, baking powder, ginger powder, zest, cinnamon, salt, and cloves in a large mixing bowl, and set aside.

3. Place the flaxseeds in a blender and grind to a powder. Add the orange juice, maple syrup, and oil, and blend well. Add to the flour mixture and stir to form a smooth batter.

4. Pour the batter into the cake pan and bake 50 minutes, or until a toothpick inserted in the center comes out clean.

5. Let the cake cool 30 minutes before removing from the pan. Slice and serve.

Yield: 8 servings

2 cups spelt flour

$1/2$ cup teff flour

1 tablespoon baking powder

1 tablespoon ginger powder

2 teaspoons orange zest

1 teaspoon cinnamon

$1/2$ teaspoon sea salt

$1/4$ teaspoon ground cloves

$2 1/2$ tablespoons flaxseeds

1 cup orange juice

$1/2$ cup maple syrup

$1/4$ cup canola oil

FYI . . .

Making your own nut or seed meal is easy. Simply place the nuts or seeds in a blender or food processor and pulse to a floury, meal-like consistency. Just be careful not to grind too long, or the meal will turn to "butter."

Raspberry-Almond Fruit Crisp

*Ground almonds replace the flour and add sweetness
to the topping for this fabulous fruit crisp.*

Yield: 4 to 6 servings

• • • • • • •

1 1/2 cups fresh or frozen
raspberries

1 1/2 cups sliced pears

1 cup peeled, sliced apples

1/2 cup fresh or frozen
blueberries

1 cup peach juice

Topping

3/4 cup almonds

2 cups rolled oats

1/4 cup plain or black
walnuts, halved

1/4 cup whole cashews

1/2 teaspoon sea salt

1/2 cup maple syrup

1/4 cup canola oil

1. Preheat the oven to 375°F.

2. To make the topping, place the almonds in a food processor and grind to a meal. Transfer to a large mixing bowl along with the oats, walnuts, cashews, and salt, and mix well. Add the maple syrup and oil, and stir until well blended.

3. Arrange the raspberries, pears, apples, and blueberries in the bottom of a 2-quart baking dish. Cover with the topping, pour the peach juice on top, and bake 30 minutes, or until the fruit is hot and bubbly and the topping is crisp.

4. Serve warm, spooned into bowls.

Cranberry-Pecan Crisp

The combination of nutty flaxseeds, rolled oats, and maple syrup provides an outstanding crisp topping for this delicious dessert.

1. Preheat the oven to 350°F.

2. To make the topping, place the oats, flaxseeds, cinnamon, and salt in a large bowl and mix well. Add the maple syrup, oil, and vanilla, and stir until well combined.

3. Place the cranberries on the bottom of an 8-inch square or 2-quart baking dish, and sprinkle the pecans on top. Cover with the topping, pour the apple juice on top, and bake 35 minutes, or until the juice is hot and bubbly and the topping is crisp.

4. Serve warm, spooned into bowls.

FOR A CHANGE . . .

• Substitute 4 cups sliced apples for the cranberries (increase baking time to 40 minutes).

• Replace 1 cup of cranberries with 1 cup sliced apples; also omit the pecans and add 3 tablespoons raisins.

• Use teff flour instead of ground flaxseeds.

Yield: 4 to 6 servings

• • • • • • •

2 cups fresh or frozen cranberries

$1/2$ cup pecans, halved

I cup apple juice

Topping

2 cups rolled oats

$1/2$ cup ground flaxseeds

I teaspoon cinnamon

$1/2$ teaspoon sea salt

$1/3$ cup maple syrup

$1/3$ cup canola oil

I tablespoon vanilla

Blueberry Crumb Pie

*This fabulous dessert is the perfect finale to any meal.
The delicious crust, made with cholesterol-free
roasted almond butter, is simple and quick to make.*

Yield: 6 to 8 servings

2 cups fresh or frozen
blueberries

1 tablespoon honey

1 tablespoon kudzu or
arrowroot

2 tablespoons cold water

Crust

2½ cups whole wheat
pastry flour

½ cup maple syrup

¼ cup corn or
canola oil

2 tablespoons roasted
almond butter

½ teaspoon sea salt

1 tablespoon vanilla,
optional

1. Preheat the oven to 375°F. Lightly oil a 9-inch pie pan and set aside.

2. To make the pie crust, place all of the crust ingredients in a large bowl and mix to form a moist dough.

3. Reserving ⅔ cup of the dough, press the rest over the bottom and sides of the pie plate with your fingers. Poke holes in the dough with a fork, then bake for 10 minutes, or until the crust is lightly browned.

4. While the crust is baking, prepare the filling. Place the blueberries and honey in a 1-quart saucepan over medium-low heat. Gently simmer 1 to 5 minutes, or until the blueberries are soft.

5. Dissolve the kudzu in the cold water, then stir into the simmering blueberry mixture. Stir for a minute or two, or until the mixture thickens a bit. Taste and add more honey for a sweeter flavor, if desired.

6. Pour the filling into the baked crust, crumble the reserved pie dough on top, and bake 12 minutes, or until the crumbs are slightly browned.

7. Remove from the oven and let sit at least 30 minutes. Serve warm or at room temperature.

Apple-Blackberry Crumb Pie

Maple syrup, teff flour, and ground flaxseeds create a delightful graham cracker-like crust for this delicious pie. Sometimes, I top a slice with yogurt and enjoy it for breakfast along with a cup of tea.

1. Preheat the oven to 375°F. Lightly oil a 9-inch pie pan and set aside.

2. To make the pie crust, place the flaxseeds in a blender or seed mill and grind. Transfer to a large bowl along with the remaining crust ingredients, and mix to form a moist dough.

3. Reserving ²/₃ cup of the dough, press the rest over the bottom and sides of the pie plate with your fingers. Poke holes in the dough with a fork, then bake for 10 minutes, or until the crust is lightly browned.

4. While the crust is baking, prepare the filling. Place the apples and water in a 1-quart saucepan over medium-low heat. Gently simmer for 5 minutes, or until the apples are tender.

5. Pour the cooked apples into the baked crust, cover with blackberries, and crumble the reserved pie dough on top. Bake 10 minutes, or until the crumbs are slightly browned.

6. Remove from the oven and let sit at least 30 minutes. Serve warm or at room temperature.

Yield: 6 to 8 servings

• • • • • • •

3 ¹/₂ cups peeled, sliced apples

¹/₄ cup water

³/₄ cup fresh or frozen blackberries

Crust

¹/₃ cup flaxseeds

1 ¹/₃ cups ivory or brown teff flour

¹/₂ teaspoon sea salt

1 tablespoon vanilla

¹/₃ cup maple syrup

¹/₃ cup canola oil

Vegan Chocolate Mousse Pie

*Chocolate mousse is one of my family's dessert favorites.
It makes a heavenly filling for this luscious pie,
which has an extraordinary exotic crust. You can also
enjoy the filling as is or use it to frost a cake.*

Yield: 6 to 8 servings

• • • • • • •

1 3/4 cups dark chocolate
chips or chunks

1 pound silken tofu

Crust

1 cup Bhutanese
red rice flour

1/4 cup teff flour

4 tablespoons maple syrup

3 tablespoons hazelnut
butter

2 tablespoons canola oil

1 tablespoon vanilla

1/4 teaspoon sea salt

1. Preheat the oven to 375°F. Lightly oil a 9-inch pie pan and set aside.

2. To make the pie crust, place all of the crust ingredients in a large bowl and mix to form a soft dough.

3. Press the dough over the bottom and sides of the pie plate with your fingers. Poke holes in the dough with a fork, then bake for 10 minutes, or until the crust is lightly browned.

4. While the crust is baking, prepare the filling. Drain the tofu, transfer to a food processor, and purée until smooth.

5. Melt the chocolate in a pot or double boiler over low heat, and add to the tofu. Blend until thick and smooth. Taste and add more melted chocolate, if desired.

6. Pour the mousse filling into the baked crust. Chill for 2 hours before serving.

Lemon Tart

Brown teff flour gives this lemony tart its chocolate-colored crust. Serve topped with whipped cream or Strawberry Cashew Cream (page 209) for a show-stopping dessert. You can also enjoy the lemon filling on its own.

1. Preheat the oven to 375°F. Lightly grease a 9-inch pie plate with a little butter and set aside.

2. Bring the apple juice and agar to boil in a 1-quart saucepan. Reduce the heat to low and simmer 5 minutes, or until the agar is dissolved. Add the lemon juice, sugar, and zest.

3. Dissolve the arrowroot in the cold water, then add to the simmering mixture. Turn off the heat, and let sit.

4. To make the pie crust, place all of the crust ingredients in a food processor and blend to form a moist dough.

5. Press the dough over the bottom and sides of the pie plate with your fingers. Poke holes in the dough with a fork, then bake for 10 minutes, or until a bit puffed (it will become crisp as it cools). Do not overbake!

6. Pour the filling into the baked crust, and let cool about 4 hours on the counter or 2 hours in the refrigerator. (If placing the tart in the refrigerator, allow it to cool about 30 minutes first.) Cut into wedges and serve.

Yield: 6 to 8 servings

• • • • • • • •

2 cups apple juice

1 1/4 teaspoons agar-agar granules, or
2 1/2 teaspoons flakes

1/4 cup lemon juice

3 tablespoons maple sugar, or organic cane sugar

1 teaspoon lemon zest

1 tablespoon arrowroot powder

1 tablespoon cold water

Crust

1 1/2 cups teff flour

1/4 cup organic cane sugar

6 tablespoons salted butter, softened

1/3 cup water

FYI . . .

You can use the cookie dough from any recipe in this chapter for a pie crust. And you can use any pie crust dough to make cookies!

Pumpkin-Pecan Pie

*This delicious dessert combines two classic pies in one!
It calls for a cheese pumpkin, which is sweeter than a
pumpkin and almost as sweet as butternut squash.*

Yield: 6 to 8 servings

• • • • • • • •

³/₄ cup pecans

2 cups cooked cheese
pumpkin

3 tablespoons maple sugar

1 ¹/₂ teaspoons cinnamon

¹/₂ teaspoon nutmeg

¹/₂ teaspoon ground
ginger

Crust

2 cups spelt flour,
or whole wheat
pastry flour

¹/₃ cup canola oil

¹/₃ cup maple syrup

1 tablespoon vanilla,
or ¹/₂ teaspoon
almond extract

¹/₄ teaspoon sea salt

1. Preheat the oven to 375°F. Lightly oil a 9-inch pie pan and set aside.

2. To make the pie crust, place all the crust ingredients in a large bowl and mix to form a moist dough. Press the dough over the bottom and sides of the pie plate with your fingers. Poke holes in the dough with a fork, then bake for 10 minutes, or until the crust is lightly browned.

3. To prepare the filling, place the pecans in a food processor and grind to a meal. Add the pumpkin, maple sugar, cinnamon, nutmeg, and ginger, and purée until smooth. Taste and add more maple sugar or spices, if desired.

4. Pour the filling into the baked crust, return to the oven, and bake for 5 minutes. Turn off the heat and let the pie remain in the oven for 10 minutes.

5. Remove from the oven and let sit at least 30 minutes. Serve warm, at room temperature, or chilled.

FOR A CHANGE . . .

• Replace the cheese pumpkin with 2 cups cooked yam, delicata squash, pumpkin or butternut squash.

Pumpkin-Date Pie

This delicious pie has a scrumptious pecan cookie crust.

1. Preheat the oven to 375°F. Lightly oil a 9-inch pie pan and set aside.

2. To make the pie crust, place the pecans in a food processor and grind to a meal. Transfer to a large bowl along with the remaining crust ingredients and mix to form a soft dough.

3. Press the dough over the bottom and sides of the pie plate with your fingers. Poke holes in the dough with a fork, then bake for 10 minutes, or until the crust is lightly browned.

4. While the crust is baking, place all of the filling ingredients in a food processor and purée until smooth. Adjust the spices, if desired.

5. Pour the filling into the baked crust, return to the oven, and bake for 5 minutes. Turn off the heat and let the pie remain in the oven for 10 minutes.

6. Remove from the oven and let sit at least 30 minutes. Serve warm, at room temperature, or chilled.

FOR A CHANGE . . .

• Substitute butternut or delicata squash for the sugar pumpkin.

Yield: 6 to 8 servings
• • • • • • •
2 1/2 cups cooked
sugar pumpkin

1 1/2 cups cooked yams

1/2 cup vanilla soymilk

1 1/4 cups pitted dates

1 tablespoon vanilla

1 tablespoon cinnamon

1 teaspoon ground cloves

1 teaspoon ground ginger

1/2 teaspoon nutmeg

Crust

3/4 cups pecans

1 1/4 cups teff flour

1/3 cup maple syrup

1/4 cup canola oil

1 tablespoon vanilla

FYI . . .

Although all pumpkin varieties are edible, the sugar pumpkin is smaller and sweeter than the types commonly used for carving into jack-o-lanterns.

Ginger Lover's Cookies

Spelt flour adds nutty goodness to these cookies.

Yield: About 3 dozen

3 cups spelt flour

1 teaspoon cinnamon

$1/2$ teaspoon sea salt

$1/2$ cup canola oil

$1/2$ cup molasses

$1/4$ cup honey

2 tablespoons grated
fresh ginger

1. Preheat oven to 375°F. Lightly oil a cookie sheet and set aside.

2. Combine the flour, cinnamon, and salt in a large mixing bowl and set aside.

3. Place the oil, molasses, honey, and ginger in a blender. (If the ginger is too fibrous, gather it in your hands, squeeze the juice into the blender, and then discard the grated fibers.) Add to the flour mixture and stir to form a moist dough.

4. Knead the dough for a minute, then shape into walnut-sized balls. Place on the cookie sheet about $3/4$-inch apart. Flatten gently with a fork.

5. Bake 15 minutes, or until lightly browned. Remove from the oven, and cool at least 10 minutes before serving.

Honey Ginger Cookies

Honey and teff have starring roles in these gingery treats.

Yield: About 3 dozen

3 cups teff flour

$2/3$ cup canola oil

$2/3$ cup honey

2 tablespoons grated
fresh ginger

1 tablespoon baking powder

1 tablespoon arrowroot
powder

1 teaspoon vanilla

1 teaspoon cinnamon

$1/2$ teaspoon sea salt

1. Preheat oven to 375°F. Lightly oil a cookie sheet and set aside.

2. Place all the ingredients in a large mixing bowl. (If the grated ginger is too fibrous, gather it in your hands, squeeze the juice into bowl, and discard the fibers.) Stir to form a moist dough.

3. Knead the dough, then shape into walnut-sized balls. Place on the cookie sheet about $3/4$-inch apart. Flatten gently with a fork.

4. Bake 15 minutes, or until they lose their shine. Remove from the oven, and cool at least 10 minutes before serving.

Peanut Butter– Chocolate Chip Cookies

Tasting mildly like chocolate, teff flour has plenty of natural sweetness and blends well with nuts and chocolate. These cookies, a classic combination of peanut butter and chocolate, are delightful treats.

1. Preheat the oven to 350°F.

2. In a large mixing bowl, combine the teff flour and salt, if using. Set aside.

3. Place the peanut butter, maple syrup, oil, and vanilla in a food processor, and blend until creamy. Add to the flour along with the chocolate chips, and stir to form a moist dough.

4. Shape the dough into walnut-sized balls, and place them on an ungreased cookie sheet about $3/4$-inch apart. Flatten gently with a fork.

5. Bake 15 minutes, or until they lose their shine. Remove from the oven.

6. Cool at least 10 minutes before serving.

FOR A CHANGE . . .

• To make Hazelnut Butter-Chocolate Chip Cookies, use hazelnut butter instead of peanut butter. You will also have to increase the teff flour to 2 cups and use $3/4$ cup chocolate chips.

Yield: About 2 dozen

• • • • • • •

1 $1/2$ cups teff flour

$1/2$ teaspoon sea salt, optional

1 $1/8$ cups peanut butter

$2/3$ cup maple syrup

$1/4$ cup corn or canola oil

1 tablespoon vanilla

$1/2$ cup dark chocolate chips

Mocha Chocolate Chunk Cookies

Yield: About 1 dozen

• • • • • • • •

2½ cups teff flour

¼ cup ground coffee beans (such as an espresso) or grain coffee powder

¼ cup cocoa powder

1 tablespoon arrowroot

1 tablespoon baking powder

½ teaspoon sea salt

1 tablespoon vanilla

½ cup canola oil

¾ cup maple syrup

⅔ cup dark chocolate chips or chunks

Teff's high calcium and iron profile leads me to believe that for better or worse, these delicious cookies are a healthy indulgence. Its naturally dark color and subtle chocolate flavor add to the fun! You can use chocolate chips or small chunks of chocolate.

1. Preheat the oven to 375°F. Lightly oil a cookie sheet and set aside.

2. In a large bowl, mix together all of the ingredients in the order listed to form a smooth dough.

3. Shape the dough into 3-inch rounds about ½ inch thick. Place on the cookie sheet about ¾-inch apart. Flatten gently with a fork.

4. Bake 10 minutes, or until they lose their shine. Remove from the oven.

5. Cool at least 10 minutes before serving.

FOR A CHANGE . . .

• Replace the canola oil with ½ cup coconut oil. (As coconut oil comes in a solid form, you'll have to melt it over medium-low heat before adding it to the other ingredients.)

FYI . . .

The greater the percentage of cocoa, the darker, more bitter the chocolate.

Strawberry Cashew Cream

*Spoon some of this irresistible topping onto pies
or short cakes, or use it as cake frosting.*

1. Place the cashews in a food processor and grind to a meal.

2. While the processor is running, gradually add the soymilk through the opening at the top. Then add the maple syrup and vanilla. When the mixture is well blended, add the strawberries and continue to blend until the mixture has the consistency of whipped cream.

3. Taste, and add more maple syrup, if desired.

4. Use immediately.

FOR A CHANGE . . .

• Use cherries or blackberries instead of strawberries.

• Substitute almonds for the cashews, and increase the soymilk to $\frac{1}{2}$ cup.

• Replace the fresh strawberries with frozen. The consistency will be more like a sauce, but still very tasty.

Yield: About 1 cup

• • • • • • •

1 cup raw, unsalted cashews

$\frac{1}{4}$ cup vanilla soymilk

3 tablespoons maple syrup

1 tablespoon vanilla

1 cup fresh strawberries, stems removed

Metric Conversion Tables

COMMON LIQUID CONVERSIONS

Measurement	=	Milliliters
1/4 teaspoon	=	1.25 milliliters
1/2 teaspoon	=	2.50 milliliters
3/4 teaspoon	=	3.75 milliliters
1 teaspoon	=	5.00 milliliters
1 1/4 teaspoons	=	6.25 milliliters
1 1/2 teaspoons	=	7.50 milliliters
1 3/4 teaspoons	=	8.75 milliliters
2 teaspoons	=	10.0 milliliters
1 tablespoon	=	15.0 milliliters
2 tablespoons	=	30.0 milliliters

Measurement	=	Liters
1/4 cup	=	0.06 liters
1/2 cup	=	0.12 liters
3/4 cup	=	0.18 liters
1 cup	=	0.24 liters
1 1/4 cups	=	0.30 liters
1 1/2 cups	=	0.36 liters
2 cups	=	0.48 liters
2 1/2 cups	=	0.60 liters
3 cups	=	0.72 liters
3 1/2 cups	=	0.84 liters
4 cups	=	0.96 liters
4 1/2 cups	=	1.08 liters
5 cups	=	1.20 liters
5 1/2 cups	=	1.32 liters

CONVERTING FAHRENHEIT TO CELSIUS

Fahrenheit	=	Celsius
200–205	=	95
220–225	=	105
245–250	=	120
275	=	135
300–305	=	150
325–330	=	165
345–350	=	175
370–375	=	190
400–405	=	205
425–430	=	220
445–450	=	230
470–475	=	245
500	=	260

CONVERSION FORMULAS

LIQUID		
When You Know	Multiply By	To Determine
teaspoons	5.0	milliliters
tablespoons	15.0	milliliters
fluid ounces	30.0	milliliters
cups	0.24	liters
pints	0.47	liters
quarts	0.95	liters

WEIGHT		
When You Know	Multiply By	To Determine
ounces	28.0	grams
pounds	0.45	kilograms

RESOURCES

Having access to a good selection of organic foods—whether fresh or dried, cultivated or wild—makes it easier to be creative in the kitchen when preparing healthy, delicious dishes. Most of the ingredients called for in this book are available at natural foods stores, farmer's markets, and major grocery stores. Your own organic garden is another great source. If, however, you are unable to find a particular item, you can order it from one of the following fine companies.

Blessed Herbs
109 Barre Plains Road
Oakham, MA 01068
800-489-HERB (4372)
info@blessedherbs.com
www.blessedherbs.com
Full line of dried herbs, edible flowers, mushrooms, and nettles.

Bob's Red Mill Natural Foods
5209 SE International Way
Milwaukie, OR 97222
800-349-2173
www.bobsredmill.com
Stone-ground whole grains (including ancient grains) and grain products, nuts, and seeds.

Coombs Family Farms
PO Box 117
Brattleboro, VT 05302

888-266-6271
info@coombsfamilyfarms.com
www.coombsfamilyfarms.com
Organic pure maple syrup in various grades, maple sugar, and other maple products.

Coonridge Organic Goat Cheese
47 Coonridge Dairy
Pie Town, NM 87827
505-250-8553
888-410-8433
organicgoatcheese@yahoo.com
www.coonridge.com
Organic goat cheese in a wide variety of flavors.

Dagoba Organic Chocolate
1105 Benson Way
Ashland, OR 97520
541-482-2001
800-393-6075

oracle@dagobachocolate.com
www.dagobachocolate.com

Fine-quality organic milk and dark chocolates, including varieties with exotic ingredients such as lavender, rosehips, chilies, ginger, lime, and chai spices. Many are fair-trade certified. Sold in bulk and bars.

Delftree Corporation

234 Union Street
North Adams, MA 01247
413-664-4907

Fresh shiitake mushrooms.

Diamond Organics

Highway 1
Moss Landing, CA 95039
888-ORGANIC (674-2642)
info@diamondorganics.com
www.diamondorganics.com

Full line of fresh organic produce, herbs, spices, edible flowers, dried fruits, nuts, nut butters, cheeses, oils, vinegars, chocolates, fresh and dried mushrooms (cultivated and wild), fresh and dried pastas, wine, and ales.

Earthy Delights, Inc.

1161 East Clark Road, Suite 260
DeWitt, MI 48820
517-668-2402
800-367-4709
info@earthy.com
www.earthy.com

Fresh wild mushrooms and other seasonal wild harvested products, edible flowers, beans, ancient grains, pastas, and goat cheese.

Four Chimneys Organic Winery

211 Hall Road
Himrod, NY 14842
607-243-7502
ssmith@htva.net
www.fourchimneysorganicwines.com

Red, white, fruit, cooking, and dessert wines; champagne; grape juice; and wine vinegars. No added sulfites.

Frey Vineyards

14000 Tomki Road
Redwood Valley, CA 95470
707-485-5177
800-760-3739
info@freywine.com
www.freywine.com

Organic and biodynamic red and white wines. No added sulfites.

Frontier Natural Products Co-op

PO Box 299
3021 78th Street
Norway, IA 52318
800-669-3275
customercare@frontiercoop.com
www.frontiercoop.com

Full line of dried herbs and spices, dried edible flowers, sea vegetables, coffees, and teas; also flaxseeds and dried burdock.

Gaeta Imports, Inc.

141 John Street
Babylon, NY 11702
631-661-2681
800-669-2681
g@gaetaimports.com
www.gaetaimports.com

Extra virgin olive oil, light olive oil, capers, balsamic and aged balsamic vinegars.

Gold Mine Natural Food Company

7805 Arjons Drive
San Diego, CA 92126
858-537-9830
800-475-FOOD (3663)
sales@goldminenaturalfood.com
www.goldminenaturalfood.com

Full line of organic and macrobiotic products—whole grains (including ancient varieties), flours and other whole grain products, beans, oils, sea vegetables, miso, dried fruits, noodles, nuts, kudzu, mirin, umeboshi products, sweeteners, and dried shiitake and wild mushrooms.

Green & Black's
Belgravia Imports
1430 East Main Road
Portsmouth, RI 02871
401-683-3323
800-848-1127
www.greenandblacks.com
belgravia@greenandblacks.com

Fair-traded cocoa; full line of organic milk, white, and dark chocolate (with up to 72-percent cocoa) in plain and flavored varieties.

Living Tree Community Foods
PO Box 10082
Berkeley, CA 94709
510-526-7106
800-260-5534
info@livingtreecommunity.com
www.livingtreecommunity.com

Nuts, seeds, nut butters, dried fruits, dried shiitake, dulse, raw honey, olives, and raw olive oil.

Lotus Foods
866-972-6879
info@lotusfoods.com
www.lotusfoods.com

Exotic rices, including Bhutanese red, Chinese "forbidden" black, basmati, jasmine, and carnaroli, and a variety of rice flours.

Maine Coast Sea Vegetables
3 Georges Pond Road
Franklin, ME 04634
207-565-2907
info@seaveg.com
www.seaveg.com

Full line of high-quality sea vegetables and sea vegetable products.

Maine Seaweed, LLC
Larch Hanson
PO Box 57
Steuben, ME 04680

207-546-2875
www.maineseaweedcompany.com

Line of high-quality Atlantic seaweeds, including kelp, alaria, digitata, dulse, bladderwrack, and nori.

Marché aux Delices
New York, NY 10028
888-547-5471
staff@auxdelices.com
www.auxdelices.com

Wide variety of fresh and wild mushrooms, as well as seasonal wild foods, such as ramps, fiddleheads, mache, and dandelions.

MycoLogical Natural Products
PO Box 24940
Eugene OR 97402
541-465-3247
888-465-3247
info@mycological.com
www.mycological.com

Complete line of fresh and dried wild mushrooms.

O Olive Oil
1854 Fourth Street
San Rafael, CA 94901
888-827-7148
mail@ooliveoil.com
www.ooliveoil.com

Imported extra virgin olive oils; California citrus-flavored olive oils; and wine and rice vinegar varieties.

Ocean Harvest Sea Vegetable Company
PO Box 1719
Mendocino, CA 95460
707-937-0637
ohveggies@pacific.net
www.ohsv.net

Sea vegetable varieties, including sea palm, silky sea palm, Pacific and ocean ribbons kombu, Pacific wakame, and wild nori.

Old Chatham Sheepherding Company
155 Shaker Museum Road
Old Chatham, New York 12136
888-SHEEP-60 (743-3760)
cheese@blacksheepcheese.com
www.blacksheepcheese.com
Wide variety of sheep's milk cheeses and yogurts.

Omega Nutrition
1695 Franklin Street
Vancouver, BC V5L 1P5
800-661-FLAX (3529)
info@omeganutrition.com
www.omeganutrition.com
High-quality flaxseed, coconut, extra virgin olive, pumpkin seed, sesame, and sunflower oils; and apple cider and balsamic vinegars.

Organic Choice Teas
Granum, Inc.
2414 SW Andover Street, C-100
Seattle, WA 98106
202-525-0051
800-882-8943
choice@granum-inc.com
www.choiceorganicteas.com
Complete selection of certified organic teas, tea blends, and infusions. Many are fair-trade certified.

The Organic Wine Company
1592 Union Street, Suite 350
San Francisco, CA 94123
888-ECO-WINE (326-9463)
cs@theorganicwinecompany.com
www.theorganicwinecompany.com
Red, white, vegan, sparkling, and dessert wines with minimum added sulfites.

The Organic Wine Works
Hillcrest Vineyards
379 Felton Empire Road
Felton, CA 95018

831-335-4441
800-699-9463
owwwine@cruzio.com
www.organicwineworks.com
Red and white organic wine. No added sulfites.

Pacific Botanicals
4350 Fish Hatchery Road
Grants Pass, Oregon 97527
541-479-7777
www.pacificbotanicals.com
info@pacificbotanicals.com
Extensive selection of fresh and dried herbs, edible flowers, nettles, burdock, and orange and lemon peels.

Purity Foods
2871 West Jolly Road
Okemos, MI 48864
517-351-9231
800-99-SPELT (997-7358)
purityfoods@voyager.net
www.purityfoods.com
Spelt and spelt products, including pastas and flours, as well as a wide selection of grains, beans, and dried fruits.

Ryan Drum
PO Box 25
Waldron Island, WA 98297
206-499-0994
www.ryandrum.com
Variety of fresh and dried herbs and sea vegetables, including kelp.

South River Miso
888 Shelburne Falls Road
Conway, MA 01341
413-369-4057
mail@southrivermiso.com
www.southrivermiso.com
Mellow and aged misos of all flavors; tamari, tahini, maple syrup, and more.

The Spice Hunter
184 Suburban Road
San Luis Obispo, CA 93401
805-597-8900
800-444-3061
www.spicehunter.com
Dried wild mushrooms, and line of herbs and spices.

Sunnyland Mills
4469 East Annadale Avenue
Fresno, CA 93725
559-233-4983
800-501-8017
info@sunnylandmills.com
www.sunnylandmills.com
High-quality bulgur wheat, wheat berries, and grano.

Suzanne's Specialties
40 Fulton Street, Unit 7
New Brunswick, NJ 08901
732-828-8500
800-762-2135
info@suzannes-specialties.com
www.suzannes-specialties.com
Natural and organic grain-based sweeteners—rice syrups, nectars, barley malt, honey, and molasses.

Taylor Maid Farms
6793 McKinley Street
Sebastopol, CA 95472
707-824-9110
info@taylormaidfarms.com
www.taylormaidfarms.com
Coffees varieties; black, green, and herbal teas (some with wild herbs and edible flowers).

The Teff Company
PO Box A
Caldwell, ID 83606
888-822-2221
teffco@earthlink.net
www.teffco.com
Brown and ivory teff grain and teff flour.

Twin Valley Mills
RR 1 Box 45
Ruskin, NE 68974
402-279-3965
sorghumflour@hotmail.com
www.twinvalleymills.com
Sorghum grain flour.

If you are interested in purchasing locally grown fresh produce from a nearby farm or becoming involved in a Community Sustainable Agriculture (CSA) partnership (see page 130), the following contact information will help you in your quest.

Community Sustainable Agriculture
Hotline: 800-516-7797
Website: www.nal.usda.gov/afsic/csa

Farmer's Markets
National map website:
www.ams.usda.gov/farmersmarkets/map.htm

INDEX

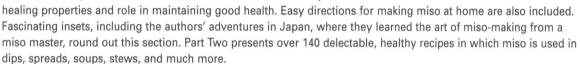

THE MISO BOOK
The Art of Cooking with Miso
John and Jan Belleme

For centuries, the preparation of miso has been considered an art form in Japan. Through a time-honored double-fermentation process, soybeans and grains are transformed into this wondrous food, which is both a flavorful addition to a variety of dishes and a powerful medicinal. Scientific research has supported miso's use as an effective therapeutic aid in the prevention and treatment of heart disease, certain cancers, radiation sickness, and hypertension.

Part One of this comprehensive guide begins with miso basics—its types and uses. A chapter called "Miso Medicine" then details this superfood's healing properties and role in maintaining good health. Easy directions for making miso at home are also included. Fascinating insets, including the authors' adventures in Japan, where they learned the art of miso-making from a miso master, round out this section. Part Two presents over 140 delectable, healthy recipes in which miso is used in dips, spreads, soups, stews, and much more.

Whether you are a health-conscious cook in search of healthful foods or you simply are looking for a delicious new take on old favorites, *The Miso Book* may be just what the doctor ordered.

$15.95 • 192 pages • 7.5 x 9-inch quality paperback • ISBN 0-7570-0028-2

TOMMY TANG'S MODERN THAI CUISINE
Tommy Tang

Tommy Tang, celebrated chef and owner of Tommy Tang's restaurants in Los Angeles and New York, shares his flair for creating unique, delectable cuisine from his native Thailand. In *Tommy Tang's Modern Thai Cuisine*, Tommy presents over ninety of his signature recipes, which combine elements of Japanese, Indian, American, and European dishes with traditional Thai flavor. Enjoy delicacies like Thai Egg Rolls, Red Curry Shrimp, Soft Shell Crabs with Ginger-Garlic Sauce, Lemon Grass Chicken, and Tommy's special sushi. Easy-to-follow instructional illustrations guarantee professional results, while beautiful full-color photographs help you choose the perfect recipe for your next cooking adventure.

If you love Thai food, but have always thought that it was beyond your culinary reach, Tommy Tang is here to change your mind. Let *Tommy Tang's Modern Thai Cuisine* bring the joy of Thai cooking to your home.

$16.95 • 172 pages • 7.5 x 9-inch quality paperback • ISBN 0-7570-0254-4

KITCHEN QUICKIES
Great, Satisfying Meals in Minutes
Marie Caratozzolo and Joanne Abrams

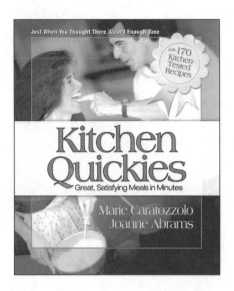

Ever feel that there aren't enough hours in the day to enjoy life's pleasures—simple or otherwise? Whether you're dealing with problems on the job, chasing after kids on the home front, or simply running from errand to errand, the evening probably finds you longing for a great meal, but with neither the time nor the desire to prepare one.

Kitchen Quickies offers a solution. Virtually all of its over 170 kitchen-tested recipes—yes, really kitchen tested—call for a maximum of only five main ingredients other than kitchen staples, and each dish takes just minutes to prepare! Imagine being able to whip up dishes like Southwestern Tortilla Pizzas, Super Salmon Burgers, and Tuscan-Style Fusilli—in no time flat! As a bonus, these delicious dishes are actually good for you—low in fat and high in nutrients!

So the next time you think that there's simply no time to cook a great meal, pick up *Kitchen Quickies*. Who knows? You may even have time for a few "quickies" of your own.

$14.95 • 240 pages • 7.5 x 9-inch quality paperback • ISBN 0-7570-0085-1

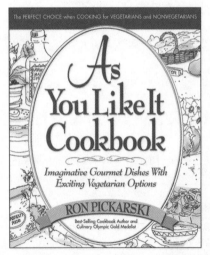

AS YOU LIKE IT COOKBOOK
Imaginative Gourmet Dishes with Exciting Vegetarian Options
Ron Pickarski

When it comes to food, we certainly like to have it our way. However, catering to individual tastes can pose quite a challenge for the cook. The *As You Like It Cookbook* is designed to help you meet the challenge of cooking for both vegetarians and nonvegetarians alike. It offers over 170 great-tasting dishes that cater to a broad range of tastes. Many of the easy-to-follow recipes are vegetarian—and offer ingredient alternatives for meat eaters. Conversely, recipes that include meat, poultry, or fish offer nonmeat ingredient options. Furthermore, if the recipe includes eggs or dairy products, a vegan alternative is provided. This book has it all—delicious breakfast favorites, satisfying soups and sandwiches, mouth-watering entrées, and delectable desserts.

With one or two simple ingredient substitutions, the *As You Like It Cookbook* will show you how easy it is to transform satisfying meat dishes into delectable meatless fare, and vegetarian dishes into meat-lover's choices.

$16.95 • 216 pages • 7.5 x 9-inch quality paperback • ISBN 0-7570-0013-4